ADELAIDE LITERARY AWARD
ANTHOLOGY
2018

ADELAIDE LITERARY AWARD
ANTHOLOGY
2018

ESSAYS

BOOKS

Adelaide Books
New York/Lisbon
2018

ADELAIDE LITERARY AWARD ANTHOLOGY 2018
ESSAYS
Special Issue of the Adelaide Literary Magazine

September 2018

ISBN-13: 978-1-949180-57-2

ISBN-10: 1-949180-57-3

Adelaide Literary Magazine is an independent international monthly publication, based in New York and Lisbon. Founded by Stevan V. Nikolic and
Adelaide Franco Nikolic in 2015, the magazine's aim is to publish quality
poetry, fiction, nonfiction, artwork, and photography, as well as interviews,
articles, and book reviews, written in English and Portuguese. We seek to
publish outstanding literary fiction, nonfiction, and poetry, and to promote
the writers we publish, helping both new, emerging, and established authors reach a wider literary audience. We publish print and digital editions
of our magazine twelve times a year. Online edition is updated continuous-
ly. There are no charges for reading the magazine online.
(http://adelaidemagazine.org)

EDITOR IN CHIEF / EDITOR-CHEFE
Stevan V. Nikolic
editor@adelaidemagazine.org

MANAGING DIRECTOR
Adelaide Franco Nikolic

GRAPHIC & WEB DESIGN
Joana Cardoso
Vesna Trpkovska

Published by: Adelaide Books LLC, New York
244 Fifth Avenue, Suite D27, New York, NY 10001
e-mail: info@adelaidebooks.org
phone: 917 477 8984

Best essays by the Winner, seven Shortlist
Nominees and thirty Finalists of the second annual
Adelaide Literary Award Competition 2018,
selected by

Stevan V. Nikolic
editor-in-chief

Contents

FINALISTS

THE WINNER

On Beauty

By Wally Swist

Beauty is relative—however, it is also abundant and perennial. One type of beauty may diminish and morph into a deeper philosophical truth. Beauty can take the guise of morality and define the outer reaches of what it means to be fully human—to grow into that.

The film *Amour*, directed by Michael Haneke, which was made in 2012 and won the *Palme d'Or*, is, ostensibly, all about beauty and what is beautiful about life, as well as what are intrinsic elements of living that may be seen as being opposite to beauty. The film's characters are a husband and a wife, two former music teachers, in their twilight weeks and days. Jean-Louis Trintignant is Georges and Emmanuele Riva is Anne. They are retired. They are cultured. They read, go to concerts, enjoy each other's conversation, and still love each other—for the most part. Anne once shocks Georges by saying, as wives often enough stun their husbands by their appraisals of their characters, "You're a monster sometimes." However, she clarifies that declarative sentence by adding: "But very kind." That *is* beautiful.

After a lifetime of marriage to each other, Anne suffers two strokes and Georges cares for her throughout her decline. He bathes her, feeds her, exercises the leg on the side she can no longer feel, practices speech therapy with her. Many men, or wives, for that matter, would never have the wherewithal or the courage to brave such lengths—of true *amour*. Georges may be guilty of being a monster, in Anne's experience, but he is the precipitant in furthering the spark of *beauty* between them. The drama may seem very French, something Camus or Sartre would have taken delight in, with both Georges and Anne seeing the end of their lives in plain sight; however, instead of being grim, they rise above the end of life, in uncommon transcendence. In their *amour*, and its tacit veracity—there are several touching scenes regarding Georges physical care for Anne, which are truly heartrending in their depth of humanity and active loving—the viewer is offered the essence of what love is and what having an affair is not. Hence, the irony in the film's title. In today's world where greed, sex, and narcissism are common, the beauty of Georges and Anne is exemplary as not only a moral and cultural pedagogy without pedantry but, quite aesthetically and humanely, one act of *beauty* after another. Through another's lens this might be seen as hardship and turmoil, unimaginable spousal duty and death in life.

At the film's end, without giving anything away, Georges is clipping the flower heads from a bunch of daisies he has just purchased at the florist. He fills the kitchen sink and scissors the flowers into the water, then throws away the stems. These are meant for his Anne. Often we need to practice the art of discernment in order to see clearly. Sometimes we need to ruin the flowered stalk to create a ritual for celebration. As Anne says, in one scene, over dinner with Georges, while looking through photograph albums, "It's beautiful." Georges responds, "What?" Anne answers, "Life. So long."

That is what constitutes perennial beauty *and* remains *beautiful*. If we allow ourselves to discover the epiphany in the commonplace in our lives, we realize, to our astonishment, that all along, through every disappointment and affliction, we can say, "it's beautiful."

Wally Swist's books include *Huang Po and the Dimensions of Love* (Southern Illinois University Press, 2012); *The Daodejing: A New Interpretation*, with David Breeden and Steven Schroeder (Lamar University Literary Press, 2015); *Candling the Eggs* (Shanti Arts, LLC, 2017); and *The Map of Eternity* (Shanti Arts, LLC, 2018). His poems and prose have appeared in many publications, including *Appalachia, Anchor: Where Spirituality and Social Justice Meet, Arts: The Arts in Religion and Theology, Commonweal,* and *North American Review.*

SHORTLIST WINNER NOMINEES

An Ascent:
Considering the Shadows
of a Stone Staircase

By Allison M. Palmer

If the woods are haunted, but the forest merely enchanted by shadows and soft light, into which realm does the stone staircase lead? And who will follow?

In a different era, as industrial wealth of the twentieth century flowered into great family fortunes, workmen were transported to a distant location and ordered to arrange a pile of rocks. It was an interesting task. Their employers—the founding fathers of our city—were determined to build a grotto in what was then wildland, something of a monument to affluence and ambition, a hint of things to come. Although, at first glance, it seemed like nothing more than a curiosity, the project had obviously been calculated, its site chosen with something in mind; the location was a place set apart from prying eyes and gentility, a place where the activities of a grotto could go unchallenged and remain hidden—never to be seen in newspapers or history books. Even now, long after the age of discretion and propriety has faded, the grotto remains a signif-icant destination. Although suspicion has given way to appreciation over the years, something of the original aura persists; the structure still engages travelers as they explore pathways and wander in the shallow woods.

Every aspect was designed with care. Gray and orange rocks form not only a fount but also a series of walls and a staircase, steps that gently descend into an entanglement of oaks.

Allison M. Palmer is a municipal park ranger, writer and copyeditor living in San Diego, California. She is currently the editor of Footprints, the publication of the Japanese American Historical Society of San Diego. Allison is also the founder and director of the Palmer Memorial Humanities Library.

Resilient Love

By Andrea Cladis

Protective paralysis overwhelmed my body the day my Mom was first diagnosed with cancer. I was fifteen years-old.

Resilience has as much to do with the body as it does the mind. We have a physical attachment to this world and the things it contains. The physical bond we have with our own bodies determines how our nerve endings perceive the world and experience life. Yet, what drives all of the physical sensations is our perception of what they are and how they feel. It is our mind that determines our reactions to these sensations and ultimately controls them. Sometimes they can be more intense than others. And often they cannot be tamed as we wish. Resilience is earned over time and through experience. If we are not resilient in our minds or able to practice resilience through that channel, we will not exhibit any sort of physical shrewdness within our lives. Yet through faith, hope, and deliverance, we can grow and persist.

Twelve years following my mother's very involved and traumatic breast cancer treatment, and fifteen years to the date of her initial diagnosis, something went terribly awry. Perhaps it was coming on slowly and we were all naïve to it. Or maybe it happened suddenly, as our minds would like us to believe, so we can avoid the blame of impending responsibility. But something horrific happened. My mother woke up one morning and the haunting scars across her chest were swollen and red. The right side of her chest was much larger than the left and it appeared a balloon was growing rapidly in her chest. Burdened by this new pain and discomfort, the taut skin of her scars appeared to frown as the swelling beneath her skin continued to overwhelm the barren space on her chest. With each shallow breath she took, she cringed and she cried. My mother, the once all-courageous cancer survivor, was fearful.

"What's wrong, Peter? What's happening?" Mom pleaded with my father, a physician, who always wished to deny the reality of medical problems ever involving those he loved and cherished.

"Honey," he responded softly. "Let's wait a few days and see what happens. Perhaps it is swelling or aggravated tissue," he said.

"But this pain, this pain," she replied. "I can't handle this pain."

As I observed their exchange, witnessed Mom's fear and encouraged Dad's embrace of her, I felt paralyzed. My mind felt as though it lacked any capacity for resilience. My mother's pain, her fear, and the discussions of possible unknowns left me in heightened state of unease.

The surgeon who had performed her double mastectomy ten years prior instructed Mom, in her new condition, to wear a sling to rest her left arm and restrict most movement through her chest and upper body for a week. The hope with this mild treatment was that perhaps the swelling would dissipate and the pain would lessen if the tissues were not being consistently aggravated by movement. I watched her, stubborn as ever, not wanting to rely on anyone but herself for anything, doing dishes and folding laundry with one hand, while her other arm remained situated in a sling. She took to cooking and cleaning

and making all sorts of phone calls. She was not exactly immo-
bilizing her chest. As I witnessed her obstinacy in movement,
however, my thoughts wandered to my high school years and
her original battle with breast cancer. The very same illness that
took her mother's life was perhaps again re-surfacing in ours as
a sort of reincarnated plague.

I reminisced on the morning of her double mastectomy,
when my older brother was abroad studying in Guatemala,
my younger sister, in eighth grade, was at school because Dad
demanded she be near others that day, and I, in obedience and
anxiety, took the day off of high school classes to be with my
Dad. That very day I witnessed the strongest man I have ever
known weakened, falling to his knees in despair.

The decision at the time for Mom to undergo a mastectomy, followed by an oophorectomy, hysterectomy, and more
chemotherapy medication was an unsettling, but we were confident it was the right thing to do. We were informed that the
mastectomy would take place right after Christmas. At the
beginning of January, when my older brother left to spend his
college's January term doing a service-learning trip in Guatemala he was reassured by my Mom that everything with the
surgery would go well. She didn't want him to worry, and I
was amazed at how well she held it together as we said our
goodbyes at the airport.

My Mom's mother lost her battle with breast cancer in
1995 and I was not at all prepared to lose my mother. Each
day as the surgery approached, we prayed together as a family.
Our nerves were mounting, sleepless nights endured, and fear,
overcome with worry, was our chief burden. Mom worked to
ready herself for the surgery and Dad, the doctor who knew
too much about her exact type of breast cancer, survival rates,
complications with surgery, etc., kept relatively quiet, but he
did not stop encouraging, loving, and praying for Mom.

January 10th, 2008 was surgery day for Mom, and the day when the culmination of fear, anxiety, and stress came to a head. Through my father's actions and reactions during the day, I finally came to fully understand the meaning of resilience in love. Though Dad had considered working on the day of Mom's surgery, probably to distract himself from the reality of the situation, and because he's never missed a day of work in his life, all of the other doctors and nurses he worked with counseled him to take the day off. He needed to get some distance from the hospital and not be confronted by people he knew all day. My Dad knew the surgeon performing the double mastectomy well and he was told he'd be updated as the surgery progressed. The most important piece of information my Dad was waiting for was whether or not Mom's cancer had spread into her lymph nodes and thus further into her body. If the cancer, which was present in both breasts, had not spread, my mother would have a much better chance of survival. But if the cancer had spread to the lymph nodes, we all knew what that meant, even though my Dad refused to say anything to that effect.

That morning as Mom was undergoing a lengthy, seven hour surgery, we sat together, Dad and me, at a breakfast diner where we normally chowed down on stacks of fluffy pancakes with sugary maple syrup cascading down the sides. Dad would drink copious cups of coffee and I would complain of being "stuffed." But that day, we both sat in silence and stared at an untouched stack of strawberry pancakes neatly dusted with powdered sugar accompanied by an ice cream-sized scoop of creamed, whipped butter. The pancakes were not very fluffy and the powdered sugar did not dance on the heated plate as it normally did. The syrup I tried to pour barely slid off the pancakes. It looked more like molasses sludge than anything else. Dad's side order of rubbery sausage did not sizzle. The coffee was cold, without any wisps of steam. Gray hairs I had never noticed before aggressively lined the crown of Dad's receding hairline. His watch battery had died and the clock face mocked us at 9:05 AM. And it continued to do so for two hours of empty stares, untouched pancakes, and a crusty, burnt piece of uneaten toast that I compulsively smothered with orange marmalade. We both hated jam, especially textured marmalade.

When the check came, we remained motionless at the table. "Would you like a to-go box?" The waitress inquired. Neither of us responded. She walked away, not expectant of any form of tip from us. Waiting on a phone call from the hospital regarding updates, Dad checked his watch.

"Still 9:05, kid. Did anyone call you?" The time warp reminded it was perhaps too soon to know anything. I reached into my pocket and pulled out my phone. It was nearly noon. There had been no calls from any hospital or surgeon made to my phone.

"Do you think Mom is going to be okay?" My teenage pimples and near-anorexic body feared the worst. Dad opened another little carton of marmalade and spread it onto the edges of the same sad piece of burnt toast.

"Pray. All you can do is pray," he said. I looked into his oversized coffee mug. Still no steam, but for some reason I expected there to be some. Instead, I saw the reflection of two gaunt faces shattered by emotional anguish, suffering from a most hollow devastation.

When we arrived home after our time at the diner, we walked our dogs, who also sensed our tension, and continued to wait. Pacing back and forth in our kitchen, shaking, crying, holding hands with me and not knowing how to handle himself, Dad finally got the call he'd been waiting for all day. A call he should have received by 12:00 PM and it was late afternoon. He picked up the phone. His face looked as though it had aged ten years in one day.

"Yes. Okay. Thank you," he said. "When will she be done?" Tears immediately began streaming down my father's face as the disjointed conversation continued. I feared the worst. I thought the dreaded news was now official. Dad hung up the phone in silence. He didn't say a word. My eyes started watering and I sat motionless on the floor near his feet looking at him to move his lips. I wanted him to say something, anything! After taking a few wobbly steps forward, he fell to his knees in the middle of our kitchen and sobbed uncontrollably. I didn't know if the news was good or bad, but I had only seen my father really cry that way one other time in my life, which was when he lost his father. I couldn't help but cry when I looked at Dad; it was good to relieve all of the pent up emotions I had experienced that day.

Through somber eyes Dad finally looked up at me and whimpered, "The cancer has not spread. There was only a microscopic amount in the lymph nodes on the right side, but it has not spread to her body." I wept with joy as Dad kept saying, "Thank you, God, thank you, God, thank you God! He pulled himself from the ground and with a surge of adrenaline flowing through his body, literally started jumping for joy. He bounded about the kitchen, picked me up and swung me around, smiling and repeating, "Yes! Yes! Yes! Woo!" He filled our house with shrieks of joyous, passion, and sheer, unbridled emotion.

A few fist pumps later, he ran out the front door and started doing laps around our home. He was overwhelmed by elation, relief and the deep love and devotion he felt towards my mother. I had never seen him respond to anything in such an emotive way. I was incredulous. I cried for my mother. I cried just watching my father and knowing how much he loved and cherished his wife. Seeing him react that day, I did not just feel love or have the experience of love – I actually came to fully *understand* what love is.

Love is not just the warm, fuzzy feeling you get when your dog lies by your feet, love is not just the simple hug from a friend at the end of a long day – love is not just pancakes in bed on your birthday. Love is resilient. Love is an indescribable emotion that transcends feeling. It is the quintessence of compassion and the utmost desire of the human spirit to be connected to others. On that cold, January day, I learned just how much my father loves my mother. I learned how much he needs, respects, admires and cares for her. She is everything to him – a part of his world he cannot imagine being without. In the spectrum of human emotion, love is perhaps the most powerful and zealous one of all. No form of cancer can destroy that love.

Folding my Dad's socks and undershirts against the counter with her right hand – a sling occupying the left – I told myself that Mom needed me to be strong for her. Though it felt as if no time had passed since I was sitting in that diner awaiting her sentence, a lot of time had. My pimples were gone and only faded scars remained in their place. Muscular development from my work as a fitness trainer disguised my formerly emaciated frame, and a few gray hairs had begun to surface in my thick, brown hair. My brother was married and considering having children, while my sister had recently completed a doctorate in Physical Therapy. Dad was still lively, but overworked and getting older. Mom looked shorter than I remembered her to be and her shoulders hunched over further than when I was in high school. Her face was thinner and the coloration of her skin was duller. Life had changed, but in many ways we had not. The fearlessness I craved was nowhere to be found. I did not want the doctor to again sentence my mother to cancer.

Over ten years later and I felt the same child-like weakness I had known the first time around. And this time I was not a kid, but rather an adult-daughter. It was different. Mom could rely on me in ways she could not before, but I felt helpless to fix anything. Out of pride, Mom tried to refuse my help with laundry or making dinner, or walking the dog, but I helped where I could and as she would allow.

Mom's condition gradually worsened and a few days later, Dad ordered me to help more and informed me that I would be attending an appointment with Mom at the local hospital's cancer center the following week. Baldness had absorbed the place where those gray hairs once crowned Dad's forehead. But his affirmative tonality in speaking to me was exactly as it had been ten years prior.

"You take care of your mother. You be here for her. Listen. Be present. Do that for me," he cried through cracked, tired lips. He wanted me to fill in all the gaps where he fell short. He wanted me to emotionally support Mom in ways he could not. He wanted me to sacrifice my own work and obligations when his were too demanding to neglect. For his shortcomings as a husband, I was to fill in as her daughter. I could not replace the role her husband needed to play no matter how hard I tried. Mom needed me, but she needed him more. That fact would never change.

The following week as I sat in the waiting room for nearly two hours as Mom was being evaluated for her chest pain and swelling, an enormous pocket formed in my own chest. I did not want to lose my mother. I did not want her sentenced again. Flashbacks taunted me and nerves made my stomach bounce uncomfortably. Mom and I were in the midst of planning my wedding. I needed her around. There was no way she could be sick. This was *not* happening again.

When she returned to the waiting room two hours later, I was informed that the results were inconclusive. Further tests were ordered. I wanted to know what the doctors were doing to her for those two hours, but rather than pester her with questions, I distracted her thoughts with a discussion about my latest graduate school project. Mom was always interested in my school achievements. She had been in support of education my whole life. I drove her home listening to instrumental Christmas music on the radio. She was quiet. It was early December and my Christmas present was a mother in the passenger's seat moaning in harrowing pain.

"Honey, can you make dinner tonight?" she asked, not wanting to afflict me with the responsibility. "Can you prepare something for Dad and your sister?" I saw her struggle to relinquish control as some care-taking was being placed on me again. Mom was hurting and I quite simply, I was capable to take care of things, but I was more than scared.

I steadied my quivering lip and cleared my throat. "I will make dinner, okay? Don't worry, Mom. Don't worry." She closed her eyes and rested until we arrived at home.

It is mystifying the way our minds work in moments and in flashbacks. In points of fast-paced movement and isolation. Mornings of frozen pancakes and hours of waiting and then ten years of gray-hair-producing-awareness that time has passed. There was no mistaking that Mom and Dad had aged during that time, but the feelings were all the same. I had to be responsible for Mom's well-being and that of the family. I had to make sure our family still had a Christmas. I had to step up and grow up and be the adult I never wanted to be as an innocent high school teen awaiting Mom's sentence.

Driving to work in the dark at 5:00 AM the next day, immersed in the silence of the morning, tears welled my eyes and I thought of how all I wanted was to go back in time. I wanted to go back in time to those family road trips that took us to nearly all 50 states, to the young, healthy parents I took for granted, the endless laughter, dinners with grandparents, and the lack of any worry about money or bills, travel plans, or if Santa was real or not. A swarm of warmth flooded my mind. All of the moments that became the life memories Mom and Dad had created for me and my siblings. And all of the time I spent wishing to be older, wishing to grow up, and wishing to do all the things I now despised. Those times with Mom, Dad, and our family together were the best, most meaningful moments of my life. They brought me to back to a place of familial love and hope. I wanted it all once again. My hands trembled on the steering wheel, but my tears dried as I focused on the classes that I was scheduled to teach that morning.

Though I could not recognize it in that very moment – a cold, dark Monday morning – it was all of those moments and memories I recalled that had given me the resilience I needed at that point in my life. That strength of our familial bond of love had deep roots that would not be easily supplanted. And that is what made me feel wholeness in the hollowness of the almost frozen, day-old coffee that occupied my cup-holder and sloshed around in my flittering tummy. The bliss of the Christmas season was tangible, but the anxiety of the unknown was upsetting. We recognize feelings through how our minds perceive the moments of life we endure. The lesson I am still learning is how to channel that perception towards the creation of inner strength in the present moment.

In the paralysis I felt after I finished work that day, I remembered what a missionary friend of mine told me about life and the continual struggle between joy and grief. She said to me that we spend much of our lives balancing joy in one hand and grief in the other. The metaphor worked well for me. The joy, she explained, is to remind us of why we live. The grief is what keeps us humble. So much of life involves trial and struggle. God gives us an abundance of joy, but He doesn't promise us a life free from pain. It is our blessing and our journey. And we have to delicately maintain that balance to temper the sadness or grief while not forgetting about the joy of life's blessings. I was cradling both that Christmas, and was prepared to give Mom some of the joy I knew she needed to balance out the hefty weight of her own personal sorrow.

I blurred the lights on the Christmas tree at my parents' home with my eyes each time I looked at it. It had been decorated during an evening of agony, impatient argument, and yelling. But through my mind's eye, I only wanted to see the delightful memories of past Christmases. That is of course what they were there for. Firmly planted. Aptly welcomed and received. You can't have joy without sorrow. You can't have life without loss. In a strange way I felt that the Christmas tree radiated the love of Christ my family needed.

Mom went for an MRI and other testing a week later. Joy and grief were solemnly resting in equal balance when we got the test results back. Mom's sentence would remain unknown. She would go for surgery to have her chest cut open, cleaned out, and examined the week before Christmas. She was a fighter and we would not let go of the hope, the love, and the memories that knit our family together.

The fuzzy, polychrome lights on the tree gave me faith that as God had done the past, He would grant Mom resilience in mind and in body as she faced surgery and a period of renewal in healing. And that Christmas, as Mom recovered, God would once more gift our family newfound patience, grace, and eternal understanding.

"When you pass through the waters, I will be with you; and through the rivers, they shall not over-whelm you; when you walk through fire you shall not be burned, and the flame shall not consume you."
(Isaiah 43:2)

Andrea Cladis, holds an MFA from Fairfield University and is a Summa Cum Laude graduate of Elmhurst College with degrees in English Writing, Interdisciplinary Communications, French, and Secondary Education. A former journalist and High School English teacher, she currently works as a freelance editor, writing consultant, and fitness professional. She has worked for Delnor Hospital's Marketing and Public Relations Department, for neighborhood magazines, and as a feature writer for Shaw Media. She has been published by SAGE Academic, The Greek Star, various literary journals, and online publications including Thought Catalog, Elite Daily, and Patch.com. She is also the author of Finding the Finish Line: Navigating the Race of Life through Faith & Fitness (CrossLink Publishing, 2017). She has written extensively for online news websites, print magazines, local newspapers, and social media blogs. Known for her local opinion columns, Andrea's writing has been described as "emotive, yet brazen, seasoned with thinly veiled cynicism, and a pinch of sarcasm." Andrea is an Advisory Board Member for Cambridge Scholars Publishing and maintains a personal site about faith, fitness, and writing which can be explored at www.andreacladis.com.

Time and The Predicament of Enrichment

By Esteban Garcia

The Universe

Everything in the universe has a counterpart and for every action there is a reaction, and they can be in balance or unstable. A duality that is the result of a three-dimensional universe bound by mathematical relationships that give meaning to the information, which can only be changed or transformed. A permanent universe made of particles and a pressure and similar repulsion that produce a predictable rate of decadence and a tendency to balance, a performance we also know as energy, gravity and matter. A structural integrity that is true for all systems and consistent with the three parts atom and determines the properties of the elements and a spectrum that goes from heavy to light, solid to gas, uncompromising and flexible, permanent and fleeting, slow and fast, a pace we also know as time.

Time is not a predetermine line just like space doesn't fold, time is gravity and acceleration, a diminishing return produced by space negation of energy, which produces a sequence that increase in frequency the smaller the event. With space as the absolute the past remains fixed somewhere generating a memory although the cause is constantly turning into the effect, it is projected to the generalization. Starting from the smaller scale time would seem to slow down until there is no point of reference, the cycles become slower and there is nothing to compare it with, big and small become one. Our energy-time awareness is a matter of scales and quality, and a performance that improves with society.

There is only a big permanent universe that changes little, yesterday and tomorrow are patterns, one, two, three, four can only have a relative relevance and reflect proportions, they don't have an inherent value and need points of references. Time is normally restored in cycles (or statistical associations). If you stretch the information it twists, and if you twist it accelerates, if it accelerates it melts and if it melts it accelerates. A Tension determines the interaction between the demand and the capacity, meaning things tend to agglutinate and the capacity generally chases the demand losing ground, moving faster increases the time deficit.

Reaching down for and absolute and catching up with itself defines time and everything else, generating pressures and a diminished return that can produce an explosion. Energy and time are generated by a capacity-demand coefficient that shapes the information which in turn defines a quantity, producing a moment with relative and absolute speed. These are tension variations caused by structural parameters and the absolute value of pi. Horizontal is a degree of certainty, you cannot separate sideways; separation is always in an angle generating a deficit or demand, which is why movement comes at an energy cost. The error is loss of traction and energy, slipping or dismantling the information; concentrating on the wrong subject, focus becomes friction and pressure. It is the necessary contact and connections in the right areas that produce the performance, the sensors, the legs and the functions; different rhythms that through an evolution work together to produce stability, which is the objective – This produced complex individuals very light and nimble in the group.

The tension generated between space and energy produces the agglutination and binding connections, it can result in many relationships and compromises. It generates energy cycles below certain levels where pressure remains stable, which means when not competing for essential resources but for a mutual capacity, a predisposition also known as cooperation. Above that level energy becomes uneven and the connection breaks down, the capacity reduces and the demand goes up until the system short circuits. The success of the species depends on the ability to reduce conflicts, the more effective the communications the more stable the platforms reducing the energy fluctuations and friction. Competition at that level is nothing but antagonism and corrosion.

Positive enrichment requires the potential that produces the relaxation displacing the vertical acceleration and reducing the interaction and "the cost", which happens as the subject of repetition reaches maximum possible certainty becoming the object of repetition, although it doesn't always produce more certainty. These layers are defined by a pressure that generate the patterns; first they accumulate information then start disappearing as the parts become more uniform, then other layers might start forming distending the tension until it stops or collapses, going round and round in cycles. The energy cycles produce all kinds of relationships and have byproducts, excess that is eliminated; gravity which life reflects through pain when the energy lacks and the head can't meet the tail, when the orbit strays from a destiny. It produces the articulations and absolutes, the end of one cycle and the beginning of another.

The universe is naturally in focus, so everything must be; a minimum common denominator corresponding to the superlative system tying everything together. Everything that can be "fixed" then is and agglutination happens within certain parameter. Without the qualitative transformation which becomes increasingly rare with the variables energy only produces a distortions of the information stretching and interrupting the cycles, unnecessary movement and erosion. This vertical limit or breaking point produces the black holes and other phenomena in smaller scale; it produces different densities and the rings of the tree, the atmospheric layers and the Earth's strata.

The Antagonism is occurs when the action and the reaction oppose each other, which causes the capacity and demand reaction. It can generate resonance where the energy bounce out, and a cycle when there is enrichment and a qualitative step takes place. As long as there is traction the system is moving forcing the performance to adjust until energy dissipates, generating the contraction; back and forth or in circular motion. Random antagonism is the "error" or defects that life reduces through trial and error, selecting the information to improve communication and generate more certainty, concentrating resources and reducing the energy which in turn reduces the trial and error per-capita and the speed of the processes, which also means friction is going down making it progressively more loosely connected too, so the moment starts coming around.

Quality is traction, a change or movement caused by isolating the repetition and displacing the ambiguities (outside), definition determined by a trajectory and a historical development, which is why information stays together and things upright, and why the bigger the concentration of energy the higher the tension that makes things move and spin, and the lower the concentration the larger the volume (needed for stability). Everything in the universe is then caught in a balance between precision and a momentum, context and friction, between the smallest point and the whole, a compact positive and a fluid negative, mass and energy, setting up the structural layers and agglutinating patterns. Everything becomes a dot of a larger system and a whole of another located by a history and itself caught between its smallest and largest parameters, its properties and priorities. Movement reconciles the need for focus and precision, for minimum certainty, it's the compromise that yields the dominant and recessive and sets up multiplication patterns, proportions, growth and bonding.

The behavior of a geometric sequence depends on a common ratio, which expresses distance and the absolute value of space. If the common ratio is:

- Positive (convex, or subject of repetition) the terms will all be the same sign as the initial term.

- Negative (concave, hollow, object of repetition) the terms will alternate between positive and negative.

- Greater than 1, there will be exponential growth towards positive or negative infinity. (Unstable, chain reaction)

- 1 (or pi) the progression is a constant sequence (bonds, stable, neutral, no chain reaction)

- Between a1 and 1 but not zero, there will be exponential decay towards zero (Infinite geometric series, chain reaction, hooks, and perpetual contraction)

- a1, the progression is an alternating sequence (ideal negative orbit, ties up, bonds)

- Less than a1, for the absolute values there is exponential growth towards positive and negative infinity. (Unstable, chain reaction)

Mathematical relationships generate a cone of certainty and an algorithm. A place of relative stability fixes the trajectory as the variables resume to one location or answer, the longer the trajectory the more predictable the curve. A reaction negates the pressure forcing the constant transfer of information and producing the resistance, and a negative energy field that can become a potential. It generates a capacity-demand reaction that reduces the tension attempting to restoring symmetry and disambiguates the information through a process of elimination, generating the cycles – As the elements get more complex they can produce fewer variables.

The duality between the universal symmetry and energy's inherent antagonism generates movement, areas of stability with negative and positive poles and correlating capacity/ demand performances that establish the rhythm. Information is internalized generating patterns producing matter and articulations; energy and time become the result of a constant pressure disambiguation. The significant information makes it a structural development displacing the friction or a chain reaction between the capacity and the demand that leads to extreme polarization, sort of moving in the opposite direction, unfolding or fading, it determines degree of certainty and volatility - A potential is what is possible but still uncertain. It could be energy or virtual knowledge.

It generates a tendency to efficiency, the 45 degree angle of maximum certainty, the wheel and the learning curve, meaning the friction that produces the grip on the environment causes the erosion, and aggregating value reduces the friction and opens the scope. Life also has stability as the target and reacts similarly to pressure, accelerating and fragmenting, the environmental demand stimulates genetic processes that introduce more variables and mutations and as stress is relieved they slow down. The more specialized they become the less energy needed, and it can carry on to a point of saturation first, or balance. For life, also, the inability to meet the demand is uncertainty which causes hyperactivity and erosion, the vacuum of information that stretches the environment and in excess breaks it apart. The universe disambiguates pressure, life manages pressure to learn and buy time.

The algorithm is the result of a symmetrical three dimensional space with unique locations, one single shortest distance between two points and energy's duality. The stage is set by the absolute value of pi, leaving us with a statistical certainty, speed and the light spectrum, and the X factor. Empiric generalization and geometric reductions that generate a capacity and an event horizon defining space and energy's properties. Mathematically as long as there is a conflict the solution hasn't been found, but the negation takes place on a scale where movement becomes predictable and information takes the path of least resistance, the shortest possible route between point A and B. The polarization grabs and information moves in both direction creating questions and answers and subliminal pressures. The vertical displacement in the loop generates the movement and a spiral, the more compact and uniform the information the longer the trajectory, like the DNA string, becoming exponentially shorter and fast with each variable. The resistance is determined by the structure which is determined by pi, the angle closes with every cycle because there is a diminishing return in the mass/volume ratio, it cannot reach the absolute vertical line. The nucleus or center of gravity should get ahead of the mathematical ability to compensate, sustain a volume.

The antagonism and decadence are inversely related to the degree of certainty shaping a universe of proportions and lightings. Speed is flexibility and polarization, the faster a system the worse the return until it reaches critical mass and the connection is broken, the disintegration makes the information part of a larger event's frequency. Perfect symmetry would negate the negation stopping everything but that's impossible, causes the heating up and exponential inflation (only social reciprocity can fully negate this area). Certainty is predictability, uniformity and recognition and uncertainty is unpredictability, ignorance and volatility, it opens a passage to the unknown and causes erosion, therefore any incursion or reach into the unknown generates proportional instability and vulnerabilities to a general integrity.

Acceleration makes the negation area expand increasing the resistance; the subject occupies more space which requires the critical mass to adjust. Like a sound barrier, time and energy start moving in opposite directions generating the energy vacuum until there is no time between point A and B. Pressure has to add up, speed changes the equation and the subject is crushed or floats up decompressing (in the absence of learning). The event stretches until the stability band breaks, literally producing a tear in the energy-time continuum, a place that heats up as the boundaries that define the event meet in a single point. Time shrinks and stops, the energy ceases being part of the system's life and its aging process, and becomes part of a different event. The demand gets farther ahead the faster you go and overwhelms the capacity causing the system to lose integrity releasing energy.

This forces things to internalize the environment or be absorbed by the environment, setting the stage for chemical reactions, synthesis, digestion, etc. Consequently manipulating critical mass in reference to a performance horizon generates movement; reducing the mass produces acceleration and adding mass slows it down, basically controlling volume and contractions.

Energy, friction and decadence are connected very tightly, in fact they are part of all information cycles, friction locates balance and generate energy, like a universal molecule. That is because it is all the effects of pressure and the antagonism, the negation of the negation and the recovery of time. This also means that the environmental demand is proportionally adjusted curving the performance and slowing down the displacement of energy (reducing resistance, making things easier, etc.). Energy always generates a demand; the bigger the structures the bigger the energy required, which defines resistance and forces everything to precision, and when it is fixed in place with purpose becomes function, energy cycles we know as cooperation, symbiosis and agglutination…generating traction with minimum antagonism.

It forces life to get just what it needs, build it only as big as necessary, the more successful species eliminating most unnecessary antagonism, as opposed to using maximum energy to generate traction. Therefore evolutionary adaptations only work within a margin of error, otherwise generating a loss of energy and diminished capacity. The capacity and the demand could enter into the negative chain reaction that produces the abnormal developments and decadence (which is unresolved antagonism).

Without the resistance to curb the performance energy is spent, accelerated by forward momentum and pulled back by gravity, and generally falling behind the pace, which generates a tendency to pick up dead weight. For life that means deformities rather than growth, and moving in the wrong direction. Since everything is interconnected stability is a statistical percentage, human society makes the species an organism without an inherent rate of decadence. The mathematical principle is locating the target of stability by adjusting the center of gravity which improves with certainty and definition. For life enrichment is generally the manipulation of energy in anticipation of a degree of difficulty which also becomes growth.

The significance attached to the relationships generates pressure and produces the structures. It displaces energy looking for stability and can focus within a margin of error defined by the relevant information. The target moves and the focus closes or more energy is necessary to provide the flexibility (widen the scope to more variables). Extreme specialization removes more variables but severs other relationships, takes them out of the range of possibilities, so it only makes sense if is necessary, after all it is the result of instability, and more energy comes with other liabilities. It is, like everything, always bound by the universal performance which we have also identified as the learning curve and diminishing returns.

Agglutination allows for growth within critical parameter, incorporating information with minimum effort and taking advantage of enrichment and momentum, so it could only happens within structural limits. It is determined by degree of compatibility, a positive energy ratio in relation to the friction produces the demand, the bigger the discrepancy the stronger the pull or contraction. When bonding occurs energy is released or absorbed bending the trajectory until the head meets the tail again. The performance adjust to resets the energy-time ratio that is essential for all things to function, process information and sustaining life. It dictates the properties of the elements and life's behavior, and generates a pattern of agglutination throughout the universe. The reaction is modified in the interaction according to structural boundaries, too much energy generates more antagonism and the system loses integrity, not enough and it loses connectivity and information comes to a halt; it's "freezing" on one side and "combustion" on the other. Restructuring occurs on the edges of these relationships, these walls" will force everything back to efficiency, reorganize or be grinded, shift the weight or shed the weight, there is no rupture of the universal laws. It is the area where permanent cycles and life happen.

Oxygen as a simple element at the bottom of the pyramid has more bonding capacity and energy potential but is also equally corrosive. The Oxygen CO2 relationship is balanced in cycles between animal and plant life. This also gives water is properties and makes it ideal for synthesizing energy.

For life it means movement and managing resources, and specific ratios between a capacity and the demand. The target of stability is turned it into a purpose and the demand becomes a necessity, making the mathematical laws and focus work its favor, determining the inevitable and turning the energy adjustment into the ability to perform a well-defined task, precision and repetition into process, and specialization into a learning ability. This produces forms and priorities which is what generates the capacity reducing friction and the liabilities, (and the innumerable adjustments involved in a free throw in basketball).

Energy comes at a stability cost; in general it is deflected, absorbed or dispersed to relieve tension; agglutination and fragmentation are the ways energy is general adjusted. It allows living organisms to extract energy from the environment and balance the equation over several steps, using mechanisms like procreation and larger societies to achieve stability, therefore individuals have a rate of decadence not the human species. Life manipulates pressure, space and time to expand and grow, using energy only in that context.

This creates horizontal cycles in relative stability, like human society and cooperation and others faster geometrical relationships like selective breeding all the way up to a vertical limit where the connection breaks and the environmental demand is displaced generating the capacity-demand chain reaction where it falls to the next generalization. Achieving balance which comes in many forms; we also know it as quality, longevity and justice. Human's moral conscience and assessment is one of the best exponents of the tendency to balance in behavior (A unique adaptation that makes integrity especially important)

Sustainability is finding the area where information doesn't have to change form due to friction or is returned to its original state, and life is a constant struggle between retaining the significant information and learning. There is a line where the loss of energy that cause the inflammation of soft tissue, brittle bones, arthritis and other signs of aging or even disease is reduced, which has to do with diet, weight and level of activity, too much sugar generates friction and not enough activity reduces the capacity to process energy for instance. This reactions end up generating progressive structural decay and morbid relationships.

There are more constants than variables in the universe, which is consistent with structural boundaries and the parameters that order and connect the information. This generates clusters of information that take on a more or less absolute value and define the systems. Agglutination acts as a spring board and produces energy pulsations due to capacity demand relationships, which probably makes life part of the general condition of the information, a reaction produced by the diminishing return and the need for balance which generates a pace. The structure determines a positive ratio in the transfer of energy with critical negative parameters, tension, temperature and boiling points.

Tension is the universal coagulator, friction causes the information bend in a kinetic contraction releasing energy. Capacity- demand dynamics manifests as a pulse around areas where certainty is shared to a certain degree correlating the mass. These cycles reflect the superlative pressure but are also connected to imperative cycles. This is consistent with the heart critically located about two thirds of the way up in the body, at that level the heart is linking everything to a predominant rhythm for optimal performance. This systems supersede others to form a new unit with more absolute value, like the electrical impulse and the planets orbits the proximal and distal demands are equally relevant. Other systems achieve more certainty and agglutinate around values that provides a wider range of motion, like human society.

Some phenomena just happen in the same relative areas generating similar patterns, but we are constantly suppressing pressure and moving between nodal points. Life reaches out only for consistency and grows when there is a qualitative development, where the relative tension is reduced in relation to a general performance. During each heartbeat, blood pressure varies between a maximum (systolic) and a minimum (diastolic) pressure, reflecting a general environmental demand and a capacity largely dictated by its own integrity. Pressure generates an expansion of the volume forcing information to be absorbed, when the polarization changes and the capacity and demand reverse trajectories the tension causes to release energy, generating more capacity if learning occurs or increasing the pressure. A qualitative change along this line might've started life itself when it internalized the instinct to curve the diminishing return, which also stablishes another cycle in the genders.

The tendency to balance generates a center of stability and critical boundaries, the capacity, or response time, is the result of these relationships. That is, the maximum amount of energy that can be invested within the ability to restore stability, concentric cycles that produce movement. This process creates multiple loops of information, complex relationships and priorities subject to a general tension, resulting in physical and emotional pain thresholds, nodal points and parameters of equilibrium reflective of stability. This makes the species only as strong as their weakest connection, combining several sources of energy generates more flexibility and capacity, becoming one of life's tendencies as is climbing the evolutionary latter tapping into more efficient and permanent cycles. But these are sensitive systems which take millions of years to evolve and when energy is introduced in unnatural ways whole ecosystems can be destroyed, balance is literally broken.

As you get away from any point in space in every direction the variables multiply exponentially and information loses meaning; one cause produces multiple effects and no permanent systems. Only in increments of about fifty percent we can produce enough certainty, and end up with eighty to ninety percent for minimum structural integrity. At a sub-atomic level the information can potentially spread every directions and it does not have an internal source of energy, so it starts from zero to infinite. Energy has to come from an external source which should generates two trajectories, a very short trajectory determine by the systems particles and a long trajectory determine by other universal constants. This negation takes place on a larger scale where the event is more predictable, and subject to a critical mass.

It's the formula leading to a single point that makes information take on a meaning and materialize, definition is stability and focus, generating context and the points of references, and turning symmetry into equilibrium. Antagonism is ambiguity, it blocks the information which breaks up and bounces back splitting in two first and in multiple pieces later, producing the expansion of the environment. Excessive antagonism is unsustainable, it nullifies, blocks and holds in place, and can produce catastrophic results. Everything would just collapse without circling around to release pressure. The need for precision and the unity of opposites produces the basic performance with the three points of contact, and the neutral area with space absolute value connected to the positive, the center of gravity that also creates the articulation to a larger system. This makes things generally unfold in three stages producing the universal dynamics, things that stay in one location with more absolute value, others that remain part of the environment only by alternating positions, and a more random movement or shuffling of information.

The cone of certainty and balance make precision the only way to incorporate information creating platforms and generating cycles and dualities; the dominant X containing over ninety nine percent of the information, and the recessive y for the flexibility, the population's gender then remains around fifty percent. This performance is the only way to exercise any concept of democracy, the consistency makes it close the cycle, the percentage is the manifest reciprocity, the result of the uniformity or symbiosis that makes it come around, versus polarization which displaces certainty up and down to the fratricidal individual producing the free radical, and sets it on the decadent spiral.

Agglutination is a numerical progression caused by the displacement of resource generating a demand and the gravity, a form of polarization. If pressure continues and the system cannot support the weight the polarization starts reversing, enters into a negative relationship with the environment and information start flowing mostly outwards. Concentrating efforts reduces the activity and generates volume slowing the system down, which translates into more certainty. The resulting structures determine the conductivity; less friction gives the system more capacity and allows it to grow, energy is more evenly spread out.

Matter is an area of condensation that pulls on the environment opposed by the larger systems tension. The center of gravity moves generating pressure on the structures forcing the performance to adjust and generating pressure. Mathematical relationships within the system give it a shape and ground it keeping it connected, which is why everything in the universe looks similar. It also keeps life connected to reality and produces selective systems and economic hierarchies, and potentially loss of balance and integrity when the "cord gets too short", or gravity becomes too strong, which is the result of extreme displacement of energy. Selective breeding can compensate for the environmental demand, stimulating movement and activity.

Gravity is the force generated by the pressure differential which is absorbed by the more flexible environment first. This causes tension variations that can make the smaller system spin faster, and can also generate magnetic fields, not unlike that of Earth, which happens because the pressures are generally pointing in two directions. The environmental demand or gravity is actually a degree of instability, a diminishing return that generates movement and must be cancelled, which is what causes the agglutination. The tendency to balance is the negation of the negation, the capacity-demand interaction produced by the antagonism, the relation between pressure and repulsion, and poses a natural limit on gravity, (although the atom reaches a vertical limit first). Because the atom has a positive gravity all subsequent systems do, there is only balance in relation to. This generates dynamics between systems of different densities; the environment attempts to equalize the tension while the smaller system tries to maintain its integrity. The forces are equal in all points of contact unless it is disturbed, and therefore if it has mass it has to be moving. This generates a tug-of- war where the mass determines the influence; cycles, approximation, loss of information, breaking up, etc…

Pressure is mass specific and particles bond accordingly, the atom is also a critical point in that process; mass of the nucleus gets relatively high but under this pressures the approximation of the environment doesn't compensate and its volume is not enough to generate stability, which creates the big negative differential and the electron emission. Electronic pulsations adjust the performance and the mass, although the atom retains a positive "gravity". In general as the mathematical relationships are stretched energy stabilizes the systems, this makes what we know as the "atomic clocks" vary with conditions. Electromagnetism expands the performance horizon further, and other circumstances like temperature and speed can cause the loss of integrity.

This is probably the reason for the immense amounts of energy concentrated in the atom; maximum energy is captured when the small atom is formed by pressures from the clusters of new starts. Because of the tendency to balance as mass increases the energy multiplies exponentially. The atom is a double duality convection point, an articulation. One relationship generates most of the mass from the proton and neutron which remain in relative balance with each other, and the other balances the energy link to a distal pressure. Those two relationships are also bound by balance, but as the mass increases so does the differential in reference to the volume, the pressure expanding the wall of the atom, creating a force field around the nucleus and the need for another electrons, which is most likely expelled from the proton, and would pulsate between near the nucleus and the outer wall generating tension, without a set trajectory probably. The capacity is expanded as the neutrons balance the mass until the maximum possible combination is reached within a margin of error. Just like tension thins out possibly causing contractions of the universe, or the volume, as the mass is reduced, on the other side, repulsion increases the volume when the mass increases overlapping the nucleus in the case of the atom and causing other phenomena like the event horizon in black holes.

A negative capacity-demand coefficient is the lack of mass that is pulled by the environment or consumes itself, a potential differential generally produced by the energy and space relationship, is more unstable, a positive charge has more mass and absorbs the information. Positive and negative are relative but have absolute manifestations, like electricity and magnetism. More repetition generates more contact and other proportions, two to one, three to one, twenty five percent, ten percent, and so on, which also means higher levels of tension, volume and mass need to expand or a meltdown can occur. Excess repetition produces a negative charge and information turns back into energy producing the contraction, a chain re-action of these dynamics can cause the environment to soar and the eventual explosion.

The atom makes a connection between the two worlds with the properties to bond and produce the elements, gasses, liquids, and solids are the result of the tension, and a capacity that generates different molecular tensions. This is the most important duality, the relationship between mass and energy, the mass differential generate the forces that define both which produces the tendency to balance; the astronomical mismatch allows the elements to re-stabilize without complete annihi-lation, and create permanent cycles. It is in the duality with matter that energy takes on its properties and vice versa; the ultimate mismatch that causes and absorbs all others. This in-teraction could be the reason for the possible expansions and contractions of the universe, which would affect tension and probabilities causing stability cycles.

The tendency to balance causes all-natural phenomena on earth, chemical reactions, temperature fluctuations and (ocean) currents that look to re-stabilize the balance. The bigger the discrepancy the bigger the amount of energy displaced and as the numbers approximate the systems slow down. Earth's own material is caught up in cycles set up by gravity between the core and the surface. But as greenhouse gasses and the disappearing ice caps even out the surface temperatures of the oceans some cycles, like ocean currents, are interrupted and others and other accelerated into the dynamics chain reaction, generating also pressures on all encompassing systems and compensating factors. For the earth's surface temperature to go up one degree the equivalent to millions of centigrade would have to be absorbed by the whole atmosphere.

Information shapes everything, it made the Colorado River carve the Grand Canyon. The canyon itself then contains information, a historical account of those forces that leads future waters, and any change in conditions alters the rivers behavior, the water's density, volume and intensity, the rocks properties and so on....These dynamics also shape all species, they convey information and the interaction keeps them on a path carved by evolution. They have a purpose, to anticipate the road that's being travelled before, always attempting to take the path of least resistance. Friction shapes the terrine and allows life to deal with pressure and generate an "image" of the environment.

Rationalizing the environment which means filling in its three-dimensional spaces and generating movement that is compatible with the environment. It projects into a future with an economic coefficient filling in the spaces and finding the refuges. For us this potential grows with cooperation slowing the acceleration and producing a better coefficient. Agglutination into larger platforms such as societies are part of a universal formula to reduce the deficit and enhance a performance, dynamics that generate many patterns and forms of collaboration. The universal constants and variables end up reflected in basic structures with functional degrees of flexibility and critical dew points, enough definition with the necessary range of motion, true for shape and behavior, and specialization without mutilation. Electricity produces an arc that is always the same and always different depending on environmental conditions, no unlike the properties of the visual structures. These are permanent patterns and a metric that is also true for human behavior, as a matter of fact it is a characteristic of the whole universe, mostly constants with some variables and two critical points; nothing can exist as an absolute or variable, a consistency that produces life and time. The information's relative relevance will give meaning to form and behavior.

Interconnectedness is the essence of everything including life. The Energy-Matter relationship is the foundation, the ability to generate energy from relatively small amounts of matter and reconstitute it, the tendency to balance fuels evolution, the need to meet the environmental demand, and genetic processes are the result of action reaction and the universal duality. Life is the product of stabilizing the capacity-demand equation and symbiosis is the only way to transfer information and distribute energy in sustainable cycles, from single organisms to societies and whole ecosystems practicing this economy is essential.

Sustaining life is the purpose, recognition and anticipation is the method. Life attempts to neutralize the liabilities and extract a "benefit" in the chain reaction of an interconnected universe. This generates a "know how", which becomes instincts and in humans a values system and culture, eventually certain clusters of information produce self-awareness.

Life agglutinates as a result of friction the tendency to balance in order to save energy and produce certainty. It displaces the resistance improving the energy-time ratio and extending the trajectory.

Cooperation is agglutination as part of the cone of certainty, increasing the numbers and providing more definition.

Sharing results nullifies variables improving the odds, expanding the time horizon and spreads the field.

Social Reciprocity is a specific form of sharing where the benefits of cooperation are maximized in a group. It is another form of cooperation.

Life anticipates cause and effect to better manage risk, produce an outcome and secure as much time as possible, which creates a general tendency to awareness in order of relevance (chemical reactions, energy sources, whether cycles, other life forms etc.), less evolved species anticipating fewer relationships. Being proactive defines life and generates a spectrum from inert to maximum perception, from minimum to greater ability to predict and control the inevitable. In this curve some things remain always constant and others present options that in turn affect the trajectory. Human society has a wider range of motion, ability to predict and affect the circumstances, but since precision requires focus it is always a constant struggle between the fixed and the flexible, saving energy and moving.

Humans were able to reach further as a result of a values system that becomes the filter and source of certainty; it conditions the expectation reducing the error and the liabilities, the traps and the viruses, the disruptive connection and undesirable information. It's the eyes and hands, additional precision is circumstantial. Real time discretion is the difference between grabbing and being grabbed, getting stuck on the environment and disambiguating the information. De-specialization is not lack of precision; we focused on cooperation and benefit from the best of both worlds, making us complicated and heavy individuals but very light and nimble in the group. The moral imperative reflects the biggest pattern of all, the energy bias, the relaxation and elongation of the information with the proportional capacity and super sensitivity, represents an expansion of the performance, understanding better, reaching across time and seeing beyond a barrier.

Most natural patterns of relevance to humanity develop relatively slow and humans are equipped to predict them in a large degree. That is because we are part of the information not just interpreting it. Human nature evolved as a result of an increased awareness of the same environment that produces the body, and in that sense absolute integrity of the information, connections and layers. We have come to understand most of the universe; we can predict weather and crop cycles, population growth and productivity potentials, and hurricane and tornado seasons. Undisturbed we could predict ninety nine percent of all natural patterns for the next thousand years and more, but we cannot anticipate one Wall Street day, or one year of the financial economy. All the species that survived for thousands of years and even millions have successfully predicted the environment. The ability to anticipate is life itself, which is why it needs a minimum level of stability to thrive. The more efficient it is at simplifying and ordering the information the better the result and clearer the picture, it generates a capacity and a potential.

A connection is also a bind, anticipation is a concession, a turn where something is left behind, focus is tension, hope is apprehension, a potential has to be positive, and stimulus is decay, a revelation is a memory, recognition is anticipation, and every action is a question. Displacing the ropes and holding the resources ransom is commoditization.

In Chinese culture the concept of yin yang is the notion that one can see a dynamic duality; male, female, active and passive, dark and light, forceful or yielding, in all things. How contrary forces are interconnected and interdependent in the natural world, and gives rise to each other in turn, opposites thus only exist in relation to each other.

Dialectical Materialism teaches about physical laws and universal dynamics like ossification, the significance of the relationships and quality of the information. It talks about historical development, a performance, opposing forces and the inherent decadence contained in every economic system as well as decadence and "fixed, fast frozen relations".

"Contrary to metaphysics, dialectics does not regard nature as an accidental agglomeration of things, of phenomena, unconnected with, isolated from, and independent of, each other, but as a connected and integral whole, in which things, phenomena are organically connected with, dependent on, and determined by, each other.

The dialectical method therefore holds that no phenomenon in nature can be understood if taken by itself, isolated from surrounding phenomena, inasmuch as any phenomenon in any realm of nature may become meaningless to us if it is not considered in connection with the surrounding conditions, but divorced from them; and that, vice versa, any phenomenon can be understood and explained if considered in its inseparable connection with surrounding phenomena, as one conditioned by surrounding phenomena.

Contrary to metaphysics, dialectics does not regard the process of development as a simple process of growth, where quantitative changes do not lead to qualitative changes, but as a development which passes from insignificant and imperceptible quantitative changes to open' fundamental changes' to qualitative changes; a development in which the qualitative changes occur not gradually, but rapidly and abruptly, taking the form of a leap from one state to another; they occur not accidentally but as the natural result of an accumulation of imperceptible and gradual quantitative changes.

The dialectical method therefore holds that the process of development should be understood not as movement in a circle, not as a simple repetition of what has already occurred, but as an onward and upward movement, as a transition from an old qualitative state to a new qualitative state, as a development from the simple to the complex, from the lower to the higher"

Dialectical materialism also proposes that every economic order grows to a state of maximum efficiency, while simultaneously developing internal contradictions and weaknesses that contribute to its systemic decay.

Man and The Evolution of Care

The mating system of the species was changing…were being replaced with something much more monogamous … "The habit acquired through the sexual division of labor had spread to other aspects of life. We had become compulsively good at sharing things, which had the new benefit of allowing each individual to specialize. It was this division of labor among specialists unique to our species that was the key to our ecological success, because it allowed the growth of technology - The Genome.

There were certain behaviors that provoked qualitative changes in our evolution and separated us from all other species. Compulsiveness to share and more "monogamous" behavior are the result of a unique specialization that separated us from all other species; it precedes man as it made us human. Self-preservation instincts where modified by the introduction of "empathy" as a practical adaptation, recognition of others basic needs as a function of our own survivor, giving us the advantage over the environmental demand. The original values system is the result of the disambiguation of time in the context of agglutination, a new event that establishes society as the species main survival mechanism and generated a new gravity center. Costumes and cultures contain a historical account of the human experience, but only remain consistent when the performance adjusts to reflect the human condition.

Organisms that take fewer steps to perform a task become more efficient and have an evolutionary advantage. They do this by detecting patterns in the environment and generating form and behavior, always attempting to find the most beneficial formula. Adding, over millions of years, pieces of tested genetic logic to a permanent structure, and eventually incorporating principles of order to an innate common sense that in man laid the foundation for language.

Cooperation or the concentration of simpler life forms into increasingly complex organisms turned out to be the most efficient way to survive, the performance is adjusted to the larger group and the energy-time ratio improves exponentially, generating certainty. These relationships produce life's tendency to agglutinate, highly specialized species as well as social ones are both the result of concentrating efforts, grouping and regrouping to achieve more balance. All societies are based on a level of cooperation; human society expresses this development in very specific ways, producing the areas of economic certainty and relaxation and preserving other relationships for political structures and hierarchies, with the resources implications. It is at the bottom the right simplification which generated the potential and complexity; an adaptation that opened up the possibilities to new variables and placed us on a natural growth trajectory.

"In an experiment set up to study human nature whenever people were asked to play a test game, they proved remarkably likely to try cooperation (it was attributed to irrationality and inexplicable niceness) – but in the late 1970's something rather disturbing began to happen, when Computers started using their cold, hard, rational brains to play, they began to do the same as those foolish, naïve human beings, to be irrational keen to cooperate" - The origins of Virtue –

The game was call "Tit for tat", it proved mathematically that cooperation and joining forces prevails over competition in the game of survival. It also attempted to find the answers to man's tendency to cooperate in reciprocity, a well-recognized behavior in primates where a favor is exchange for another one later from the same particular individual. But this kind of reciprocity always included exchanging food for sex, and friendship for protection and other benefits, and in humans, this instinct like many others was modified and the favor is not necessarily returned by the same individual always. Helping becomes part of a longer curve, sharing information in the context of more general expectations becomes an existential priority.

Reciprocity is the half-way point between two locations, the perfect cycle and the stability measure, but stability can only be found in the movement therefore takes on the shape of many cycles and complex structures. This provided the flexibility for economic hierarchies and idiosyncrasies that linked to the resources would cause a relative loss of energy limiting the species; it facilitated growth. Social reciprocity is the function of the new organism that produces the development of virtue and generates the capacity.

Reciprocity as part of the collective bargaining becomes social reciprocity, the feelings and emotions is how we perceive the new time continuum and what makes it work, the motivations generated by the energy relationships. Environmental pressures are reset to the new event validating the empathic resources and transcend time the only way possible; making the environment available everywhere and giving us the ability to regenerate, the capacity to recover the ambiguities and the common ground. It freed the species form the smaller event and the dead-end corners to become part of a larger ecosystem and reflect a more general condition of the information. The smaller variable can be easily replaced which yields the statistical advantage synthesizing energy, becoming indistinctive for all intents and proposes of the new certainty and reducing the environmental drag. In the context of a learning curve and technology no demand is ever above the performance, and every person becomes aggregated value as part of a negation.

It stimulated the development of "care", establishing a performance that defines the social environment, a political condition that provides a range of motion in the context of the empiric negation, allowing for the learning and providing the traction. Conditioning some relationships to the empathic event where they yield a better economic coefficient and others to the faster movement of a higher demand. In general, widening the stand and lowering the center of gravity.

Evolving from cooperation a platform remains better define as other relationships take on a value as part of a historical developments, which consists of needs and specialized structures that build the body out the awareness, giving us the capacity to recover time and "understand". Human's social deference and moral self-awareness are not antagonistic, in fact they are the result of the social evolution and part of one another, and can only exist in that connection.

It created a memory that could absorb the growth without the need for the restructuring caused by enrichment; the internal tension that forces the reduction of cost and contact or subverts the energy (focus). It achieved maximum possible certainty generating moral structures and the emotional articulations. A social performance dominated by values, with stimulus and motivations that provided context for the socio-economic activity, with the resistance reversing direction to reflect the empathic resources and the social expectations of the new body, the gratification pointing at giving and sharing.

"Care" is the negation of movement that allows us to move and consume, a manipulation of place and time and the process of ossification, what is rigid, soft and more fluid. An enhancement of the performance that allowed us to incorporate more information and absorb the fluctuations of a longer trajectory; like being young or old, tall or short, pregnant or nursing, sick and hurt, and many other unpredictable variables. It is the quantitative easing that generates the expectations that allow us to comprise the resources and produce the positive range of motion, and the most defining human function. The expansion of the time horizon generated assumptions that allow us to grow in the context of a cultural legacy, the sensitivities constitute a subconscious awareness of time and mathematical relationships. We developed a conscience that defines a path and asks the question; what are these feelings for?

As part of a general refocusing it is based on social reciprocity, redistributing the energy and sharing information in all directions which reflects the environmental demand also being displaced and similar. It reconciles many conflicts and antagonistic relationships, like the restrictive essence of the agglutination process itself, producing two areas that would complement each other and enhance a general capacity. A time window urged by the emanation of empathy resets the speed coefficient, setting up the virtualization of resources that produces the understanding and the panoramic view of the universe. Similar stabilizing mechanisms have been appreciated in nature, organs and floating bladders that get around structural limitation, but none as complex as human's moral negation, which reflects the energy projections of a single organisms that changes the way we count and multiply. We can internalize quantity as part of a larger time abstraction and reflect pressure in a much distant future.

Chimpanzees already start relaxing some of the hierarchy when sharing food to make sure all individuals eat, and isolated primitive human societies share up to ninety percent of all the meat the hunt, even cultures that haven had contact in thousands of years. Social reciprocity is the resetting to the larger organism giving us the longest reach and the most freedom of movement.

All societies have been formed through various mechanisms that facilitate agglutination process and guaranty order, such as the queen bee, the alpha couple or extremely patriarchal and matriarchal societies, etc. All elitist systems that usually involve extreme compromises in the reproductive system that force collaboration. A modification of procreation predispositions human empathy was eventually incorporated into our genetic blue print. It expanded from maternal instincts and generated monogamous behavior and the rest of the original values system. At the same time selective breeding is eliminated and equal reproductive responsibilities spread out to all individuals and a family nucleus evolves. The division of labor between man and woman is not found in any other primates though there were additional benefits in sharing the burden of survival further.

In general, the force that brings human society together is replaced by a new connection as the energy is spread more evenly adjusting the performance to promote the flow of the significant information and a social environment. This happened in a very small group of individuals, a bottle neck that causes humans to be genetically more similar than all other apes of the same species are to each other. When we see the obvious differences in appearance we can only see one single destiny, the numbers cannot work otherwise.

Women's reproductive cycles reflect human's unique requirements. Unlike most other species which procreate until near the end of their lives women reproduce for only half of theirs; reflecting the huge significance of a learning culture since nothing usually takes precedence over procreation. It provides the necessary time for nurture and education, determining society's age demographics and emotional composition with very profound socioeconomic ramifications. It guarantees the process of passing down knowledge and a balanced work force, establishing also an age hierarchy. In general, we reach our physical prime much earlier than a psychological or intellectual maturity, showing also the performance and shifting of the burden to society.

These are some the dynamics generated by agglutination and the transfer of responsibilities to a larger more efficient system, energy adjustment in exchange for a longer more secure existence, with the human bond being the coagulators. Men goes out of his way to help which can only make sense as a function of a superlative system, a different context and the only one where it become the shortest possible distance between point A and B, is the performance of the part that "sacrifices" certain things for the body. The smile for instance, which is a unique human characteristic, is the stabilizing calling of a new certainty, with the reassuring, invigorating, calming and soothing potential... little sacrifice, it at all, with incredible redeeming value. (When society takes the longest route for the sake of another entity it is sacrificing itself to its forces and trajectory)

Human's agglutination mechanism transformed the old self into a new species with unique adaptations to experience the surroundings, which is how the task is accomplished. The individual is shaped in function of a new and unique mating system, receptiveness to empathy and new ways of interacting that define the human condition. Obvious physical barriers like hair are lost, and facial expressions developed during retrofitting cycles of sensory transformations and emotional awareness that shaped the human body and the brain. The smile for instance, which is a unique human characteristic, is the stabilizing calling of a new certainty, with the reassuring, invigorating, calming and soothing potential.

The complexity brought about by society generated the exceptional expansion of the brain and stimulated the abstract thought that allows us to communicate, but it needs language to express the potential and exercise the condition, the tools and the vocabulary. There is a direct correlation between the size of the brain in land mammals and their societies; in fact, the number of relationships is mathematically predictable, human have the largest relative brain capable of recognizing over 250 individuals. In addition, the emotions are contained for the most part in the frontal lobe where the decision making and rational thought take place, and there is proof that damage to this area and the reduction of emotions in general produces irrational behavior.

Specialization comes with attachment to specific resources and other restrictions, by specializing in cooperation humans are able to get around the inevitable focusing attached to evolution and achieve actual de-specialization, as well as the flexibility to solve conflict that limit other species. Man then gets maximum benefit from both cooperation and the ability to specialize on a cultural level. But this is not a unique concept in nature; humans were just able to reproduce some of the same attributes of the stem cell within the proportions of a longer learning curve; Stem Cell research is based on the fact that cells in embryonic state are generally de-specialized and when placed in a specific environment can learn to perform different function.

The lack of selective breeding is a result of the extraordinary efficiency of this system; mating is based on other mechanisms that included a more distinctive individual. Sexual dimorphism starts disappearing with selective breeding and the processes that generate constant reproductive changes are suppressed or turned off. It produces a little bit of a hybrid, extremely social being with great awareness and range of motion, reflecting the displacement of the variables, speed and the movement.

The SRY gene, which is related to masculinization, is one of the fastest evolving and active ones, but in the human race it is a variation free gene, there are virtually no point mutations since the last common ancestor of people 200,000 years ago, and there is ten times more variation between humans and other apes as it is typical for other genes. In addition, there was between 500 and 200 hundred thousand years ego an unusual high number of mutations in a gene called SLC2A1 which builds proteins for transporting glucose from blood vessels into cells, vital to the brains wellbeing, in humans there are about 2.5 to 3 times as many copies of this gene as there are in chimp's brains. At the same time the gene for the glucose transporter in the muscles called SIC2A4 also underwent natural selection but in the opposite direction; human's muscles contain fewer glucose transporters than chimp's.

Not coincidentally the human brain took on its current form and size about 200.000 years ago when Homo sapiens emerged. Women's immune system in the womb also restricts the masculinization of the brain by a series of genes in the Y chromosome, but not that of the reproductive organs. In addition, scientists have found that the whole assault on the Y chromosome and aggression in general intensifies with each pregnancy, and that it might extend to the nursing period. Furthermore, the levels of testosterone have be linked to the economic activity, cultural development and population, hunter gatherer societies and agriculture, proving the humbling effects of the socialization process, the retroactive nature of the system and unique relationship with technology. While there is a manifest destiny the interaction with the environment determines some of the movement.

There is proof that a process known as Sexual Antagonism slows down the introduction of fresh genetic material,
variations and mutation through a sort of evolutionary trial
and error known as Genetic Sweeping, and that the more social the species becomes the more likely this antagonism is to
show up. Ninety seven percent of the human genome, which
has been described as "Selfish DNA" or "Junk DNA", is probably the result of this process. The genders secondary function,
replacing the genetic material that is constantly eliminated
through selective breeding, is largely replaced with genetic
shuffling, transferring a good portion of the ability to adapt to
a single organism. This means the responsibility of specialization goes to the culture and the socioeconomic infrastructure
depend on education, making seniority a corner stone of the
evolution, in fact defining the moral structures.

This could be the reason for the very existence of the genders. It is itself a mechanism that generates movement and
guarantees genetic variety, extending the curve and creating
also a control in the sexual antagonism, which eventually reduces the Y chromosome to extreme levels due to the need for
precision. This need is so strong it further favors one side of
what's already an extremely well adapted body generating the
right or left-hand bias.

Genetic predisposition and processes that take place
during the gestation period are geared to eliminating the old
selfish and aggressive tendencies as well; human culture can
only be the third phase of that process rather than oppose it.
"Junk DNA" which is more likely to be a filter of information
rather than useless historical data, if not the information would
be tested over and over. What doesn't work is as important
as what does; we are defined as much by what we are not as
what we are, what we negate or turn away from. It is also safe
to assume at this point that social structures guaranteed access

to food and other resources since this is usually determined by the species reproductive needs.

All species calibrate the three-dimensional world around them and balance capacity with possibilities through experience; depth perception, range of motion and speed. They fill in particular measurements into hard wired evolutionary adaptations, genetic formulas that approximate the information to the limits of the specialization and calibrate only the variables, allowing them to make instinctive risk and efficiency assessments but they are always caught between the restriction and the need to be better. In humans these abilities are transferred to the social context and turned into a moral intuition that is connected to an emotional structure and constitutes the center piece of man's social brain.

The emotional spectrum evolved to reflect human empathy as part of the new social dimension. This form of communication developed from behaviors previously preserved for procreation as a result of the need to coexist. Eventually instinctive reactions were transformed into behavior directed at group cohesiveness and reducing tension which produced a new compulsive need for the group. As the values system emerges it suppresses most instinctive behaviors transforming them into strong suggestions, somewhat insulated from the compulsive animal instinct, allowing for patterns that develop over longer periods of time to produce more deliberate behavior. This should also have influenced the evolution of the intellect and emotional outlets unique to humans, like laughing and crying.

It generated a pause that facilitated the expansion of awareness and the transition from subconscious to conscious behavior, a social conscience that requires calibration to the group, reflective of cultural idiosyncrasies and more general expectations. As a function of certainty and the evolution of responsibly it becomes a sort of echolocation system, generating an image of the environment and the significant information. The emotional system retained behavior conditioning properties while creating the capacity to process more complex information, remains strongly connected to the heart and other bodily functions, reflecting its priority status. We acquire more control over our actions within the context of a code of conduct and a moral system that seeks balance and defines the human condition, become more proactive in every sense of the word, able to articulate our spaces and comprise the resources more efficiently.

The moral assessment is the element that enabled the process of narrowing down the search while remaining in a "quality" environment. In essence prioritizing group cohesiveness and conditioning the relationships to the motivation allowing for the fusion of an emerging intellect. Empathy defines human nature and is our evolutionary solution the antagonistic essence of agglutination and the need for growth, allowing us to maximize the resources. It also reflects cooperation prevailing over competition defining a path and a very long trajectory.

A new form of communication is incorporated into our DNA as part of a new awareness and a social condition. Scientists have discovered proof of the innateness of language skills, a universal human grammar of comparable complexity even in people isolated from civilization since the Stone Ages. It has been located and identified as the "language gene", we are born with this capacity but most of the connections are made during childhood and development years. The language structure is part of the same evolution that generated the moral articulations that allow us to confine the moment and express the predisposition of the time continuum maximizing the resources.

This unique adaptation is essential to human evolution. All life forms reinforce essential behaviors through repetition, they home in their skills or evolutionary advantages to produce stability. This is even more important for humans who have more capacity to rewire and program the sensitivities to changing expectations. Language is part of a general intuition that allows us to restructure and organize information. We are able to fill in missing pieces to a greater extent due to the expansion of the time horizon and the imagination. It also allows us the ability to think, appreciate music and the arts in general.

The increased dependency on culture is the result of extreme de-specialization, which makes the values system also introspect and part of the social development, modified through the years and experience. Like the ability to speak it is a logical structure that needs the points of reference and readjustment of time to be completed. Through this system we incorporated information and generate behavior to simplify the answer whenever possible. We also form opinions, make decisions and develop concept that reflect our values.

This process is an evolutionary imperative; it is how we focus and refined the tools we use, how we adapt which is obviously an incredible advantage. It is also bound by structure well defined sense of direction and priorities. It is all around us, precision and strength, energy and function, freedom and regulations, being selective with the information which is indispensable to obtain a result. This can take on the form of selective breeding which in humans is replaced by the moral imperative. Specialization and cooperation reflect the universal tendency to beat the variables and the environmental demand, a disproportionate approach makes the performance suffer.

Under normal conditions focus reduces and places a time limit on the energy demand not on us; the right tool or a better designed one wastes less energy, and too much strength affects precision adversely (the adaptation or specialization). They are inversely proportional and in either case we don't get the right results, or answer. Like in all other social species as a result of the mutual evolution genetic predispositions determine social composition and structural boundaries, procreation, hunger and other risk and self-preservation needs are hard wired because they are uncompromising when it comes to survival. Although in humans' education shares almost equal time with procreation.

The ability to relate to suffering and the context provided by a new concept of time made us self-aware. The introspect nature of the "search" gives us a conscience, and an emerging intellect furthers our understanding of the universe. From this point on the species awareness is linked to a social evolution and a learning process. It slowed down the pace of life as the horizon of certainty expanded optimizing our capacity to capture the patterns within.

Human Empathy brought about a unique awareness that made man more efficient. This improved ability to solve problem created a protective environment to which we gravitate, a self-preservation instinct that holds it together. It changed competition into cooperation and displaced the pressures of survival of the fittest, transforming the environmental demand into reasonable expectations. In bringing more certainty to life it also provided more capacity to benefit from "trial and error" and relative freedom from the perpetual search for food and shelter, allowing time for the development of culture and making a learning imperative. It mitigated dependencies on more dynamic conditions and readjusted the species energy needs, also increasing the life expectancy. It reduced the environmental demand keeping us on the path of the never-ending quest for the most efficient ways to relate to the environment.

It is this evolutionary emancipation that allows men to specialize on activities others than food production and safety; supporting roles such as education and infrastructure which become paramount to survival, and eventually others that generated the need to trade. The fact that humans can dedicate fewer individuals than any other society to basic functions is a reflection of success not a vulnerability, and it's only made possible by the capacity to share and ability to allocate resources.

This process constitutes a substantial transfer of recognition and anticipation in terms of the species evolution from the individual to the group, a much more efficient organism. Society can manage millions of times the information and comprise a wisdom unavailable to a person, building platforms from which the specialist benefits and contributes to and making the return always greater for the species. The energy relationship is adjusted to the new unit yielding time to all the parts, the social structures and connections that ensue are restricted by these boundaries, guaranteed by the moral negation and the values system, its social reflection.

Human society is held together by structures and internal dynamics that keep it in balance with the larger environment. Cooperation and the need for recognition are the yin and yang, the same process that gives us the evolutionary equality makes us distinct individual, the moral assessment also brings about a quality of life, the affections and love generate expectations and pain, understanding is linked to the values and the social to the private, they define each other and produce the quality. Society creates the "new self" which cannot exist without society. They are not antagonistic or inconsistent; in fact, they are in specific evolutionary relationships and interactive, inseparable and only defined in reference to each other, and when isolated they become dysfunctional.

Growth and Culture

- Morality resides in the senses as a purposive set of instincts – The Origins of Virtue.

Life is part of the environment, it is organized information and its main purpose is learning and becoming a permanent cycle itself. It flows through many channels and takes on millions of forms, and in humans, a highly evolved social species, some of it becomes a "know how" shared and pass down through social structures as much as genetic ones.

The values system solves problems before we fully understand the all relationships, but it doesn't work either without strong traditions. The process that is used to extract the essence of all knowledge continues and generates the culture, therefore the institutions are not question too much. We are programmed to trust the social environment and assume some details get lost over time or remain hidden, incorporating the meaning as part of a larger legacy. It becomes an extension of human nature, a social genetics of sorts that is rounded up by specialization, and a vehicle that allows man to transcend to geography and other differences.

It created a universal system where focus is turned into learning and empiric reductions that can take hold anywhere, with the relative energy loss involved with a more interactive system. Culture is the recombination social relationships and conjugation of time. Uniformity is nature's goal and what generates the potential, virtue is expressed in the tolerance defining certainty and pain thresholds. It is projecting the resource into the future and defining efficiency.

De-specialization and equal reproductive responsibilities set us up for growth; they are the equalizers that gave us the ability to multiply and repeat the same formulas on a social scale, reorganize and restructure to produce the potential, indeed putting evolution in our hands. Socio-economic growth though involves the same principles of movement, the ambiguities have to be resolved and concentrated in areas that generate traction improving the ability to synthesize energy, following also a learning curve where they materialize into a function.

New methods and technologies can enhance our capacity helping us restructure, but they can change the frequency of certain patterns, and therefore application is very important. They can affect critical-mass and displace certainty generating the empirical pressures and an environmental reaction; working immediately on the spaces and elasticity, on the natural rhythm. They can become the focal point and generate a contraction reversing essential capacity-demand dynamics, stretching the environment and making the demand rise as they improve their own capacity, increase repetitions and raise the temperature. On the other hand growth can generate tensions, on both sides balance is lost and a qualitative change becomes increasingly less likely.

A real qualitative transformation displaces energy and the fluctuations to more specific areas reducing them and securing an advantage, developing the flexibility to deal with specific levels of uncertainty. It generates new variables as it reduces the general repetition trigger making room, opening spaces, and the patterns then repeat more often, it creates uniformity and the antithesis of change at the same time, it creates certainty. When it finds stability it locks down, if it doesn't the general cycles between movement and definition, variables and uniformity, closing and opening continue transforming the information, and with a tendency to fall back on the last reliable platform, or universal context, which could mean regressing or decomposing under the right conditions. Without relative stability nature pushes for balance with absolute disregard, the general tendencies take over and continue displacing energy.

This is the general process of enrichment and how life seg-
regates the information generating the connections and con-
tacts with the appropriate degree of intensity and repetition;
trading information and simplifying. The systems caught in
between produce economic hierarchies and selective breeding;
they are a protrusion in the environment with a time differential matching that of a relative loss of energy, and can become more or less permanent depending on the acceleration,
it must sustain a minimum level of integrity. It is adapting to
the pressures which generates the shapes with increasingly less
fluctuations towards a center left behind, which also means
that this areas are increasingly localized the more developed
the system, become part of more specific functions, they have
a relative significance with resources expectations.

It is all about energy, too much or not enough can change
the dynamics and the content of the information. Enrichment
is holding or securing a location, positive enrichment produces
a potential rather than restrain dynamics. Agglutination requires a reduction of the spaces that can affect the species,
which must again center on a smaller area of repetition, a phenomenon that could cause a form of "autism", an over abbre-
viation that displaces pressure to other functions attempting to
generate uniformity. It needs to retain a level of connectivity
that for the culture mostly means technology and socioeconomic relationships. In nature energy-time parameters determine density and force a constant reduction, which is what
makes life agglutinate to find balance.

The general tendencies are increased agitation, strata
formation and real simplification, more uniformity which
is a form of specialization. This produces the segregation of
functions; generally the variables are gradually displaced outwards to the next level reducing friction and generating the
efficiency, which requires a degree of compatibility. When the

system cannot settle the tension differentials it continues alternating between reducing the individual parts and expanding a volume searching for balance...pressure continues to produce energy starvation, distortion and interference. In other words our common denominator is not necessarily that of nature, which causes the abnormal development, instead of certain spaces or socio economic relationships determining the performance they are mostly just responding to the environment, which is responding to other factors. Similarly as long as we are developing nature would look to generalize more, a process that runs into money.

Uniformity is relative and marks the end of a cycle, it doesn't recognize a level only balance in reference to; equal parts, focus and gravity. Generally energy circulates more evenly but it doesn't care about the capacity of the parts, it doesn't stop transforming the information until balance is found. If it is not it is the end of that development. A form of antagonism shows up in the sacrifice of the parts for the whole when it does not respond to specific priorities, man is diminished and the culture breaks down, at that point society is not working for the species anymore. It stopped being the solution and we get caught in the negative chain reaction to another point of precision.

Density and size of the population determine the characteristics of all species and vice versa, from smaller groups to very large concentrations there are very distinct patterns, and it has all to do with how they relate to food and the resources. Density eventually undermines the expansion of the capacity attached to socialization, so human evolution is like a needle in a haystack, the common denominator that would stimulated the expansion of the brain, man and society itself, no more and no less; the development of virtue and a moral imperative grounding the capacity-demand connection. For humans, quantity is an environment and socioeconomic relationships, a condition that needs nourishment. For us more uniformity is also education and socioeconomic development, without either one it will take on other forms and cannot generate the quality. It cannot produce the content and potential that keep us disambiguating growth. We are on a "get smart" trajectory as part of the consolidation of a larger more permanent ecosystem that adjusts the energy.

The statistical balance can lead to maximum use of resource and transparency, the right structures and a social curb, the perfect order in agglutination which is only achievable on that scale and through the energy bias, the right articulations and the relaxation which determining the distance between point A and B. Otherwise it requires more uniformity and either a super intelligence or extreme specialization; a role we have filled with technology which when well applied complements our de-specialized condition. The natural enrichment generates a capacity and forces a development and a refocusing and often a change in paradigm. As it balances the equation environment becomes more stable, which usually requires certain also certain elasticity. If there is too much enrichment the distortion of energy defeats the purpose, it actually becomes a more dense and heavy element.

Economic hierarchies are mathematical equations that have not been or cannot be simplified further, with the proportional deficiency and rate of decadence. In general, increasing repetitions overheats the environment and reducing them relaxes it and eventually also breaks the connection. Information is only aggregated for balance, the enrichment of socioeconomic relationships works the same way, platforms where the information coming in is brought to minimum certainty and the information going out is the result of the function, supported by free exchange only in that context. The permanent record becomes part of the cultural traditions and institutional wisdom where the significant information transcend time, and the rest becomes more recessive and circumstantial, void and null, or inactive. Like the telescope the better we are at segregating the information and focusing the greater the potential, rationalizing, categorizing, grouping and simplifying. Information is usually processed by "historical currencies" that produce a positive return determining what is beneficial and negative, what remains and what is dismissed and what remains, what is transformed and functional.

Humanity has followed a growth trajectory with technology helping synthesize energy and acting as a catalyst and agglutinating factor at the same time. De-specialization forced us to think, and from that point on the integrity of this relationship was essential to our own. Technology's trajectory though is only generally connected to that of man. It is subject to a social development and other circumstances that can generate pressure if the right parameters are not understood and the function is not defined by the right development, by a performance that generate the potential. It always had limitations and very obvious impact on society which could then make the adjustments, the line between the damages and distortions seem to have been more discernable at some point. The repetition required by precision can generate a capacity, but also the displacement of energy and negate the spaces, moving in the opposite direction of our own growth.

Today is not so apparent but the boundaries still exist where certainty is displaced, and the technology becomes alienating. It has a tendency to continue constricting the event, although it should become increasingly less transcendental as part of the empiric generalizations, generating the exponential growth, which depend on default values, like the body to the arm to the hand. It has done the opposite; a different technology affects the most intimate moment and breaks down an economy on a molecular level, not showing the social repercussions for a long time.

Technology is, after all, a manipulation of size and proportions, an accelerant, speed increases as the duration of the event decreases and the relationship with energy and resources start reversing until the capacity and demand cross path responding to distal performances, causing the temporal disturbance. The energy relationship and a level of stability with society and the environment makes it a support point, a spring board, hub, or step, or a sink hole, a positive point of reference or a question. It only works when we simplify the information as part of a natural ossification process and organic relationships, getting what you need and otherwise corrupting the whole system. It reflects the connections' duality, capacity and resistance, supporting beams and weight. They are themselves a concentration of information, a short cut and manipulation of focus which is what allows it to multiply the energy; they improve their certainty and reduce the environment's, which means time.

It needs controlling just like the enzymes in our bodies, they translate information and transport energy, help in bonding and break down information, restore and have by-products, and don't always have to produce certainty sometimes we just need the energy. They are all repetition points but there is a gradual loss and decline that makes precision indispensable. Oversimplification in general can cause obstruction of functions and development, and the cultural dimorphism, we can't either withhold or deregulate technology.

From the beginning we contributed to our growth through a series of discoveries, we needed the tools to specialize and in the process stimulate our own social development. Along those lines it would seem that technology could expedite trade as the activity increased and more variables appeared, which is where money finds its niche. An empty pseudo-technology with no energy or time limitation that could speed up the process, but also reduce everything to a transactional equation, with the destructive power that entails. Money creates the short cut and closes the focus squeezing energy out of everything it touches, similar to the chain reaction caused by technology where the negative ratio changes our expectations which in turn pushes the technology.

In general a faster repetition point can create the wormhole and suck the energy out of the environment. It becomes the platform rather than working off another platform, and the variable becomes the standard. It produces the instant gratification syndrome which is a reversal of roles and the contraction rather than the simplification, the nominal minimization that shots the door on progress. Social development like agglutination requires a redefinition of spaces (we sometimes call civilization) which should evolve from old parameter set by the values system but that were not completely defined before. Technology contributes to generating room for growth only when it is at the service of society.

The idea is they go faster and we keep the pace, they suffer the erosion we don't, but we could not grow healthy without the development of technology or in its absence. As part of the algorithm it is supposed to gain more definition and capacity as trade whines down with the variables, changing form. This process is always going to be limited by the de-specialization that generates it, the compromise in the flexibility versus predetermined and simpler genetic functions.

Anticipating is the essence of life, in the measure we lose control of the circumstances the chances of survival decrease. Restructuring is made easier by virtue and human evolution, the ability to predict and get ahead of the curb actually paving the way. As circumstances take control the options are reduced to simple more drastic solutions that have the potential to destroy society, and although they justify themselves they are not necessary related to an inevitable trajectory, but rather lack of recognition and anticipation, picking up the pattern. Life loses interest with degree of uncertainty avoiding being pulled into the unknown or stretched too thin, but also has to incorporate information to reduce friction.

De-specialization meant we had more choices and became more proactive and deliberate, which distinguished us from all other species; our destiny was more in our hands since. Certainty became relative to an intuition and grounded by a values system, extending proportionally the awareness that is linked to a social development that allows us to synthesize more energy, a capacity that can also expands as the information becomes more difficult. These parameters are relative to the resources available and the effort put forth; dynamics are not much different than those of the brain and the learning curve. The values system and a moral imperative expressed the dynamic potential of what is possible which allowed us to venture into every corner of the world.

An increasing awareness is also part of the performance adjustment in human socialization and a learning curve that helps maximize our potential and forces us to find the ideal social environment. Redefine the spaces involved in the human condition as part of the exponential growth and empiric reductions, the energy adjustment that demands restructuring and our ability to affect the circumstances that in turn can change us. Where are these conflicts and natural friction triggers and that force the focus to shift or the structure to weaken and crumble? Where is the definition that slowly turns into repeating patterns generating certainty and facilitating actual growth, where the flexibility is not tested and our essence changed?

We once solved the problem through despecialization and a dual performance, maximum flexibility to absorb the environmental fluctuations and protect the integrity of other mechanisms. This had to both generate a very high tolerance and establish the boundaries for the process of cultural specialization and ossification. It requires resources and efforts to train and develop skills, and educate a person, more time to displace the energy properly. It requires a movement that become too protracted for the individual and only society can produce, a restructuring that takes place from the bottom up as much as from the top down and defines the resistance.

The same flexibility that promotes the growth creates the human event with the individual variable, therefore the universal tendency to trade the muscles for intelligence, space and quantity, have to be limited by the human condition. In other words the organism has a capacity to process x amount of information and potential for enrichment, and needs to spread out in the measure it depends on trade and more activity to deal with friction and difficulty. Agglutination is the transfer of energy to a much more efficient system; a collective intelligence which is contained in the values system, which potential we haven't discovered.

In general the enrichment that generate the efficiency is bound by a historical development that curbs the performance producing the potential. The complexity of the human condition suggests that the simplification process has to be limited by the evolution of language. even though uniformity makes everything more efficient in absolute terms. For instance, any species is a variable as part of an ecosystem that defines what is functional. It has to be a true common denominator but the closest to a minimum denominator the more efficient it becomes, which reflects also the dynamics involved with the learning process. Going up can only mean going to basics and enhancing the foundation, it generates maximum definition for that specific system, making everything else a distortion.

Enrichment generates a capacity and forces a refocusing, it produces platforms and eventually shuffling of information. The balance is then in the access and free exchange of the significant information, and the variables supported by the evolution. We constantly move between environments generated by parameters established by a more general one, which is always attempting to absorb the information and make it more uniform, like gravity, becoming saturated and with more absolute value eventually. Despecialization produced a fluid environment transforming the areas that have a tendency to fold under pressure generating a spectrum or strata, generating in man a performance that only has meaning in the context of human empathy.

Men put a lot of stock on movement and the diversity that produces the ecological success, but an increased predictability must match the growth as the recombination of values takes place reducing the movement. Recovering time on a social scale would produce the necessary adjustments but should also run into the boundaries that force the restructuring and sometimes multiplication. The occasional qualitative step opens the possibilities to new variables, but the waters always have to calm down, a capacity and demand that should be marching in unison.

The question remains what are the effects of the environmental pressures on the species collective trajectory? The answer is we were built for multiple environments and many levels of cooperation and a predisposition for growth, and that generally socioeconomic hierarchies could extend or cut short a trajectory depending on other dynamics, that all systems tend to come around full circle to a place of stability and that we are not exempt from these laws. So how much is too much, and can we produce the transformative development without a drastic assault of the human condition, are we there in that other generalization?

We started with a dual performance and an advantage, the consistency and the flexibility. The essence of the problem is the evolutionary predispositions that shape the human condition come from de-specialization with the inefficiencies of the universal system. They are all connected and through the learning and specialization process which generates a relatively high breaking point. The good news is much of it is cultural and when the expectations are adjusted the flexibility is just right, similarly the expectations that shape our condition and emotional make up are affected by the movement.

We can only make society more uniform in the context of language and the "false labor" that produces man to begin with, no more than we can eliminate diversity or the need for education, particular talents and vocations, they are in relationships and affect one another, the cultural component that resumes generating a potential, the final connections and attachment. True growth happens through the exercise of purpose in the social structure, more certainty is always relative because is in the quality and redefines quality. The cause comes from evolution, and since it is a form of kinetic development it has a tendency to replace other patterns, therefore preserving essential human qualities becomes imperative. It's all about the things that are uncompromising and the ones that can move and then how much do you really want to change those, it is all about the feedback and the expectations, finding out what the order and symmetry that generates the capacity mean to society. At some point is we have to ask are we producing more certainty or are we just stretching?

Human's advantage was harnessing the kinetic contraction though, and turning it into the evolution of cooperation and equality, in other words real time assessment without other preconceived limitations. The prevailing development is de-specialization which generated the absolute and relative values and capacity to grow. Care and virtue are the yin and yang, not exclusive, not antagonistic; they gave rise and exist in reference to each other. It found and defined a common de-nominator and the equation cannot be reduced further while obtaining the right answer. It's the evolutionary memory and the cultural development, the emotional awareness binds the species and the intellectual capacity generates a contribution that only has value in the social context. Unfortunately the long reach and strong grip also made us vulnerable to a very fast chain reaction and abnormal development taking advantage of strong sensitivities and a cultural essence.

The concentration of efforts is ultimately the stabilizing potential that forces us to find new patterns, specifically those that apply to the human condition, as well as the general tendency to scale down the activity and spread the horizon, the structural boundaries. Agglutination has a trajectory improving the energy-time coefficient until it reaches a point of optimal performance, and then friction starts undermining the purpose and the environmental demand begins to rise. The capacity for enrichment is limited and at some point the activity generates pressure, the pace accelerates causing the system to expand displacing energy and bouncing back out, reflecting the end of the cycle.

Things grow but tend to go back to the single point where everything starts from as a result of the energy fluctuations, contracting and relaxing, in and out, between enrichment and reduction. This creates articulations, determines proportions, size and reach, generating the leverage and flexibility, but also become rigid and dysfunctional under extreme conditions. Economic hierarchies are a form of environmental enrichment and a lockdown of movement and the learning process, a sign of inefficiency, when the restructuring or qualitative transformation needed for more stability is not occurring, information is blocked or there is too much friction. The system cannot return to an internal state of symbiosis because the need to maintain a precarious balance with the environment. It is itself a level of decay that requires constant new information constantly, a test of the elasticity and an inflammation of the tissue. The energy eye opens to absorb more information, it could settle back down but continues to increase with pressure, eventually the cycle brakes and a passage or tunnel opens and information starts flowing in the opposite direction.

In the degree the economic hierarchies develop and the system gets more inverted learning becomes more difficult and the information moves faster consuming more energy. But this also means that they are a conditions of materialization and stages of evolution which life can only eradicate mathematically at the social level. These relationships set the stage and the options, drastic transformation of the information, shuffling (holding your position) and somewhere in between, ways to solve the antagonism.

Nature's solution is always maximum reduction, but life uses a combination to find balance since it needs more energy, and we find it everywhere in that spectrum, as well as some extreme adaptations around the edges. Improving the performance can generate more energy and on the flip side energy can help improve the performance, but it generates a demand. This generally keeps life simplifying and restructuring to compensate for the resistance, using more energy only as a last resort. These dynamics generate the tendency to the essentials and bring us back to cooperation among specialist, which is part of the re-measuring involved with agglutination, a redefinition by definition. As a matter of fact it is just a universal formula that humans take to the next level.

It is agglutination again and again to create a more efficient coherent system, parts joining for mutual benefit and an easier to meet stability target. In survival of the fittest the purpose is fitness not competition itself, a reduction of the variables in a given direction. Competition for survival accomplishes that but also reduces population in the process, which is a liability. So evolution walks a tight balance between fitness and numbers and produces a spectrum with all possible combinations. As some species move to cooperation competition takes on other forms. Highly specialized forms of cooperation, like in some insect species, displaces competition through the distribution of labor but also restrict the movement through some other form of procreation, like a queen bee for instance. Humans take it a little further and displace some other functions to culture and traditions, education and social structures giving us a better chance.

Human evolution solved the problem transforming the empiric reduction into the ability to learn and specialize, an expansion of "awareness" and an awakening of the species that is in a big part the code of conduct itself. Man was able to simplify and become more complex at the same time avoiding the limitations of extreme specialization by concentrating in the process itself and developing a strong bond in the place of rather restrictive functions. This freed the main adaptation for maximum definition, which is the objective, and still allowed man to specialize on other goals. A socio-economic system would have to reflect such structure, specifically the fusion of heart and mind, the flexibility of the coagulation around the ability to care and the consistency of tradition and respect it demanded, the moral discretion and values that justifies the affections.

Once again, the target is determined by the answer to the environmental demand, but this time with a sense of purpose and direction. We have a series of priorities that share our attention and have emotional and socio-economic implications, they are relatively flexible and the results come from the combination, they are points of references and triangulation, and require equal tension to be stable or in focus, that means a relative significance attached back from the source. These are the proportions and context of our lives, the spaces in our relationships. Men then has the ability to re-focus in one or even several areas more or less intensively for shorter or longer periods of time, which like training could become second nature and, in some cases, even tradition. Intensive focusing looks for higher performance and like a muscle contraction is time sensitive and supposed to re-stabilize a system, solve a problem or capture a moment.

Growth as part of the natural trajectory reduces stress, which means less relative energy consumption and more security. The variables have been reduced by an evolutionary trajectory but the scope opened up when we de-specialized to give us more range of motion, capture the useful information and dismiss the rest. It's the head lights and the road, background and focus for a clear picture. Certain dynamics therefore in human society are inherently contained in a performance which reflects the degree of difficulty. It mirrors the universe, meets a "demand" and connects the dots.

It creates dualities and sets the pace; focus and tension, resistance and bond, difficulty and stress are the same. The efficiency produced by reciprocity sustains reciprocity and the lack thereof generates competition and a refocus that could produce a reduction of the awareness. Extreme pressure causes repetition to concentrate in undesirable places restricting our function and the areas of uniformity that have already been defined, therefore humans as we know them stop being the common denominator and the maximum repetition point.

When the priorities drift away from evolutionary assumptions for any reason (usually having to do with resource) so does the center of gravity and a system develops with its own common denominators, areas of repetition and uniformity, and ultimate trajectory and destiny which now connect us to the universe. We become part of a new system and caught up in a less permanent condition subject the transformation that it might require as the best possible options. This looks exactly like the natural trajectory because it is the natural process. It's the environmental tug and traction of a larger event because there can be no absolute rupture due to inefficiency, although it is a departure for us. The difference is maintaining the integrity, the emphasis on the adaptations to remain more or less in a zone during our development which keeps us on a human curve, the object of repetition and the constant.

The essence of Tai Chi is practicing a balance protecting virtual and physical spaces and a form that is not impervious to change and the environment's influence. It is sending a signal through repetition validating the human condition and a capacity that due to despecialization needs more exercise. Generally what is not practiced tends to atrophy. The concept of the taiji, supreme ultimate, in contrast with wuji, without ultimate, appears in both Taoist and Confucian Chinese philosophy, where it represents the fusion of Yin and Yang into a single ultimate, represented by the taijitu symbol. T'ai chi ch'uan theory and practice evolved in agreement with many Chinese philosophical principles, including those of Taoism and Confucianism.

Humans like everything else are bound by structural parameters, compulsiveness to share and social reciprocity set us up for growth at the same time that transcending specialization created the capacity to sustain balance in the context of a learning curve. It generated a larger tolerance area, a wider "stability band" that

is part of a general potential and the universal connection necessary for recognition and anticipation. Growth is an adaptation
anticipated by evolution that coexists with other necessities, it is
procreation to nutrition, education, research and investigation,
technology, etc. These are actually energy cycles that feed of each
other and can produce the expansion determining each other's
environmental demand and a stability area.

Morality and human concepts such as pride, dignity and
respect have an original function related to structural integrity and allocation of resources. They are human's molecular
tension; the interaction, the balance, common denominator
and bonding capacity. It is the substance to the negation that
in conjunction with the culture and the traditions puts life in
perspective, the continuity of structures not unlike language
and the ability to speak. It is the reciprocity and integrity that
is preserved, the behavior matching the expectation for which
some spaces might require redefinition, like clothing and what
is private have a cultural component.

We are moral beings, it distinguishes us from other species giving us a sense of direction. It is the result of the new
certainty and prioritizing cooperation. It goes back to dialectics
of movement; respect is the cost that justifies the motivation
defining a performance and the conditions where the species can thrive. Differing cost to the virtual spaces sets up the
learning process and makes socialization the manifest destiny.
It defines the moment and the power of discretion, the immediate goals and the long term evolutionary objectives engrained
in our nature. Some species eat their young in a bad season,
some will push the weakest one out of the nest, or provide
their own bodies as a food source, and some die in the process
of reproducing. The supper objective has to prevail in a series
of priorities in order to preserve equilibrium, the center of
gravity which provides the continuity. For humans the moral

and economic relationships generate the boundaries and natural inhibitors we gradually lose around the edges producing all kinds of social mutations with a tendency to "snow ball", where information loses its meaning.

As population grows and the numbers change basic parameters are determine by the original values system, the proportions that kept us living and multiplying within the laws of efficiency, allowing us to adjust the performance and get a better return. Certainty is displaced in time and space to reflect a new center defined by collaboration to a degree that becomes more evident with population growth, generating also the strain on the environment. Exercising this condition and range of motion is necessary since we continue to adjust to the environmental demand, singularly and collectively. This also means the capacity can be enhanced and reduced by manipulating the demand, like the lungs and heart is the result of an adaptation that make us more efficient, but it is limited by structural parameters with an "idle" point for longevity. Huge muscles beyond a functional degree generate a disproportional demand causing multiple health problems including an enlarged heart, no balance and the tug of nature, at that point the return is diminished.

The difference is that for humans balancing the energy equation is mostly a social responsibility, and that we agglutinated around an intuitive values system, the connections, the cognitive and non-cognitive reactions, more or less localized for efficiency. Focusing becomes a matter of social recognition, preserving the spaces and integrity of the system, opening and closing, extending and retracting are more the result of a social DNA. Tradition and cultural legacy can become very specific but also readily available in evolutionary terms, which also means the implicit uncertainty of the flexibility (and fast reactions) that requires enrichment to reduce the error, we also know it as common sense.

Other systems combine extreme simplification of functions and uniformity to reduce friction, limiting the variables and the possibilities; the objectives and super-objective almost become one, the load is not shared necessarily equally and some individual are more expendable than others. In some cases not only are they genetically predispose to do a job, the numbers are also "measured", which we lack precisely as a result of a much more complex society, they lack the discretion. We incorporate information faster, develop agriculture and technologies, find new sources of energy and manipulate natural cycles in order to keep up with the demands of growth. But success depends on structural integrity, if the right priorities are not driving the intentions the capacity can never find stability and slowly wastes away, the curve doesn't adjust and the head never meets the tail. We can exert ourselves with purpose and accelerate within critical mass restrain and a minimum degree of certainty.

The truth is we got some control over time as part of a social awareness that is the key to the ecological success. Understanding complicated relationships is part of internalizing the energy as part of a general performance, allowing us to find solutions to bigger obstacles with a special purpose anticipated by evolution in the values system, they are meant to work together and cannot be separated either. It makes the priorities match the imperative providing a range of motion that requires the right measurements for a walking motion. As we grow and the walking becomes more of a social responsibility the knowledge platforms play a bigger role, which also means that the social awareness and sensitivities have to develop proportionally as part of our social brain expansion.

There is always a tradeoff involved, which makes the universe move between precision and agglutination and life between function and simplification. When the performance is adjusted it reduces consumption and saves energy, but it requires minimum certainty to begin with. As human population grows new conflicts arise; cultural differences and resources that are naturally scattered around the world are used to undermine the instinct to cooperate, which is replaced by competition. We get further away from the next junction and the recovery, a quantity with the energy correlation that produces a positive generalization.

Specialized structures produce the performance rationalizing the articulations society grows into and materializing a purpose in a rhythm, which become products with a negative coefficient and more questions than answers, inverted articulations where we become incongruent. Government and social institutions are supposed to transcend the culture, which cannot transcend itself, setting standards based on values that define the questions that remain to be answered and the reproof-negation process, preserving the integrity and a range of motion. The empiric generalizations that expressing basic assumptions generates uniformity and produces growth displacing the ambiguities. They generate time to deal with the uncertainty which expands the smaller the moment (or the longer the time elapsed).

Focus is the reason why we couldn't live in isolated nation-cities today, and in truth why we require a minimum degree of certainty to enter into certain economic alliances, and even why most people would not be able to survive in complete isolation. The absolutes are always true and the problems get worst as long as we remain on the wrong track. The empiric negation is the recovery of time depends on the resources and cultural development, socioeconomic awareness and technological advances that are all part of the same process, the trajectory with the potential to takes us to a higher level of cooperation among specialist as we exercise the human

condition and fill the promise of growth and ecological success. But certainty has been displaced by the dogmas and Glo-
balization is preempting the natural process and taking us
down a dead-end path, where we are never ready to meet the
demand of the moment and a different set of assumptions
resonate throughout the environment.

Esteban Garcia was born in Cuba in 1964 where he remained
until 1985 when he migrated to the United States after graduating from college with a bachelor's degree. He studied Computer Programing and System Analysis at United Business Institute from 1985 through 1988. After graduating he worked
at an Interior Design company as a System Annalist for about
three years, until he decided to start his own business and become an entrepreneur. He has been working on this book for
the last ten years as a result of a very confounding experience
involving Secret Societies and have done extensive research on
every angle associated to the subject.

"Schindler's List at 25, or Why I (Still) Don't Like This Film"

By Robert Cardullo

I am not one of those who believe that the enormity of the Holocaust is above and beyond presentation in artistic form, except in the most indirect or metaphorical way. I have never believed this, and maintain that those who do wish simultaneously to apotheosize the victimhood of the Jews (but what about the millions of victims of the Holocaust who were not Jewish?) and to deny the edifying powers of art. After all, if Christ's crucifixion can be depicted on film, so too can that of twentieth-century Jews. The ultimate question in art, of course, is not so much *what* you present as *how* you present it. Some have chosen to treat the Holocaust in documentary film form, such as Alain Resnais with *Night and Fog* (1955), out of the apparent belief that no one could quarrel with the unvarnished truth. But Claude Lanzmann implicitly quarrels with Resnais in *Shoah* (1985), his nine-and-one-half-hour documentary on the Nazi extermination of European Jewry, by not including any imagery of his picture's central subject. We see interviews with survivors, with former Nazis, with Holocaust historians; we see the sites of the concentration camps today. We do not, however, watch footage of the Jewish ghettoes, of the emaciated camp survivors, or of the piles of corpses, as we do in *Night and Fog* and numerous other films about the German atrocities. Which is one way of saying that these atrocities are beyond representation, even in documentary form, and that to represent them is somehow to endorse them; that before as well as after the Third Reich, such brutality was and remains unimaginable, or, conversely, is conceivable only in the moral imagination. (Indeed, Lanzmann himself has said that "fiction about the Holocaust is a transgression; I deeply believe there are some things that cannot and should not be represented.")

Other directors have elected to treat the Holocaust in fictional form (if that is the appropriate term), going as far back as Wanda Jakubowska's *The Last Stage* (1948), Aleksander Ford's *Border Street* (1949), and Jerzy Zarzycki's *Unvanquished City* (a.k.a. *Warsaw Robinson*, 1950), continuing with Andrzej Munk's *The Passenger* (1963), and stretching into the 1990s with Andrzej Wajda's *Korczak* (1990) and Agnieszka Holland's *Europa, Europa* (1991). Each of these films, with the possible exception of the documentary-like *Last Stage*, is marred by broad or monochromatic characterizations and empty rhetorical gestures; each was also made in Poland, where today only 8,000 Jews are left out of the more than three million who lived there before Hitler's arrival in 1939. To this list of motion pictures were added, in 1993, Steven Spielberg's *Schindler's List*; in 1997, Roberto Benigni's *Life Is Beautiful*; in 2002, Roman Polanski's *The Pianist*; in 2005, Lajos Koltai's *Fateless*; and, in 2008, Edward Zwick's *Defiance*.

At the time of its release, *Schindler's List* was trumpeted as "the first Hollywood movie to depict the horrors of the

Holocaust." (What happened to *The Pawnbroker* [1965] or even *Sophie's Choice* [1982]? Neither of these two films takes place during the Holocaust, yet both of them depict its horrors in flashback.) *Schindler's List* was also made by the most commercially successful director in the history of cinema. Commercially successful this film was, as well, for it was not the start of a new, "adult" period in Spielberg's career, as a number of critics once argued—they made the same argument after the sanctimonious *Color Purple* (1985)—but instead a redeployment in ostensibly serious form of his crackerjack formula for entertaining the masses. That formula is at work in such superficially different yet essentially similar pictures as *Jaws* (1975), a horror movie; *Raiders of the Lost Ark* (1981), an adventure flick harking back to the Saturday-morning serials of the fifties; *E. T.* (1982), a science-fiction fairy tale; and *Jurassic Park* (1993), a sci-fi thriller: an Everyman protagonist has his conception of the world dramatically enlarged as he comes face to face with some extraordinary, generally non-human antagonist often hidden from the rest of the world—and the audience—until the film's end.

Spielberg's vision, then, is that of the child-artist whose innocent imagination can, on command, summon up primeval dread from the deep as well as transcendent wonder from the sky, and *Schindler's List* proves no exception. Indeed, it exemplifies that vision, which twice before used, and once more will deploy, World War II as a backdrop: in the crazy (stupid?) comedy *1941* (1979); in *Empire of the Sun* (1987), *Schindler's List*'s nearest relative in the Spielberg canon, in which an eleven-year-old English boy gets his sentimental (not sentient) education amidst the random brutality of a Japanese internment camp; and in *Saving Private Ryan* (1998), whose mawkish title tells you all you need to know about this graphically realistic yet historically inaccurate, emotionally dishonest war film. In fact, historical inaccuracy, if not outright distortion, political tendentiousness, and emotional dishonesty or manipulation have grown more prominent in Spielberg's work subsequent to *Schindler's List*: witness only *Amistad* (1997), *Munich* (2005), *War Horse* (2011), *Lincoln* (2012), and *The Post* (2017).

Schindler's List is based on the "documentary novel" of the same name published in 1982 by the Australian writer Thomas Keneally, which is to say it tells a true story that is somewhat touched up. The hero of the tale is Oskar Schindler, a Catholic businessman from the German Sudetenland who, when Hitler conquered Poland, moved to Kraków to strike it rich. He opportunistically joined the Nazi Party, spent what money he had on treating German officers to food, drink, and women, then was permitted to take over an enamelware factory confiscated from its Jewish owners. Staffing the factory with unpaid Jewish workers, Schindler quickly achieved huge profits by manufacturing metal pots and pans for the German troops. His chief assistant in this enterprise was a Jewish accountant named Itzhak Stern, who discreetly turned "Emalia," as the factory became known, into a haven for Jewish refugees, kept track of which official needed bribing in what way, and generally managed his boss's business affairs. His domestic affairs Schindler could manage for himself: in short, by leaving his wife, Emilie, behind in the Sudetenland, becoming intimate with a number of young Polish women, and living the life of a *bon vivant*.

Then in the winter of 1942 Schindler's antagonist or alter ego arrived in the person of SS Commander Amon Goeth, whose mission was to set up the nearby Plaszów forced labor camp and liquidate the Jewish ghetto in Kraków's Podgorze district. Horrified by the murderous treatment of the Jews as well as by the disappearance of his labor force, Schindler cultivated a friendship with the bestial yet suave Goeth, persuading him by means of gifts and geld to authorize the building of a sub-camp at "Emalia" so that Schindler's workers could resume production. By 1944, when orders came for the removal of all Plaszów Jews to Auschwitz, Schindler had decided it was time to leave Kraków for his hometown of Brünnlitz on the Czechoslovakian border.

In Brünnlitz, reunited with his wife and assisted by the trusty Stern, he opened a munitions factory staffed with 1,100 "essential" Jewish workers, whose lives he had purchased from Goeth at great cost and risk; and here he ensured, again at great cost and risk, that for seven months his work force would produce nothing of military value to the German army. At the end of those seven months Oskar Schindler was broke but the war had ended, his Jews had survived, and the Nazi Goeth had been executed. Leaving his employees to their newfound freedom, he fled to the West and died in 1974 at age sixty-six, a complete failure at every business he tried after the war. Nonetheless, over 8,500 "Schindler Jews" remain today, survivors from his list of "essential" workers together with their descendants.

What's wrong with this picture, or what makes *Schindler's List* in the end an artless film? First, only eight years after *Shoah*, there wasn't any need for another movie about the Holocaust, and certainly not for the $22 million this one cost (nearly $40 million in today's money). Put another way, if you're going to make such a movie, you had better have some light to shed on the subject, something to add to all that has already been said, thought, felt, filmed. Spielberg has nothing. He's a popular artisan, not a serious artist, which means that he's interested not in expanding viewers' minds, in challenging their views or unsettling their emotions, but in reconfirming their prejudices, in reinforcing their received ideas—especially their feelings—about history and the world. All that *Schindler's List* does is congratulate its audience for not being anti-Semitic, for deploring the evil of the Nazis—an evil that such an audience, in its virtue, would of course never be capable of. In its mission to sanctify the Jews and the "good German" who helped them, at the same time as it puts money into its director's purse, Spielberg's film is similar to two other contemporaneous, high-profile releases from Follywood: *Malcolm X* (1992), a bit of hagiography for all those who deplore racism, and *Philadelphia* (1993), a charmer directed at that segment of the American population which thinks it has never had a homophobic thought, or has long since cured itself of any homophobia it might once have felt.

Schindler's List, then, is a sentimental melodrama, nothing more, and as such takes its ignoble place alongside all the other anti-German, pro-Ally (or pro–Occupee) propaganda films made during the Second World War and long after it. It is technically well made and acted, yes, but that's like saying a book has been beautifully printed and handsomely bound, then concluding that its content must therefore be of equally high quality. The content of *Schindler's List* is *clichéd*, that's what it is, beginning with screenwriter Steven Zaillian's decision to focus primarily on Oskar Schindler's story, on the metamorphosis of his character from self-regarding opportunist to self-disregarding savior, and to juxtapose it against the static malevolence of Anton Goeth. What we get as a result is the Hollywood practice of showing catastrophe, or deliverance therefrom, from the point of view of the perpetrators; what we lose in the process is the Jewish perspective on events, the genocide of the Jews as seen through *their* eyes.

Lina Wertmüller tried something like this in her 1975 tragic farce *Seven Beauties* (as Benigni did later, in the same genre, in *Life Is Beautiful*), where she followed the "adventures" of an Italian deserter in a German prison that reeks of murder. Wertmüller failed (as did Benigni), but Spielberg doesn't even try (as Koltai did in *Fateless*), except to single out the angelic Stern from the anonymous mass of Jews as the apparent agent of *Schindler's* moral awakening. I say "apparent" because, although Stern seems to have something to do with it, Schindler's change is not clearly articulated in either the book or the film. Keneally says that nobody knows exactly why Schindler did his good deed, and Spielberg more or less takes the Australian at his word. Some have seen this absence of explanation as the picture's virtue, arguing that *Schindler's List* is in fact about the mystery of the titular character's goodness, which finally is as inexplicable as the mystery of Nazi savagery. However, this is to give too much credit to the movie, which is really about Schindler's goodness, wherever it comes from—and one can make the argument, for which Spielberg does not merit mention, that it is gracefully heaven-sent to the Catholic profligate—in a battle against diabolical evil in the form of Goeth.

So much is Spielberg's film a stereotypical allegory or anachronistic morality play on the division of the German soul between the absolute good of Schindler and the absolute evil of Goeth, as opposed to a character study of the dialectical, inner struggle between these two contradictory impulses in one human being, that *Schindler's List* resorts to the moral conventions of Hollywood movies of a bygone era in order to divide the world into black and white. Hence Nazi criminality, including Schindler's, is regularly associated with promiscuous sexuality and revelrous gluttony, while Jewish innocence—especially the ascetic Stern's—is directly connected both to ethical purity and to lethal starvation. For example, at one point Spielberg heavily intercuts among scenes of Goeth's near-rape, then vicious beating of his young Jewish housekeeper, Helen Hirsch; a Jewish marriage ceremony, performed by a woman, in one of the camp huts; and a nightclub party at which a *chanteuse* simultaneously serenades and seduces Schindler. Shortly thereafter, we watch Goeth's doctor warn him against his overindulgent lifestyle during a physical examination, then watch camp doctors examine Jews to decide which ones are healthy enough to remain slave laborers and which are so sick or undernourished that they must be exterminated. These are not isolated instances, but rather regular manifestations of an editorial mode that Spielberg establishes early in the film, when the sybaritic Schindler moves into a luxury apartment in Kraków with the words "It couldn't be better" while the married Jewish owners of the apartment resettle in a crowded ghetto rat-trap with the words "It could be worse."

Even Schindler's transformation from cynical war profiteer into empathetic human rescuer is portrayed in terms of his sensuality, or rather his renunciation of it. Once he enigmatically makes the decision to save the lives of the Jews working for him—while he paces the floor to the tune of Billie Holiday's "God Bless the Child" playing on his phonograph (how's that for subtlety?)—Schindler stops the rampant womanizing and extravagant living that had marked his earlier existence and rejoins his wife. The fact that they agree to get back together in a Catholic church is Spielberg's ponderous way of telling us that theirs will now be an essentially spiritual union. Yet it's not as ponderous as his and Zaillian's decision to have Schindler forswear his adulteries in the first place, just as he forswears them in Keneally's novel—but not according to the real-life Emilie Schindler's best recollection.

The reborn Schindler then complements his winning over of his wife by winning Helen Hirsch in a card game with the devil himself, Goeth: that is, he wins her life, her soul, for transport to Brünnlitz whereas, like the SS commander, he had previously desired only Helen's body. Next he miraculously rescues a trainload of his women workers (297 of them, in fact, as opposed to 801 men), including Hirsch, mistakenly routed to Auschwitz, even as he had earlier saved his accountant, Stern, from a similar fate. And once ensconced in his new factory, Schindler is virtually deified by Spielberg in a low-angle shot as he sermonizes to the awestruck Jews down on the workroom floor. (For similar scenes, see such Bible-in-pictures spectacles as *The Ten Commandments* [1956], *King of Kings* [1961], and *The Greatest Story Ever Told* [1965].)

What about how *Schindler's List* looks, in contrast to how it tells its story? The movie looks great, as I've hinted, and that's part of the problem. Except for an epilogue and a few other moments (more on these exceptions later), *Schindler's List* was shot in black and white by Janusz Kaminski. Spielberg argued at the time that since our visual knowledge of concentration camps comes from black-and-white photographs and newsreels, a film about the Holocaust should have such a documentary look as well. Fine. The problem, however, is not that Kaminski's superbly shaded cinematography is too beautiful, too "artistic," too undocumentary-like, as some have argued, but that it stands in aesthetic contradiction to the narrative line of the picture it adorns. In the images, there isn't a Manichaean division between angelic white and infernal black; instead, there is a relativistic gradation from black to gray to white that is sometimes augmented by mist or dust, and regularly underlined by a handheld camera that destabilizes the frame. There *is* such a Manichaean division between the characters in *Schindler's List*, whose Jews are all decent, noble, generous, saintly, and wise, and whose Germans are naturally just the opposite, with Oskar Schindler in the middle ready to exchange one extreme for the other, or suddenly to discover the inherent goodness in himself that has been obscured by his sinful (from a Catholic perspective) actions in the past. One therefore feels a kind of cognitive dissonance while watching the film, and that dissonance is not relieved by the screenplay's halfhearted attempts to "complicate" its antagonists.

To wit, the German officer who sits down to play the piano in a room "cleansed" of its Jews during the obliteration of the Kraków ghetto, and the two soldiers who argue over whether his music is by Bach or Mozart, are clumsily meant to tell us that even Nazis can have an appreciation for classical music, which is to say a human face beneath their monstrous mask. And the Jews who, after a good deal of hard bargaining, agree to finance Schindler's kitchenware factory are cursorily meant to tell us that there were black marketeers and collaborators even among the sacrosanct *Juden*. But these Jews, like those Nazis, should have been the subject of—not a footnote in—any latter-day Holocaust film, in order to reveal the Nazi and the Jew, the money-changer and the art-lover, the wolf and the sheep in all of us. Obviously, this is not to deny the historical fact of the Holocaust or to make a case for National Socialism; it is to insist that, even among the victims of German butchery, there were sinners as well as saints, bad people along with the good, other people besides Jews (including thousands of homosexuals together with the inmates of Germany's prisons and mental hospitals). I want to know about all of them in all their human complexity, not just their innocent victimization, and I want to see genuinely humanized German soldiers, not smoothly or even banally wicked Nazi oppressors, committing acts of violence—toward Jew and Gentile alike—against their will or to avoid their own execution.

What I do not want to see, after a three-hour sermon accompanied by the woebegone violin of Itzhak Perlman, and culminating in Schindler's anguished cry that he could have saved more Jews had he not been such a spendthrift, is an epilogue shot in constrained color in contemporaneous Israel. Here Oskar Schindler was buried at his request, and at his graveside on Mount Zion in Jerusalem, a number of actors from the film are partnered with the aged survivors they have been impersonating—just in case we still doubted the truth (cinematic or otherwise) of their story—together paying silent homage to the man who rescued 1,100 Jews from Hitler's ovens. I nearly groan at the unabashed bathos and forced obeisance of this sequence, which is connected to a prologue to *Schindler's List* where, once again in color, candles are lighted during a Jewish religious ritual only to have their flames successively die out (symbolism, anyone?).

The prologue itself is connected to a scene from the annihilation of Podgorze. As Schindler observes the destruction of the ghetto from a hillside above the city, the camera—*the camera*, which assumes his point of view, not Schindler's naked eye, which is too far away—picks out the red overcoat of a little girl wandering in black and white among the carnage-cum-wreckage. Later the child's body, still clad in the red that makes her stand out among the other corpses, turns up on a cart that passes underneath Schindler's gaze. Spielberg is straining in this instance to plant the seed of his hero's epiphany, his metamorphosis into a moral man, but he does so at the expense of all the other victims we, and Schindler, have seen. Or is the Spielbergian child-artist up to his old tricks here, fatuously arguing that unspeakable crimes become expressible or comprehensible only when they are being perpetrated against children?

Fortunately—or is it unfortunately?—the three principal actors are so good that, like Kaminski's cinematography, they make *Schindler's List* seem better than it is, almost enabling the picture to transcend its naïve vision of people and the world. How do Liam Neeson, Ben Kingsley, and Ralph Fiennes, as Schindler, Stern, and Goeth respectively, do this? Not merely by committing to the external actions of their characters—to Schindler's sensuality or Goeth's sadism or even Stern's impassivity—but also by creating inner lives for them in a form, the melodrama, that does not really call for consciousness of self. This was especially an achievement in the case of the Nazi villain, who, although here based on fact, has become such a filmic cliché that Fiennes had to invent a fiction beneath the reality of Goeth, an imaginative truth beyond the truth of his existence, in order to make him horrifyingly believable rather than comically implausible. I don't find it accidental that none of these men is American (though Kevin Costner himself wanted to play Schindler!), or that there are few Americans in a large cast that includes Polish, German, and Israeli actors as well as amateurs. Somehow Spielberg figured out that his quintessentially American, "them-against-us" view of the world in such a film needed foreign actors if it was to be taken seriously—actors, that is, who have inherited the knowledge, the grief, the gravity of a genocidal war conducted in their own backyard.

In sum, *Schindler's List* is a serious work marred by its sentiment, its attempt to be morally uplifting instead of morally searching. Given its subject, how might it have avoided the almost ineluctable trap of cinematic sentiment? By recasting its story in the form of a black comedy, however inappropriate or offensive that may at first seem. The premise of dark comedy, as applied to Hitler and the Holocaust in works like Chaplin's *The Great Dictator* (1940) and Lubitsch's *To Be or Not to Be* (1942), is that laughter is the only sane response to the horror of modern, cataclysmic warfare, that such horror must be combated by humor. The reasoning behind such extremist comedy goes something like this: in a world that could produce Hitler, the Holocaust, and ultimately the H-bomb, nothing is sacred, nothing absolute; all values, beliefs, and truths are open to question. This questioning then logically extends itself to artistic forms, where, in black comedy, the most serious subjects are given, not a serious or tragic treatment, but a satirical, even farcical one. In psychological terms, this genre can be seen as a schizophrenic reaction, and thus as a kind of cry or plea, to an absurd world, a world itself gone crazy. Although many people find "war comedies" morally objectionable, the success of such movies as *Dr. Strangelove, or How I Learned to Stop Worrying and Love the Bomb* (1963), *How I Won the War* (1967), and *Catch-22* (1970)—as well as the long-running television series *M*A*S*H* (itself derived from Robert Altman's 1970 film of the same name) and *Hogan's Heroes*—testifies that just as many find them morally apt.

In his own sentimental melodrama, Spielberg, of course, is hoping that our sympathy for the Jews and knowledge of what happened to them throughout Europe will cause us to overlook the triteness-cum-contrivance of his film. But, I can hear some readers exclaiming, the events in *Schindler's List* actually took place! Who are you to disparage them, along with the memory of Holocaust victims? Well, first of all, I'm not disparaging the events or the victims; I'm disparaging their artistic, or rather artless, handling by Spielberg and company. Second, *some* of the events and characters in *Schindler's List* are taken from real life, not all of them. Third, who cares whether *any* of this stuff occurred in reality or whether *any* of these people really lived? Since when is art to be judged by the factuality of its contents, as opposed to their imaginative transformation? Since they started making Holocaust films, I guess.

R. J. Cardullo is the author or editor of a number of books, including *Play Analysis: A Casebook on Modern Drama* (Sense/ Brill, 2015), *Soundings on Cinema* (SUNY Press, 2008), and *In Search of Cinema* (McGill-Queens UP, 2004). He is also the chief American translator of the film criticism of the Frenchman André Bazin, with several volumes to his credit. Cardullo earned his master's and doctoral degrees from Yale University and received his B.A. from the University of Florida. He taught for four decades at the University of Michigan, Colgate, and New York University, and is now teaching abroad.

Pondering Proust, Recalling Moments

By Joram Piatigorsky

After fifty years of science with an eye toward writing a memoir, I saw Marcel Proust's monumental autobiographical novel, *In Search of Lost Time*, in a bookstore. I picked up *Swann's Way*, the first volume, and read snippets at random. The extended sentences comprised long strings of phrases separated by commas and folded into paragraphs. What sentences! One ran more than the page. I bought *Swann's Way*.

When I finished reading the book, I craved another fix of Proust and read the other five volumes. I loved the descriptive prose, similes and metaphors that transformed scenes into images, like that emerging when piecing a puzzle together. More personally, I often felt a déjà vu phenomenon, made famous by Proust's madeleine, with the elegant salons and the empty gossip of the characters trying to impress in order not to be dropped from the prestigious inner circle. This personal connection stemmed from my Parisian visits when I was a young boy to my maternal grandparents of the Rothschild banking dynasty, who had been a part of Proust's aristocratic world. I even heard, within this deep layer of myself, my mother's voice that I act with unimpeachable decorum because I'm a Jew, stained by the Dreyfus affair in Proust's era, and must remain above reproach as a shield against anti-Semitism.

It was fortuitous that I read Proust's novel before writing a memoir, when I was troubled that I hadn't done anything sufficient to attract attention. My father's brilliant journey from the pogroms in pre-Bolshevik Russia to world-fame as a cellist, and my mother's brave escape from the privileged but emotionally starved childhood in the Rothschild palaces of France to excelling in chess, tennis, and sculpting in the United States, made fascinating stories. Why would anyone want to read about me, a U.S. government scientist, who had lived a sheltered life in the United States.

Proust came to the rescue. He made his relatively uneventful life – a boyhood crush, seaside vacations, museum trips, introspective neurotic torments – momentous by filtration through his inner world. Nothing of note actually happened. What Proust did was expose his precious society in terms of his private conflicts. He showed me that writing became compelling by exposing oneself, turning inside out as it were, blending and blurring boundaries: reaching out while looking in and having the courage to be authentic.

I thought back on my life for hints on what I might write about in my memoir. What stood out? What did I remember first? What made a lasting memory?

While working as a scientist I wrote about my research projects, emphasizing what I believed were the most significant findings. As interesting as these were, or at least I thought they were, they didn't represent me. Science was what I did, not who I was. No. It was neither the projects nor their outcomes that meant most to me when I thought about my life in science. Rather, it was my amazement when I first glimpsed the clarity and magnifying power of an eye lens – a bundled group of transparent living cells – and how the lens became almost invisible when I placed it in a Petri dish; it was the awe I felt when I watched under the dissecting microscope the beating heart propelled the blood of a chicken embryo barely two days old; it was when I saw a lone jellyfish rise majestically from the depth, followed by another and then another, free, attracted to the light I beamed on the water at night by the dock in La Parguera, Puerto Rico. These were defining moments that I cannot forget or relive.

What I chose to write about in the memoir, then, were these and other special instances etched in my mind: the time Alberto Monroy, a scientist I admired, told me at Woods Hole when I was a novice graduate student, "Only *real* scientists would be playing hooky at the beach on such a beautiful sunny day"; when Professor Leigh Hoadley kindled my curiosity when he asked the embryology class at Harvard, "What do you think would happen if a beginning frog embryo would be cut in half?"; when my father touched my cheek backstage before turning his attention to a line of admirers waiting for his autograph after he played impromptu the Don Quixote cello concerto by Ricard Strauss at the Casal's Music Festival in Puerto Rico. What my research project was at Woods Hole when Monroy discovered me on the beach playing hooky from the laboratory to go for a swim, or what actually happens when a fertilized frog egg is cut in half, or why my father decided to switch the program at the Casal's Music Festival are all interesting – even fascinating – but the impact of the transient, special moments for me outlasts the events themselves.

I love opera, but when Mimi dies in *La Bohème* or when the lovers are buried alive in *Aida* bring tears and breaks my heart, not because these are sad stories, but because the music at those moments blends with everything I love and becomes intensely personal, making the difference between hearing the story and feeling it.

When I think about my high school days in Los Angeles playing competitive tennis, I remember when I was soundly beaten (oh my god, 6-0, 6-0) in my first tournament and then when I upset more highly ranked players (victory is always sweet) as I gained expertise. But my more meaningful memories, the ones that prevailed, were the feelings I had when I could hit the ball as hard as I wanted and place it on the other side of the court precisely where I chose and knew I wouldn't miss – a suspended state of confidence, whether justified or not, that arrives by chance and leaves at will, called playing "in the zone," which transcends winning or losing. Those were the moments when I became one with the sport and married to its magic.

It is these personal moments – the ones that Proust gave me confidence to focus on in my memoir – that characterize most truthfully who I am as a human being. It's such lingering memories, not the specific events, that have the most meaning and make it all worthwhile.

Joram Piatigorsky
During his 50-year career at the National Institutes of Health, Joram Piatigorsky has published some 300 scientific articles and a book, *Gene Sharing and Evolution* (Harvard University Press, 2007), lectured worldwide, received numerous research awards, including the prestigious Helen Keller Prize for vision research, served on scientific editorial boards, advisory boards and funding panels, and trained a generation of scientists. Presently an emeritus scientist, he collects Inuit art, is on the Board of Directors of The Writer's Center in Bethesda, blogs (JoramP.com), and has published a series of personal essays in the journal Lived Experience and a novel, *Jellyfish Have Eyes* (IPBooks, 2014). He has two sons, five grandchildren, and lives with his wife in Bethesda, Maryland.

Cockroaches: A Memoir

By Ron McFarland

*"When Gregor Samsa awoke one morning from troubled
dreams, he found himself changed into a monstrous
cockroach in his bed."*
Franz Kafka, "The Metamorphosis" (1913);
trans. Michael Hofmann (2007)

My obsession with cockroaches dates from when my family
moved to Florida from Ohio in 1950, shortly after I'd finished
second grade in Barnesville. The whole family seemed to go
bonkers upon confronting these insects in the Sunshine State,
because there the roaches appeared to be ten times larger and
twenty times more ominous than in the Buckeye State, probably because (technically) they weren't cockroaches at all but
palmetto bugs (*Eurycotis floridana*). They swarmed multitudi-
nously; they seemed enormous; no cookie, cracker, or crumb
of my mother's spectacular butterscotch fudge was safe. Late
nights they invaded the small kitchen of our rented, crack-
er-box bungalow. Even my fearless father decided he might
forego his midnight snack.

After a few months, we were introduced to the glories of
D-Con, which came in two attractive forms, as I recall: tablets
that looked like large aspirin or potassium vitamins and bottles
of a liquid that could be painted along the baseboards. The

tablets involved random placement, I think, whereas the liquid must have required strategy, logistics. One might slap some of the stuff across the thresholds so the critters would think twice before entering from the outer world, the new-to-us world of heat, humidity, sandspurs, and (of course) mosquitoes. We did experience most of these natural phenomena in Ohio, but central Florida opened new horizons along those lines.

When we moved to Merritt Island in 1952, our garage apartment did not insure us against incursions of the order *Blattodea*, an order which also includes, Wikipedia assures us menacingly, the termite. These ancients date back more than three hundred (300) million years, they are infamously Carboniferous, and as any paleontologist will gleefully attest, they will out-survive us all. They will prove post-apocalyptic. Long after Cormac McCarthy's cannibalistic denizens of *The Road* have dwindled out of existence, the mighty cockroach will be flittering about the ashen world.

Not to be overly patriotic about this, but shouldn't I about now pen some sort of paeon to The American Cockroach (*Periplaneta Americana*)? Early on, we soon-to-be true Floridians learned to distinguish this insect from the palmetto bug, (*Eurycotis floridana*), which my brother and I regarded as, technically speaking, "gooshier." The palmetto bug does not fly, and it is smelly when smooshed. Although I have not pursued the matter, I believe this scientifically sound observation can be replicated under laboratory conditions. I should point out here that while I have dwindled to the point of being an English professor, I did begin my academic career as a biology major. This unwarrantedly optimistic digression lasted all the way through Chemistry 101.

Flash forward to 1965, when our sister Susan came onto the scene not long after Mom and Dad moved us into the cement block tract house in grand-sounding Broadmoor Acres, two small bedrooms and one very small bath. Tom and I shared one of the tiny bedrooms, but when Susan came onto the scene, Dad decided to turn the carport into a third bedroom and add a shower, toilet, and washbowl to the utility room. Dad had worked at a lumberyard as a young man, and he'd helped his father build the simple frame cottage in Belmont County, Ohio, that we called "The Camp." People who can do these things always amaze me, as I have no manual skills at all, but as Vergil wrote, "Possunt quia posse videntur": They can because they think they can. One of my favorite children's books was *The Little Engine That Could*, the originator of which might well have known his Vergil: "I think I can, I think I can," mutters the little engine as he hauls the heavy load up the hill, and then "I thought I could, I thought I could" as he rumbles down. I probably knew the 1930 version. Anyway, when it comes to small, medium, or large motor skills, I know I can't, I know I can't.

Dad fashioned a bank of windows on the north facing the street, and to the west he hung some sort of bamboo matchstick curtains that proved attractive in two senses of the term: aesthetically appealing and destined to attract cockroaches. Because our bedroom was pretty much flush with the ground, having been intended for the car, the roaches found easy entry. Almost from the first you could hear them soaring through the night air: thhhrrriiip! And upon striking the bamboo, the cockroach would alight, as often as not, on my pillow.

The first time that happened, my 13-year-old-self yelped, leapt from the bed, switched on the light, grabbed my copy of *Boy's Life*, and beat the insect to a pulp. I'm not sure how many additional times this scenario played out before I determined to get cold-blooded about the matter. Let's face it, I told myself one night after the roach missed my pillow and landed on my cheek, this is going to become a recurring phenomenon. Mind you, I hadn't the verbal sophistication at that age to phrase the dire situation in those exact terms, but it came down to the same thing. I had already taken the expedient of providing myself with a pre-rolled back issue of that Boy Scout magazine for the express purpose of dispatching the nocturnal bug, but turning myself out of bed, flipping on the light, and awakening my brother was getting irksome. I determined that henceforth, I would steel myself to the task of squishing the intrusive insect with my bare hand, wiping the icky residue on the sheet, and returning to the land of nod. What can I say from the vantage of these sixty years? It worked great. Not meaning to get overly explicit here, I should point out that (surprisingly) this process did not make that much of a mess on the sheets.

At this point I should pen a brief paeon to smug self-satisfaction. Here was rare evidence of man's (or boy's) victory over insect. Here also was testimony to my conquest of fear. No 13-year-old about to become an Eagle Scout wants to admit to being terrified in the dead of night by one of Florida's most ordinary and ubiquitous insects (among many candidates for that honor): Man vs. Insect. Man wins. Note: Somewhere amid the rubble of my boyhood resides my sash emblazoned with the Insect Life merit badge, now known as "Insect Study" and featuring what might well be a grasshopper feeding on a wheat stalk, or maybe it's a beetle crawling on a twig.

From that time onward, whilst others of my family might scurry about in search of a swatter to deal with a cockroach that had the temerity to scurry across the kitchen floor during one of our evening card games, I would fairly leap from my chair and slap the thing into submission before the amazed and grateful eyes of the adult world.

Well, perhaps the adult world was not always altogether gratified by my valorous behavior. While Mom and Dad viewed my antics with bemused detachment, or with sighs of resignation accompanied by the hope I would outgrow my aggressive impulses, they expressed, I suppose, predictable disapprobation when I flew into action when guests while present. "Ronald," my mother would say, hoping (in vain) that her tone of voice would be sufficient to restrain my enthusiasm for the kill, as my Aunt Estelle watched wide-eyed. Aunt Stell as we called her was my father's older sister, a lovely woman given to high propriety and some degree of Presbyterian religiosity. Uncle George always struck me as more philosophical. He was a quiet and contemplative pipe smoker. My mother, ten years younger than Dad, always felt herself the object of scrutiny. No amount of intense housecleaning and D-Con application could offer sufficient prophylaxis against Aunt Stell's unspoken censure: If there were cockroaches, the house must be dirty.

In an earlier time, perhaps, my mentor, some Deerslayer type converted to insects, call him "Roachslayer," would have streaked my forehead with a touch of the gore from my first triumph. Well, look up "insect blood" and you won't find much of interest, but it won't be red whatever it is—"hemolymph" apparently. It wouldn't be the same.

Flash forward now by some thirty years, the mid 1980s, and I'm back in Ohio teaching for a year as an exchange professor at Ohio University in Athens, where my father put in a couple of years as an undergraduate before The Great Depression wiped out what might have passed for The Family Fortune. The latter might also pass for The Family Myth. In any event, we swapped a year in our very nice home in Moscow, Idaho, for what turned out to be a tiny, two-bedroom, cockroach-infested apartment set back about a hundred feet from busy US 50. We had three children then aged five (son), ten (easy daughter), and fifteen (difficult daughter).

Here we encountered the multiplicitous German cockroach (*Blattella germanica*), small, tan, swift of legs. I think of them as "German browns," not to be confused with the admirable trout species. Wikipedia describes the German "brown" cockroach as "gregarious"—sociable, as it were. Think of them as the Brownshirts of the cockroach world, the *Sturmabteilung* (SA). Interestingly, per Wikipedia again, the German brown appears to have originated in Southeast Asia, and even more interestingly, or at least curiously, the Germans refer to them as Russian cockroaches. I suspect this could have something to do with *Der Zweite Weltkrieg*, Operation Barbarossa, Stalingrad, and so on. Still enthusiastic about Russian some twenty years after my last course in the subject, I prided myself on being "Убийца тараканов" (pronounced "oobitsa tarakanov") or "cockroach killer."

Those who were around during the 1960s surely will remember the so-called "beehive" hairstyle, and they will also probably recall the urban legend—if in fact it was merely legendary—of the young woman who kept spraying her beehive to keep it intact. This meant not washing it, of course, with the result that a horde of German brown cockroaches infested her beehive, necessitating the shaving of her head. "O, horrible! O, horrible! Most horrible!" wails the ghost of Hamlet's father. I confess the direness of his horror may have outstripped the one afore-mentioned.

But away from Germany, Russia, and Denmark and back to southern Ohio and 1985. Now in my forties, I am in my prime as a cockroach killer, and this proves fortunate, as these babies are everywhere. Good news is they don't fly. Bad news is they can scurry like the devil. We come in one evening after a party, flip on the light, and there they are, everywhere. Their number is legion, like Milton's bad angels. I drop to my hands and knees in a frenzy of floor-slapping that soon ends with a swarm of deceased insects. Our babysitting daughter gazes upon the carnage in mute . . . well, I'm not quite certain I can claim "admiration" here. Perhaps "astonishment," as she has witnessed nary a roach back home in the Idaho panhandle.

The dead here in Athens, Ohio, must number in the Homeric hecatombs, dread sacrifice to the gods of cockroachery. After a few more such encounters, I begin keeping tabs on my kills. Not to boast, but to keep the saga short, my record is 63 in one intense evening.

(Note: On a recent family camping trip along the St. Maries River in the Idaho panhandle, while playing cards by lantern-light, I dispatched no fewer than 40 aggressive moths. I won't attempt to impress you with statistics from my on-going battle against slugs in our yard and garden, where I've armed myself with a state-of-the-art saltshaker against that slimy enemy.)

Some skills one acquires in exotic places or long ago do not prove adaptable to one's current place and time. Here at my office in Carol Ryrie Brink Hall at the University of Idaho, a 1930's brick structure that formerly served as a men's dorm and that is distinguished by its narrow hallways, confusing corridors, and infusions of asbestos, I do encounter the occasional black cockroach, usually at the basement level, which houses one of our linguists and random mathematicians. These roaches I've found almost (but not quite) always in some stage of rigor mortis. I suspect they are the oriental or Asian cockroach (*Blatta orientalis*), most likely introduced in the luggage of international students or faculty who have indulged themselves in exotic sabbaticals to the Far East. Apparently, this species also inhabits the Southeast of the U.S., but I like to think in terms of more geographically distinct regions.

Recently, I discovered I'd once again left the detritus of my late-night snack scattered on the kitchen counter: crackers, an open jar of peanut butter, a slice or two of cheddar. These items proved to be unmolested by any of the order *Blattodea*. A similar oversight in Florida, Texas, Illinois, or Ohio, the various states where I've lived a couple of years or more, would surely have brought about an unpleasant if not repulsive scene. Years ago, when I lived in Florida, an artist friend gave me a very nice landscape he'd painted in tempera featuring the Indian River Lagoon. I made the mistake of leaving it in my closet when I went off to graduate school in Illinois, and when I returned home for Christmas, I found that much of the paint had been devoured by a horde of cockroaches, who obviously had developed a taste for art. Clearly the Idaho panhandle has proven a less hospitable venue for such insects.

Which among the various sciences might be described as the most "exact"? I suppose it is not entomological geography. Insects seem to bustle the world all too easily for entomologists to establish reliable boundaries for them. The Wikipedia folks got it right when they described German cockroaches as "gregarious." And aren't they all—all the cockroach species, that is? They do get around. Despite my fearless, indeed courageous, efforts at controlling the spread of these brutes, they appear to be almost as numerous as they were before I undertook my mission to exterminate them all.

Ron McFarland teaches literature and creative writing at the University of Idaho. His recent books include a study of regional memoir, *The Rockies in First Person* (2008), *Appropriating Hemingway: Using Him as a Fictional Character* (2015), and a biography, *Edward J. Steptoe and the Indian Wars* (2016). Pecan Grove Press published Ron's fourth full-length book of poems, Subtle Thieves, in early 2012. Chapin House Books published his memoir of growing up in Florida, Confessions of a Night Librarian and Other Embarrassments, in 2005. Current projects include a small book of his essays and poems on angling, title to be decided.

I Want to Feel Safe

By Susan M. Davis

I'm gay and I'm a teacher. Thirty years ago, I wouldn't be able to say these words and still be safe in my job. I teach English to eighth grade students in room 14 in Santa Ana, California. I have over 170 kids each year. Three classes are honor students. Some say I have the stellar job. Perhaps I do. I have earned this position. I have taught over two thousand students thus far. I live for the applause. Teaching is my passion.

On the opening day of school, I told my students my story, *I've been teaching for twenty-seven years and twenty-two of them have been in this very classroom. Room 14 has been my second home. I have a life-partner of thirteen years, so yes I am gay. Karen suffered a ruptured brain aneurysm nine years ago. I rushed her to the hospital in our car, which ultimately helped save her life. I don't stay afterschool. I need to go home and be with her.*

As you can see behind me on the white board is my placard that says: Safe Zone. I want this classroom to be safe for everyone. The kids clapped and for the first time in my career I felt genuine to who I really am.

The first week of school, three students wanted to talk to me. One confided she was gay, one said she was bi-sexual the third didn't disclose. I believe my disclosure allowed these students to feel safe. Honesty is what students want. They want their teachers to be real. When a student hears that you are being honest about who you are, it allows them to feel safe and open up.

The minute I flip my classroom lights on at 7:00 am, students arrive. A few are already standing at my classroom door waiting. Some want to come out of the cold, others want to print an assignment, others come to talk to friends, and frequently someone needs to talk with me. We have tackled abuse, sexuality, bullying, friendships, relationships or even just homework. I listen to every story. I never know if I will be the teacher that helped change that student's life. For many kids, teachers are the heartbeat of their existence. We become their source for strength, inspiration and hope.

Last year by November, I had thirty students in my room every morning before school began and again at lunch. They were with me for over 126 minutes a day, and 630 minutes a week. I think they own my time and me. They were gifted, honor students who enjoyed being in my classroom as a group. They studied together, played games and laughed with one another, some even cried together. By the end of the week I would ask, "Don't you want to go to another class?" Their response every time, "No, Ms. Davis we want to be with you." We amalgamated and became known as the Breakfast Club.

Whatever their need, a smile, a word of advice or just a hello, they know I'm here for them. My placard screams the words: Safe Zone. Everyone deserves a safe space to learn. Perhaps it is my "dare to be different" attitude that draws students into my room.

I sprout silver spikey hair with purple streaks and have seven tattoos that decorate my arms. My tattoos reveal the love and passion I feel for my profession. The Cat in the Hat sits proudly on my upper right arm holding a book surrounded with the words, "Teacher of the Year" from 2007. I'm proud to be a teacher. I'm the first in my immediate family to graduate college. As a child, I dreamed of becoming a teacher, but I dropped out of college, USC, at the age of nineteen. I was tired of studying. I became a professional bowler. I earned a trip to Japan at the age of twenty-one to open new bowling centers.

At twenty-six, I returned to school and attended junior college. I continued to the university where I earned my Bachelor's Degree, Teaching Credential and two Master's Degrees. Being a teacher has kept me a lifelong scholar. I've learned not only from books but from my students as well. They teach me as much as I teach them. I've been versed in the difficulties in their young lives. The streets are tough: drive-by shootings, a home lost to a fire, a pregnancy at the age of thirteen, parents in jail, to name a few. These things can't be taught in a Teacher's Credential Program. On the job Teaching is not for the lighthearted.

Students say I'm demanding. "She makes you write an essay every Thursday for the entire school year." *Writing is important,* I tell them. *Words are power.* Reading is important too. Students read two books a month. They win a medal if they reach 1.5 million words. Bulletin Boards in my classroom come alive with rows of certificates with brilliant hues of color for my million word readers. Books are in shambles in my classroom library from being checked in and out so often. *White Fang, Roll of Thunder, Hear My Cry, The Diary* of *Anne Frank, Freak the Mighty*, and *Night* to name a few.

I buy many of the books, but I can only afford so many. However, it means all my students have access to books. I prepare future leaders.

Former students keep in touch long after middle school and high school. They write e-mails or text me. Tim Alexander a former 8th grade student wrote, "You did more than TEACH me. You were my second period English teacher in 8th grade. A very pivotal year for me and the tough love and challenging work prepared me for high school and college. From the bottom of my heart, I am so grateful for the extra effort you put into my education and for not giving up on me. You were THAT teacher for others and me as well. My family was homeless at the time. We were living in a car. When you found out you brought me bags of groceries the next day. Thank you."

This is why I teach; To touch the future.

This year I was honored to teach our schools' first Transgender student. I asked that he be placed in my class. *Am I prepared to teach him?* Of course, I know my curriculum. What about his needs other than my mandated lesson plans? No, I don't know what a transgender boy at age fourteen needs, but I have the personality and the heart to make him feel welcome. He comes before school and often is the last one out the door when I leave my classroom. He needs someone to listen. Does it matter that I've never taught a Transgender student before? Not to him. He says, "I know your room is safe and that is what I need." He likes the placard on my whiteboard that reads: Safe Zone. "I feel safest in your room, Ms. Davis. You create an environment for me to feel safe among my peers."

The bell rings at 7:55 every morning and students file in and out as they go to other classes. Students walk to their assigned seats. They can be removed from our school for having seven tardies or more in a single class. My kids know there are others waiting to take their place if they screw up. We have over 1000 students on the waiting list each year. Homework is placed on the desks ready to be presented to me. Students know how to follow the rules, and only a few will stray.

Students, let's look at the writing prompt on the overhead. Think about a time when you were the butt of a joke because you might have looked differently than others. You have five minutes to do a quick write. Begin. This begins my tolerance and acceptance unit. I also teach a two-month Holocaust unit and anti-bullying lessons.

I walk slowly back to my desk and take a sip of my blueberry tea latte only to realize the caffeine isn't enough to last me through the morning.

These students become my kids. I do my best to advocate for my kids, to teach valuable lessons that will not only benefit them today, but for the future as well. After twenty-seven years of teaching over two thousand students, I'm still touched by how many appreciate me. When June comes, I'm melancholy as my kids graduate and move onto high school but I know I have made a difference in many of these young lives by listening and caring. My job is complete until August, when I will receive another 170 students who will also become my kids and claim me as theirs for the next 180 days.

Susan M. Davis graduated from California State University Fullerton with a degree in English. She has been an 8th grade English teacher for 27 years. She is a former Teacher of the Year. Susan also has a Masters of Science in Educational Counseling. She just completed her MFA in Creative Writing Non-fiction from Fairfield University in Connecticut. Susan resides in Southern California with her wife, Karen Kozawa and their 3 Cocker Spaniels. Her favorite color is purple. If you know her, you will know this.

FINALISTS

Stuck

By Allen Long

Seventh grade English class, autumn of 1969.

"You fucked a girl yet?" my friend Tim Rogers asked.

I shook my head, no.

"Oh man, you wouldn't believe how good it feels! I thought it might be tricky, but she guided me in, and then I figured out the rhythm to it. Everything went fine—you've got to try it!"

"How'd you get the girl to agree?" I said.

"You know Juliet Barnes?"

"Yeah. We went to elementary school together."

"Well, she's the one. Our parents are friends, and I've known her all my life. So I called her up one day and said, 'Barnes, I'm going to fuck the shit out of you the next time your parents are gone.' And she called me, and we did it!"

"Very romantic," I said.

As I headed off to Biology, I thought about Tim's story. I liked Juliet, and I could see how she'd be a friendly person with whom to lose your virginity. And I *was* really horny—I'd been having wet dreams and knew I'd soon be on a path of self-abuse reportedly leading to blindness. Still, when I fantasized about sex, it was always with beautiful lingerie models from the J.C. Penny catalog. Although I imagined taking these women gently but firmly between their silken thighs with my pulsating pillar of pleasure, the most satisfying moments of these flights of fancy always came after our lovemaking, when my lover inevitably fell in love with me and wrapped her naked body around mine in a loving embrace. I had a hard time imaging myself making love to girls from school, no matter how gorgeous or sweet; they were too young and innocent.

This reminded me of a conversation I'd recently overheard in the locker room. A rich and handsome classmate named Gary Clayton told his friend Rick Thompson that he'd arranged for them to fuck two pretty girls in their social set, even though they didn't know them well. Rick was the good-looking quarterback of our football team and a straight-arrow guy I admired. He was as appalled as I was at Gary's callous plan, although he said he'd consider it if they got to know the girls better.

This led to a final thought before I reached class. There was a girl at school named Kim Montjoy who had fabulous breasts. Most guys snickered and referred to her as Kim Mountains of Joy. While I certainly admired her full breasts, I was struck much more by her kind smile and friendly green eyes. She was one of the few knock-out girls who said hello to a crew-cut nerd like me.

At home after school, I usually knuckled-down on my homework so I later could play records or my electric guitar or pick up my place in the *Lord of the Rings* trilogy, but that day I was restless. I paced around my room until I decided to listen to The Beatles' *Sgt. Pepper's Lonely Hearts Club Band*. At first I kept the volume low, but the music felt so soothing that I cranked it up. Less than a minute into the title song, my mother flung open my door and gave me a furious look that said, I am *so* close to telling your father to pull down your pants and blister your bottom!

"Turn that thing off!" she said. "You *know* you're not allowed to play your music that loud! What's gotten in to you?"

I immediately apologized, praying she wouldn't add, "And wait until your father gets home!"

She slammed the door behind her. I quickly turned the music off, laid out my books and papers, and feverishly dove into my homework in an adrenalin-induced panic. From the time my younger brother Danny and I were small children, our father, encouraged by our mother, beat the daylights out of us with a homemade thick oak paddle at the slightest provocation. And he hit us hard about a dozen times, although he'd once struck my bare bottom a searing two dozen times over an imagined offense. So far, my parents hadn't beaten me since I turned thirteen and entered seventh grade, but there was no guarantee the violence was over. I remembered all the times I'd been physically ill with fear, hiding in my closet, waiting for my father to come home and thrash me.

The following summer, as my buddy Will and I basked in the sun at our neighborhood swim club, a young Aphrodite approached us, and I was smitten before she even spoke. Her raven hair whipped in the wind, occasionally covering her warm brown eyes. Her teeth were Mr. Clean white, unlike my own teeth, which had been stained gray by tetracycline prescribed for many childhood ear infections. She was fit and wore a hot pink bikini that showed off her tan and curves.

"Will," she said. "May I sit with you guys?"

"Sure," he croaked, blushing deeply.

She held out her hand. "Samantha," she said. "Or Sam. Will and I are in Band together at school."

"Allen," I said. "Pleased to meet you."

The three of us spent the rest of the day sunning and playing hide-and-seek-tag in the pool. At one point, after Sam excused herself to go to the ladies' room, I asked Will, "What's the story with her, and do you have any interest in her?

"She's a total fox," he said. "And you're welcome to go for it. If I tried to talk her up, I'd just stutter and drool. But watch out—I noticed she went through a lot of boyfriends last year. And I get the feeling *she* dumped *them*, not the other way around. That girl's *fast*—don't let her leave no tire tracks on *your* back." This last remark was a reference to our beloved Jimi Hendrix.

When the shadows of the lifeguard towers grew long, I offered to walk Sam home—I'd learned she lived on the same street as me, just a few more blocks down. We talked on the way, getting to know each other. Will walked silently behind us and peeled off to the right when we came to his street. Our hips kept bumping as if our bodies were magnets. I was thrilled to be walking with a pretty and apparently warm-hearted girl on a beautiful summer day after many hours of swimming, a spiritual activity for me, since it helped soothe the part of me damaged by child abuse.

I put my arm around Sam, and she snuggled into me. I felt such comfort and joy at this loving touch that I nearly stumbled. When we reached her house, she invited me inside to meet her parents and kid brother. Her father was tall with horn-rimmed glasses, reminding me a bit of an owl, especially when he sharp-eyed me, gauging my potential for getting his daughter pregnant. He seemed to decide I wasn't a threat. Standing beside her husband, Sam's mother looked short, but she was about the same height as Sam, around 5'4". She wore tennis whites, and her face was flushed and perspiring, but, even so, it was obvious she'd passed her good looks onto Sam. She smiled at me, but I caught a flash of concern in her periwinkle eyes. I got the feeling she was worried about her boy-crazy daughter and hoping neither of us would get hurt. When Sam introduced me to her little brother Mark as her new boyfriend, he smacked a palm against his forehead and said, "Not *another* one!"

"Mark, hush," said his mother.

I was ecstatic Sam considered me her boyfriend; suddenly, I felt lifted out of childhood onto a higher, joyous plane where I could finally love a woman I trusted with all of my heart, and she would love me back just the same.

I left soon after, but not before promising to walk Sam to school the next day, which was Monday. I'm pretty sure it was her idea, but I was thrilled. I was starved to be touched in a loving way again.

Thus for the next month, I walked Sam to and from school during the week, and we spent most of our spare time at the pool on weekends. Usually, the pool closed after Labor Day, but it was unseasonably hot that year, and the pool remained open until the end of September. We also ate lunch together in the school cafeteria. We never fought or argued, and Sam seemed ideal to me: beautiful, intelligent, loving, and possessing a great sense of humor. I pushed Will's warning about her to the back of my mind.

Then one day when Sam and I were hugging in the privacy of my basement, she said, "Do you realize we've been together for a month, and you still haven't kissed me?"

I hugged her tighter.

"Are you afraid of me?" she said. "I won't bite. Kissing would be nice."

"I'm not afraid," I said, although suddenly I was.

"What is it, then?" she said.

"I don't know—I just like hugging you, holding your hand, putting my arm around you, stuff like that," I said.

"But we love each other," she said. "There's nothing wrong with letting things progress—I'd really like to make out with you, and I'd like you to feel and suck on my breasts."

I could imagine myself doing these things, but my internal compass warned that sex would drag me out to sea like a rip-tide, roiling me far from where I wanted to be, which was in this chaste but comforting embrace.

I thought about how Gary and Tim at school were up for having sex with any girl who was willing, and I thought about how even straight-arrow Rick seemed to think it was okay to make love to a girl you liked or loved. But I just couldn't.

"Allen, loosen up," Sam said. "I can't breathe."

Allen Long is the author of Less than Human: a Memoir (Black Rose Writing, 2016). He is a regular contributor to Adelaide, and his work has recently appeared or is forthcoming in Broad Street, Hawaii Pacific Review, and Eunoia Review. Allen has been an assistant editor at Narrative Magazine since 2007, and he lives with his wife near San Francisco.

Have You Ever Tried to Write a War Poem?

By Faleeha Hassan

Some people believe that writing poetry requires training and planning. That if you go to school and attend poetry-writing classes or get experience by attending workshops, then you will get the ability you need to write poetry.

Honestly,

I am not totally against this idea, but there are some questions that jump into my head every time I hear it.

Such as...

Is *everyone* capable of writing poetry even if s/he does not have natural talent?

Are training and planning alone sufficient for the birth of a poem?

Even if we are convinced that training and planning are generally necessary, writing a poem about war is completely different. Going to school or workshops to gain enough experience to write a poem about war is not enough. No matter what we do to prepare, war poems remain frightening at their birth.

Let's explore that idea.

Let's say you are sitting on your rocking chair on your balcony on a beautiful quiet morning. As usual, you are smoking your cigarette. Next to you is a glass table with a cup of coffee. Suddenly you decide to write a poem. To be specific, you tell yourself, "Today I will write a war poem".

You take a deep breath and a sip of your coffee. You close your eyes to imagine a short war scene of a little girl sitting on the floor trying to hide her head between her knees. She is shaking and does not dare turn around for fear of the sound of the fighter planes. She panics as the sound gets louder.

Or…

You might imagine a group of children without shoes screaming and running in every direction, looking for a safe place to shelter. They hear the warning siren and stumble into the holes in the streets made by tanks.

Now what do you think?

Is it easy for you to find the short, concise phrases that show how you feel and what you sense to describe the panicked little girl?

Is it easy for you to find a convincing, persuasive phrase to help the reader visualize the status of those frightened children?

I honestly do not think you could write those phrases unless you were that little girl who was hiding during the raid. That girl who was watching with all her senses the death that was approaching her moment by moment. Or you would have to be one of those children who were running in every direction in order to survive.

Only then could you write a real war poem.

And in that moment--I mean in the moment of writing the war poem--you will remember how you miraculously survived the shrapnel and the missiles. How the sound of the guns and engines of the fighter craft would not go away from your ears. And you will find out that in that moment that you are reliving those dangerous memories, everything around you will turn into a war zone.

Suddenly the chirp of a bird turns into a warning siren. You see the dove that is flying over your head become a military observation plane. The tangled bushes on your balcony become barbed wire. The air almost fades around you, and the space closes in and tightens.

You want to scream but you can't, because your voice is now mingled with the muffled murmurs of that shaking girl and those frightened children.

Even your cigarette becomes a dynamite finger that is about to explode in between your real fingers. So dangerous that you need to carefully put it in the ashtray. The taste of your coffee changes to become bitter.

You try and try to find a gap through which to escape from your memories that have now turned into horrible present moments. And when you do not find that gap, different feelings start to conflict inside you. You want to cry, but there are not enough tears in your eyes to wash your soul of that terrible moment--a moment which is full of fear.

But you try and try and try anyway to find a moment of peace like you felt this morning, not so long before your poem was born-- after a very hard labor.

Yes, writing a war poem is a dangerous process. You may lose your sense of internal peace, or you may lose that moment of enjoyment that you feel when you notice the small things around you.

Maybe some who read this article will say that the writer is a plaintiff, or that her words are exaggerated, or that she is insane. But I say to all of them: No one can write a war poem where the reader can truly hear and see and feel the war moments inside it, unless s/he has actually experienced sitting on the edge of death. And has been lucky enough to survive and become a poet.

It is Easy to Be a Creative Woman?

According to traditional philosophy, woman was to be treated as objects not as human beings. For example, Aristotle believed that "women are imperfect men" and that "the function of women is limited to reproduction like animals". Jean-Jacques Rousseau said, "Society will collapse if a woman has not grown from a young age to obey a man." Freud believed that "women are inferior to men because of their lack of a biological system".

And Kant believed that "women cannot be full moral persons, because morality depends on the mind." He thought women were mentally deficient. This led to two important things--women pretending to be less intelligent, and women thinking negatively about their own creativity.

But modern philosophers have rethought traditional beliefs about women. Modern day feminists stress that "biological deficiencies" are compensated for by a woman's ability to have children. Some even believe in the idea of young male envy of women, also known as the "envy knot". Feminism has grown into a socio-political, inclusive movement that seeks social and cultural change toward gender equality. Women have become increasingly interested in feminist writing--writing from a woman's point of view-- from female and even at times male authors

Feminist writers rethink both life and society, trying hard to destroy the idea of masculine domination without advocating feminine domination as an alternative to it. On the contrary, feminists are trying to destroy the idea of domination itself

Most important is the focus widely on the experiences of women as just as appropriate and exciting and important as the experiences of men. this focus has already spread to the sphere of literary criticism for example. We might ask:

Is the author male or female?

Is the narrator male or female?

What are the roles of women in the text?

Are female characters in the text primary or secondary?

Does the text show any stereotyped characteristics of women?

What attitudes do male characters have toward female characters?

What is the perspective of the author or authors in relation to women in society?

How does the general public receive the female characters?

Does the text contain female or feminine images?

What is the importance of those images?

Do the female characters speak differently than the male characters? If so, how and to what extent?

When literary critics study the work of feminists and feminist critics and use those ideas when critiquing, they rebuild our thoughts about women being creative,

they reshape and reformulate our ideas about self, identity, and personality, and society,

Feminists seek to promote equality, but if we ask about the purposes of women's writing, the first answer would be that a woman who writes is difficult to ignore simply because she is a woman who has seen or lived and suffered difficult and horrible situations. Her writing is a valid place for her revelation.

Second, that woman is refusing to be under society's control, under unfair conditions. She will not be hybridized and she is brave because she asks for change that leads to the greater good.

Third, she may use poetry as a tool to detect and reveal the inner mechanisms of herself as a poet and a woman. This is not always available to male poets, because the they are often seeking great issues to about to keep their place in history, or to keep their poems in the mind of the readers for as long as possible. On the contrary, women's writing reveals to us so many mysteries of the human spirit. It reveals moments of sadness and joy and all of the other emotions that we ordinary people feel in different situations. These emotions appear in the poems of woman in a clear and honest manner far from intimidation and superficiality,

Unfortunately, some men, while critiquing women writers, look to take it as a document against her.

Some of these men see that a woman's poem is supposed to embody the woman who wrote it--a poem she wrote not only to other women, and some do not believe that the poem belongs to the woman who wrote it unless she shows a clear female perspective. It is as if the critic was looking to free a pent-up desire, and that he forgot that the existence of that writing is not a problem that needs a solution.

Just as a woman does not need to paint her nails to prove her femininity. Her text says, I am a woman and this is an announcement, but my poem is a reflection of what is inside me and not my outside. It is not a hole that helps you to sneak into my bed or my close,

It is interesting to note that there is a continuing witch hunt for erotic vocabulary in women's writing but not in men's writing. Some critics say that a woman writes to describe her body and turn it into an icon, but my opinion is that the words have only become erotica because of two contradictory conditions--excessive repetition and inappropriate presence. We cannot use a woman's writing against her.

Faleeha Hassan is a poet, teacher, editor, and writer born in Najaf, Iraq, in 1967, who now lives in the United States. She got a master's degree in Arabic literature, and published sixteen collections of poetry in Arabic and her work was translated into English, Turkmen, Bosevih, Indian, French, Italian, German, Kurdish, Spanish and Albanian.

Being There

By Richard Schmitt

TMI: Too much information is detrimental to recall.

June 8th 2018. Oscar Scherer State Park, just south of
Sarasota, Florida. I am here now, in my truck camper, of this
there is credit-card proof, signed and filed at the Ranger Station. That I've been here before is possible. I feel certain that I
have. But I'm not sure. What I see here corresponds to images
I've long held in memory. The lake and the picnic tables surrounding the lake, children splashing while parents loll, and
the rangy pine standing above the rest where I saw, or think
I saw, a buzzard/osprey/eagle/hawk—who knows which—sil-
houetted before a thunderhead beyond the treetops, and my
friend Dave, healthy then in bluejean cutoffs, white threads
stuck wet to skinny legs, pointing. The way I see it, we're in
the lake beneath the skyscraper-gray sky and he points to the
incoming storm. We'd better get to the tent.

I don't hear him say that and I don't recall if it rained. It
may have rained. But wouldn't I remember being in the tent
with Dave? With the water beating the canvas and the seams
leaking? I don't see that, I don't feel it. But I hear Dave mention
seams. I know he said *seams*. He says duct tape/spray sealant/
tarps. I see his face resigned to leakage. I don't think I've made
that up about the leaks, conjured it out of likeliness. I know

tents leak, and I know Dave was resourceful, so maybe I am dreaming this about the tent and the seams. Memory/seams/ leakage are all so fleeting. I cannot be sure of any of this because of the web. Recent studies claim the web contributes to memory loss. But I wonder, what might the web *add* to memory?

I fear internet memories. I've studied the park website, read brochures, and watched drone footage. Consequently, I'm stumped on what I know from experience and what I imagine knowing from looking at a computer screen. This is more than unsettling, it pisses me off. The past is gray area enough and now the information age has corrupted even what I think I know. Living with the web is living in the age of doubt. Fake news isn't relevant to me. Fake life, false memories, whether I was here or there—these things disturb me.

It was a green umbrella tent the way I see it, a worn yard-sale find. Dave had no money and was living in the state park. Site 19. That much I know. It might have been site 20, but I think it was 19. The two most remote sites in primitive camping, tents only, no water or electric. I am now in site 83, a full hookup RV site on the paved road. It is on the same winding black-water creek as site 19, which, when I go to examine it, looks exactly the way I've been picturing it for twenty years. The paved road gives way to soft sand, the picnic table, fire pit, the pole to hang food out of raccoon reach, the faded green tent possibly with duct tape patches. All of it visually intact and also called into question because of the web.

I'd come to stay at the park on a whim, for nostalgic reasons, and maybe to find an answer or two. I came seeking nothing but hope. There is always hope. Well, not always. But I believe when Dave lived at the park in the nineties he still had hope, though possibly it was waning. I knew this was the last place he lived in Florida before moving north to Illinois where he lost all hope and killed himself. I came hoping I'd

ESSAYS

see something, feel something that would connect me in some tangible way to these visions or memories I've harbored of visiting Dave in the park.

I see myself on the sandy road dipping and rocking into the primitive tent section in my 1966 Chevy pickup, which is impossible. If this visit to Dave occurred at all it was after my daughter was born in 1991 and that Chevy pickup I once owned in the seventies, when I first met Dave, had long been recycled. So what was I driving? I can't see it. I'd driven from Ocala three hours to the north, maybe. I feel the rolling and squishing of the sand under my tires. I see clearly Dave's site with the tent good for a family of four according to the smiling face of Ted Williams stitched near the zippered flap. Ted was spokesman for all things Sears then, coincidently he lived nearby in a gated community, regular sightings of him out on a golf course or fishing in the Gulf of Mexico.

Because of the web, none of this can be verified or discounted. I've sat miles and years away in front of a computer screen seeing pictures of the park and Google maps of Ted's neighborhood—his home and his neighbor's homes, the clean streets, license plates fuzzed out, and every so often the shadow of Google's mapping vehicle which they don't bother to edit out. I know there may be embellishments here. I know myself at least well enough to know that I'm prone to enhancing details, things I may be imagining, especially absurd things like Ted Williams's face on the flap of Dave's yardsale tent.

The simple truth—can there be such a thing?

Site 83 is rich with Wi-Fi. I sit in my camper sucking images out of time and space, acquiring information I may one day question. Because of the web I'm in the dark. Because of the web I'm losing my ability to discern so-called reality from so-called virtual reality. The haze grows sharp and more precise. There is no end to the misinformation age. We've all

147

seen places we've never been, but it's troubling when you're sure you've been someplace but cannot separate the actual experience from the simulated one because of the web.

I have a corporeal memory of stringing my mosquito-netted Vietnam-era hammock between two trees in site 19, one tree was a palm, the other a prickly oak, or something like that. There were bees, probably in a knothole of the oak, if it was an oak, and ants streaming along up the palm. I feel my hands lining the hammock with a lightweight sleeping bag I'd carried out of Alaska in 1976. A factual event not warped by the World Wide Web of which there was no such thing in 1976. Events actually happened then. I know where and when I got that sleeping bag. Kodiak Island, a cannery barge belonging to Pan Alaska Fisheries, a Japanese company. I traded a much better sleeping bag for the lightweight one because I knew I was headed to Florida. A kid from Oregon was happy to trade. He was freezing in his shitty bag. I can feel it now and again, my hands stuffing the orange nylon, goose-down-filled bag, into the hammock that I ordered from an Army Surplus Catalogue. These things are real. And I guess, I don't remember this part, maybe I slept blissfully mosquito free in my bag/hammock between the trees. I don't remember being drunk. Which is another problem.

Dave and I stand on the bank of site 19 feeding short white Hormel sausages to turtles. The canned sausages come in clear glutinous fluid and look like white cigar butts. These are unlikely to be found in research or imagination. The pop-top cans fed to turtles, which I've enhanced to gators, are too precise. I wouldn't have conjured them up on my own. So how have I come by these pictures in my mind? Memories, so called. Dave and Ted Williams and me in my hammock hung between the lone palm and the bee tree. Or was it ants?

I first came to Sarasota in 1972 when I was eighteen. I met Dave detailing cars and we often passed the park entrance driving on route 41 and never gave it a glance. Then one day twenty years later I heard Dave was a permanent resident. Permanent except once a month he had to get out. Thirty days maximum stay. He told me this? Anyone can read it on the park website. Check it out yourself. Once a month, Dave struck the tent, loaded up his van and drove out of the park. I see myself doing this with him. Maybe I arrived on the twenty-ninth day. Out we head, circle the sign at the entrance, one way in and one way out. We pull up to the ranger's station. "Morning," Dave says. "Is site nineteen available?"

"Let me check," the ranger says. "Yep, nineteen is open. Would you like it?"

"I would like it," Dave says.

Both of them are dead serious, as if they've never before seen each other, never in a million years, or even thirty days, played out this once-a-month charade. It's easy to picture. It's not on the web. But the thirty-day rule is. So, the whole scene is vaporous. Falling somewhere in the range of possibility between utter fantasy and verifiable fact.

Raccoons were acrobats of the hanging pole and stole Dave's can goods in the night. They had trouble opening the cans but they tore the labels off. In the morning Dave retrieved the labeless cans scattered in the scrub around the site. "Lunch is always a surprise," he said. That sounds like Dave. If you were there you'd know, that sounds like him. And how likely is that small raccoonian detail? Isn't it too true to be imagined? Labeless cans are not on the website. Did I see the cans? Hold them in my hands? I don't recall that, I don't feel them.

At site 83, I have the contents of Dave's wallet given to me by his sister given to her by the coroner's office in Illinois. There are two worn prayer cards with the name of a mission in Sarasota stamped on them. "A place to get a free meal," Dave told me. "Spaghetti or stew. You have to listen to a lecture

first." I know Dave told me this. I would not know it otherwise. I hear him say "stew" distastefully. But I don't know *when*
he told me this. It could have been when he came to Ocala
in 2004, or in a letter sent from jail. He was in jail for ninety
days for being a stubborn drunk and refusing to obey a police
officer. I can never get straight whether the jail stint was before,
after, or during the time he lived in the park. It hardly matters,
except for the drinking question.

When my daughter was born in 1991, I quit drinking.
Dave quit drinking in jail and didn't go back to it right away
when he got out. Was our visit after he got out of the county
jail? Both of us clean and sober for the only period in our entire
history? That would be a good story if I could remember it. I'd
known Dave twenty years by that point and we were always
bad drunks, smashing up cars and getting thrown in jail and
bonding each other out. Later I heard from his sister, Carol, the
only reliable source of information, that Dave started drinking
again after he was evacuated from the park due to Hurricane
Charlie in August 2004. Could he possibly have been living in
the park for ten years? What a mess this memory shit is.

I am here looking for a past I merely suspect. I see us
and hear us rising and falling in scene after scene like len-
ticular print images. Look one way, a picture appears, look
a different way, the picture changes. We emerge and recede
from the fog of doubt. Turtles become gators, ants and bees are
synonymous, raccoons steal the labels. We are primitive in our
remembrances that mean so much. That define us. Our past is
not gone but it's disfigured, because of the web.

People are always saying "in another lifetime." Looking
at an old snapshot they feel nostalgic, or some sudden longing
sparks a memory, of themselves or loved ones, long gone in
days of youth or disaster. Has the web both diminished and
expanded the possibility for those other lifetimes? Allowing en-

tire experiences that exist solely in the realm of possibility? Or maybe other lifetimes have always existed somewhere in a parallel emotional dimension or timeframe within us, these just waiting for the invention of the internet in order to emerge.

Dave shopped at yard sales, he told me. I don't know when he told me. He listened to sermons and ate bad stew. I have the prayer cards. I hear him say, "The rangers all know me." I could not have imagined or made up the Hormel sausages in the cans with fluid like grease fed to turtles that I want to be gators. The seams of the tent were sealed whether I was there or not. Did Ted Williams really live nearby? I could not have invented label-stealing raccoons that provided Dave with surprise lunches.

These are the meagre facts: Dave was in good health in the nineties. Not so good by 2004. He deliberately squatted in front of a train on July 3th 2005. I don't know why. There is no video. At a place called Merz Crematory in Salem, Illinois, they burned him up and ground his bones to dust on July 5th. Someone paid for that. There is credit-card proof. They mailed his remains to his mother. She signed for the box.

I have no idea if I ever set foot in Oscar Scherer State Park before June 8th 2018. But I feel as if I did, because of the web, maybe.

Richard Schmitt is the author of The Aerialist, a novel, and, Living Among Strangers, a short-story collection. He had published in *Art & Letters, Blackbird, Cimarron Review, Gulf Coast, Gettysburg Review, North American Review, Shenandoah, Tri-Quartely* and other places. His story "Leaving Venice Florida" won 1st Prize in The Mississippi Review short story contest and is anthologized in New Stories of the South: The Year's Best 1999. His essay "Sometimes a Romantic Notion" is anthologized in Best American Essays 2013.

Art And Poetry

By Byron Beynon

The relationship between painting and poetry, how poets and painters turn to one another for inspiration, has continued to be of interest for sometime. There are many examples of how art can inspire the writing of poetry, and the responses can take many forms.

The historian Plutarch (c.46–120 A.D.) in his essay on the Glory of Athens quoted Simonides, a Greek poet, as saying "painting is silent poetry and poetry, painting that speaks." Using art to inspire poetry is conjured up vividly in Homer's famous description of Achilles' shield in the Iliad. It appears before the mind's eye (an ekphrastic poem, from the Greek word ekphrasis, translated simply as description) as a visual representation, but also something that means so much more in feeling and depth.

A well-known ekphrastic poem by John Keats (1795-1821) is Ode on a Grecian Urn, where the stillness, the time-lessness of great art, is contrasted with the inevitable disap-pointments of human experience. Since the death of its maker, an anonymous craftsman, the urn has been fostered by time and silence. The poem appeared first in the Annals of the Fine Arts in January 1820.

Keats also moved in a circle of friends which included artists and critics such as B. R. Haydon, Joseph Severn and

William Hazlitt. It was the artist, Haydon, who took Keats to see the Elgin Marbles at the British Museum in March 1817. The Marbles had arrived in England in several shiploads from The Parthenon in Athens between 1803 and 1812. Keats wrote two sonnets soon after seeing them. Decades later William Holman Hunt's first Pre-Raphaelite work exhibited at the Royal Academy was inspired by Keats's poem The Eve of St Agnes.

The nineteenth century also saw the influential French poet and critic, Charles Baudelaire (1821-1867) publish his important essay entitled "The Painter of Modern Life" (published in 1863). Baudelaire asks the artist to capture "that indefinable something we may be allowed to call modernity.... the transient, the fleeting and the contingent". The painter Edouard Manet was his friend and was influenced by the poet. Baudelaire can be seen in Manet's painting "Music in the Tuileries Garden", along with the writer Théophile Gautier and the composer Jacques Offenbach.

Closer to our own time, a critic writing in 2009 about Gwen John's painting 'A Corner of the Artist's Room in Paris' said that it was as close to a love poem as a painting can get.

Gwen John herself said "my room is so delicious after a whole day outside it seems to me that I am not myself except in my room."

There have also been some artists who have been both poet and painter: a fusion of both skills and expression. Michelangelo started writing poetry at a fairly early age, but later in life, from 1532 until 1547 he wrote some two hundred poems.

William Blake (1757-1827) wrote, engraved and printed his first book of poems, combining great poetry with vibrant images. He was largely unrecognised during his lifetime. Worldly success was of little consequence to him. He was dedicated to his work and lived in a world of imagination and the spirit rather than the material world. Blake would have seen a real tiger at the Tower of London, and as a child he had seen images of tigers. The illustration for his poem ' The Tyger' was once described as having the expression of a stuffed toy. Blake's illuminated books are unique in that he printed both his texts and illustrations which he subsequently coloured by hand. It has been strongly suggested that Dylan Thomas would have had access to the Everyman edition of Blake's poems published in 1927. He would then have seen the frontispiece to Blake's "Gates of Paradise", and been influenced by the illustration. For example in I See the Boys Of Summer, where in the third section of the poem he writes 'Man in his maggot's barren./ And boys are full and foreign in the pouch."

Blake was probably ahead of his time, and two centuries after his first and only exhibition flopped, Tate Britain recreated it in 2009. As Blake wrote 'The eye sees more than the heart knows.'

David Jones (1895- 1974) also belongs to that line of poet-painter. His epic prose-poem of the First World War, In Parenthesis was first published in 1937 by T.S. Eliot at Faber & Faber. Eliot regarded it as "as a work of genius." Jones's art ranged from paintings, engravings and sculpture to inscriptions and lettering.

A painter who appreciated poetry was Vincent Van Gogh (1853-1890). In a letter to his brother Theo he mentions Longfellow, and reading poetry with a friend. He also wrote in the same letter "I have not read Hyperion yet, but I have heard that it is very beautiful....."

R.S. Thomas's (1913-2000) collection 'Between Here and Now' published in 1981 opens with 33 poems, each one a response to Impressionist paintings which hang in the Louvre, including paintings by Jongkind, Degas, Monet, Vincent and others. In 1985 he brought out another collection entitled 'In-

growing Thoughts', it contains 21 poems, inspired by twentieth century artists such as Picasso, Matisse, Chagall, and Paul
Nash.

The Fall of Icarus by the Flemish painter, Pieter Bruegel
(c.1525–1569) was based on the myth of Icarus and Daedulus.
The painting was admired by the poet W.H. Auden (1907-
73) and it inspired him to write the poem 'Musée des Beaux
Arts'. Bruegel was a pioneer of landscape painting, of hunts,
festivals, dances, with great powers of observation, and minute
depiction of detail. The painting was bought in 1912 by the
Museum of Fine Arts in Brussels. Auden would have seen the
painting in December 1938: he understood how the artist
showed everyday life going on steadily, unconscious that Icarus
is falling to his death.

Ceri Richards (1903-1971) held his first solo exhibition
at the Glynn Vivian gallery in Swansea in 1930. A retrospec-
tive of his work was held at the Whitechapel art gallery in
1960, and two years later he represented Britain at the Venice
Biennale, winning the Einaudi painting prize. He was also a
trustee of the Tate Gallery from 1958 to 1965. Dylan's death
in 1953 keenly affected him and although he had met the poet
only once he felt a profound affinity with Dylan, the man and
his work. This can be seen in his work based on Thomas's
poem to his father 'Do Not go Gentle into that Good Night'.

Like Richards, John Ormond (1923-1990) was born in
Dunvant, he was a poet and a gifted documentary film-maker
at the BBC. He created films on Dylan, Ceri Richards and
R.S. Thomas. He also worked for Picture Post. In his poem
'Certain Questions for Monsieur Renoir' he is inspired by
Renoir's painting La Parisienne. The woman in the painting is
an actress, a favourite model he used between 1874 and 1876.
The brightness of the painting giving it an unique vibrancy
and charm. Gwendoline Davies bought the painting in 1913.

This is just a brief glimpse through an open window at the relationship between the world of art and poetry: how close it has been and how the relationship continues to flourish.

Byron Beynon lives in Wales. His work has appeared in several publications including San Pedro River Review, Agenda, Quadrant, Poetry Pacific, London Magazine and the human rights anthology In Protest (University of London and Keats House Poets). Collections include Cuffs (Rack Press), Human Shores (Lapwing Publications) and The Echoing Coastline (Agenda Editions).

Immeasurable Greatness

By Rachel A.G. Gilman

Everything started at eight years old, with my tonsils. The year before I had them out I was ghastly white, except for my nose, which was usually bright red. The cases of strep throat and the common cold were plentiful. Watch a video from my performance as Shprintze in *Fiddler on the Roof* and hear my voice as nasal as if I were playing *Rudolph the Red Nosed Reindeer*. I was also quite thin.

After it was determined my swollen tonsils caused my illnesses, the tissues were removed. Two weeks post-op were spent in bed with a sore throat, unable to eat much and say even less, but it got better and the illnesses dissipated. My coloring came back. My voice cleared out. And the clothes that once fit me no longer did.

I recall saying my face looked like a tomato in my yearbook picture. My frame expanded first vertically then horizontally. When I wanted to wear outfits to match my American Girl dolls or to look like a Disney princess, the sizes stopped before my body did. I did not understand. Everything felt more complicated.

I quit ballet lessons a year later after growing tired of being put in the corner because I was "too big," spending productions of *The Nutcracker* in the back of the stage dressed up as a male tin soldier, reindeer, or hungry chef since the costumes for the roles of maids and snowflakes would never fit me. The costumes for the girls' parts, I understood, were small, and I was not.

In fourth grade I danced in the school talent show and had to wear a tank top with an elastic shelf on the inside underneath my clothes to hide my budding chest.

In fifth grade I hit 100 pounds before any of my other friends.

My body was too big for the instructions on the medications I took when I used to get sick, too big to go down the slide on the playground comfortably, too big for every Halloween costume in children's sizes. I did not identify with my body. Inside, I was still a rail thin little girl with the sniffles.

For a while I wondered if keeping the tonsils would have kept my original body chemistry, would have allowed me to stay the same. The change, I realize now, was inevitable.

We understand puberty as the period during which adolescents reach sexual maturity and become capable of reproduction. Marketing from beinggirl.com and girlsheath.gov, with bright colors, smiling faces, and so many flowers does not explain that everything about this time sucks.

Instead, these websites break down the process into fun steps of growing breasts and body hair, developing pimples, and eventually getting a "shape". Apparently you were a formless lump of clay before, who knew! And do not fret if you skip a step. There is no "normal."

I had these elements glossed over in an explanation to me at the end of fifth grade when the health teacher had all of the girls sit for a video from the 1990s detailing the importance of us keeping a calendar to track our cycles and how we were going to start feeling attracted to boys. We should not be upset when it happened. I had always loved my calendar and boys, but I was still upset about the talk, though not as upset as the girl the nurse embarrassed for having already gotten her period. During this talk all of the boys got to play kickball. They never had an equivalent lecture and I have never let that go.

The last few years have brought attention and research to the question of whether or not girls are reaching puberty too early. Mothers of daughters as young as three worry about their girls already showing developmental changes. The doctors have labeled any signs of such as "precocious" and "a new normal," even though they said there was not a "normal" to start. They are awfully endearing labels.

Every year in school, the nurse would take our height and weight measurements as well as blood pressure and vision. We were told it was state-mandated, but if we went to the doctor the summer before and showed we had already been through these checks, we would not be called out of class.

I went to the doctor every year, brought in the signed papers, and handed them directly to the nurse. Still, she always called me in.

In middle school, it went alphabetically by your grade. My last name happened to be sandwiched in between the popular kids. These were the boys with the toothpick legs in basketball shorts and the voices that had changed. These were the girls who flat-ironed their hair, wore push-up bras and make-up, who had just started weighing a hundred pounds and who would never weigh much more. By comparison, my frizzy hair was hapless, my glasses made eye make-up pointless, wearing a push-up bra would have suffocated me under my too big breasts, and I had not been one hundred pounds in a few years.

The nurse read all of the measurements aloud. I had gotten to 5'5" in height. I have blocked out how much I weighed. I was not so lucky to forget her shouting the number for everyone in the vicinity to hear and informing me I was "overweight".

She said it like she had never seen someone my size, someone wearing a large Abercrombie sweatshirt instead of a small.

I was sent out of her office with pamphlets on exercise and healthy snacks with tubby children pictured, feeling very bad about having what I had already subconsciously felt and known delivered to my face.

I cried a lot in middle school, like when I got my period before the mile run or when my bra broke in math class or when the boy with the rocker style hair and skinny jeans told all my friends I was ugly. But I never cried about this incident. Instead, I went on weird diets, exercised profusely, and still, looked the same.

My body had the power, so I gave in and blamed it for my other problems. I knew how I looked was somehow wrong – not petite, not pretty, not correctly feminine – but I could not find a solution.

Skater skirts. Cocktail dresses. Boyfriend jeans. The way we speak of women's clothing is composed of hybrid words that form a new language. As part of the dialect, one needs a familiarity with the way these things are sized. There are numerous articles on the subject.

"The absurdity of women's clothing sizes, in one chart."

"It's Not You. Women's Clothing Sizes Make No Sense."

"Proof that women's clothing sizes are bizarre and inconsistent."

Most people, it seems, are quite puzzled on the matter.

In the 1940s, the Works Progress Administration began to implement the "ready to wear" clothing model with a study of 15,000 American women (tiny, white women). This study involved measuring fifty-nine parts of the female body and resulted in the creation of twenty-seven unique dress sizes. A decade later, the National Bureau of Standards simplified the information and in 1958 made the system mandatory for commercial pattern makers. The mandate was dropped by 1983. Maybe they realized it was too complex, or that they should not have tossed out the measurements from the women of color, or that there was something at fault with what Julia Felsenthal of *Slate* called "the ever-expanding American woman".

The Center for Disease Control and Prevention recently found women today weigh as much as men did in the 1960s. I am not sure what disease this research is trying to control or prevent. Anxiety, paranoia, and depression are certainly not the concerns.

There have been attempts to revisit this standardized sizing system in the U.S., but companies disagree. It is far too good a marketing campaign to make the garments dissociate from the norms of numbers.

Look in any woman's closet and the sizes will confuse you. Mine includes the following. Size 8 denim mini skirt from J.Crew. Size 5 Ted Baker fit and flare dress. Size 44 vintage wool blazer with a label written in Japanese. My jeans in their many variations are as convoluted as any statistics test.

"They're just random numbers," one professor of fashion said when discussing this matter for *Washington Post*. "They don't mean anything."

I think of the Body Mass Index calculator, what is an appropriate average daily caloric intake, and all of the times when I feared a store would not carry my size, whatever it is, because they had isolated it to "online only" – heaven forbid people with my body type shop in actual shops.

The numbers may be random, but they certainly do mean something.

My Catholic high school had a "business casual" dress code. The boys were expected to have collared shirts tucked into chinos. Conversations concerning the clothing choices of the girls, of course, were far more complicated.

The first week of freshman year I wore a madras plaid dress that came down to my knees with a cardigan. My homeroom teacher (the religion teacher) asked me if I could step outside the classroom for a moment. We stood by the open door as she proceeded to tell me loudly that my outfit was inappropriate. She said it was revealing. I looked down, confused, and then saw the dress's bodice was boned around the bust. No skin was showing, but this was to which she was referring.

She did not appreciate my response of, "I don't think the dress is saying anything that isn't already obvious." But I was right. In a turtleneck, I had noticeable breasts.

"You need to compose yourself," the teacher yelled. All of the boys in my homeroom leaned forward in their desks to see out the door.

"I'm fine," I replied in a calm voice. "You're the one shouting. Maybe you need to compose yourself."

This response went over even worse. I buttoned my cardigan to my neck for the rest of the day.

Throughout high school, there were morning dress code checks from the Dean of Students, and my name frequently ended up on the list. My hemlines were wrong because they went up in the back thanks to my butt. My V-neck sweater was suggestive. My lacy tights were inappropriate since you noticed my fuller thighs. These were not problems for the girls whose bodies did not look like mine. They were able to go unnoticed. They were the same girls who once told me in art class that I could not "pull off" my outfit.

"I can't help it if I have an ass," I finally stated to the Dean after a year of complaints and ending up in his office. "It's not something to be ashamed of, and it's certainly not the most important problem in this school."

This was true, but I still hated the attention my body drew. I had hated it since I was eleven and mistaken for sixteen, when I was hit on at the beach or in stores by boys twice my age. I did not want the boobs or the butt that my friends joked came along with my brains to make me the "full package". I wanted to be able to walk in a room and not think the giggles coming from someone were in a response to my entry.

There is a test you can take online for almost anything, including helping you to determine whether or not you have a variety of psychological conditions. One test is for Body Dysmorphic Disorder (BDD), "a preoccupation with one or more perceived defects or flaws in appearance, which is unnoticeable to others". 1 in 50 people suffer, says the Anxiety and Depression Association of America.

The questionnaire for BDD is less complex than most Buzzfeed quizzes: nine questions, including how often you deliberately check your features, how unattractive you feel, and how often your features preoccupy your thoughts. It is scored out of 72 points and anything above 40 suggests you might want to speak with a doctor about the condition. Anything above 30, they say, is also iffy territory.

It is all a result of the culture. American media is plethoric with images of perfection women are meant to strive toward.

You should be tall. You should be thin. You should be poised and perky and pleasant. And you should pull off this image naturally, just like the women wearing the Lululemon yoga pants in the window ad or the blogger who is always eating pasta in Italy with ornate make-up and the perfect outfit.

But nothing about this is natural, not even the images themselves. They are hyped, staged, worked. Yet this is what we are taught to idealize, what we are pressured to emulate.

The pressure is part of the reason people go on thinking they are not good enough. It contributes to why the National Eating Disorders Foundation found that 79% of girls and 85% of women admit to opting out of important events because they do not feel their best. It is why 44% of girls in high school, according to Dosomething.org, are attempting to lose weight. It is undoubtedly the worry at the back of the minds of parents with the Google search input, "How to improve my daughter's self esteem." The figures are even more upsetting if you are a woman of color or identify at LGBTQ.

Some companies say they are working to fix this ideal by replacing it with support for embracing your actual self, and some are actually doing so, like Aerie, Modcloth, and Dear Kate who all feature more diverse models and sizes. Everyone, however, claims they are on board, which is why the sentiments in these movements remain hollow.

You still walk down the street and see willowy white women on billboards wearing clothing that does not come above a size 12. You still read articles about how to be "sexy, sculpting, and slim" when you are looking for an exercise to do for more energy. You still know that while a lot of people are telling you that you are just fine that really you are not. You can see it when you look in the reflection on the storefront window for the deliberate twelfth check of your appearance that bumped your score up a few points on the BDD questionnaire.

In college, my freshman year, I reached my heaviest weight at 235 pounds and wore size eighteen jeans that fit snug on my hips. I hardly ate, ironically, but what I did consume was sugar and fat. At my lightest, junior year, the scale finally read something considered "healthy" even though I was going weeks running on only electrolyte-enhanced water, bites of granola bars, and bottles of children's Motrin to ease the hunger ache (it did not matter if I was too big to take it anymore). I was not healthy. The feeling of emptiness, I thought, would lead to a bigger reward, though that reward I never discovered.

I eventually decided to work on figuring out how to be happy, on how to work toward greatness while finding acceptance. I discovered not where these things come from but instead from where they do not.

It is not from online articles giving steps on how to be "healthier", or working yourself into the ground on four hours of sleep and three hundred daily calories, or keeping an article of clothing simply for the sake of thinking one day you might again fit into it. It is not from measuring your limbs to see if they have shrunk when the scale reads the same number after weeks of working out, or blaming it on stress, or telling yourself there must be something wrong. It is not from an outside source. The change to accept, to find greatness, comes from within.

I still struggle to remember to eat three meals, to go to bed on time, and to wear whatever I feel comfortable in without thinking of criticism. I constantly remind myself I am and I am not the past versions of my exterior, both those I have loved and those I have hated. I am instead the culmination of everything. I am all I can be, and that, I must remember, is great.

The positive feeling in acceptance comes from removing the outside world; from realizing anything worth being is not weighed against something else. True greatness exists on an immeasurable scale. Only you can determine when something feels good, and after good it will eventually get to great – it is a process, but a rewarding one, I am choosing to believe.

Rachel A.G. Gilman is a writer whose work has been featured in Minetta Review, Verdad, and others. She has also contributed to TV Guide Magazine and Popdust. She holds a B.A. from NYU and is pursuing an MFA at Columbia University and an MSt at Oxford University. Additionally, she founded the feminist literary journal, *The Rational Creature*, and hosted the award-winning radio show, "The Write Stuff". Find out more at rachelaggilman.com.

Vanishing

By Leslie Tucker

The Anxiety of Geography and Genetics

Roots of the mammoth oak have heaved the sidewalk in front of our yellow clapboard house and two-year-old Becky rattles over the bumps on her Big Wheel, blond pigtails whipping behind her. Ten-year-old Lisa pokes her head out the screen door. "Buzzer went off. Should I take the brownies out?" She's followed the Betty Crocker box directions, greased the pan, broken the eggs and blended the brown goop.

"Toothpick test first." My wrap-around skirt billows open and I tip my head back, gaze at mounds of cumulus floating above the canopy of elms.

It's Mother's Day 1976 and unseasonably warm and sunny for southeastern Michigan. Dad's Mercury beeps twice as the car idles up the driveway and I see his high beam grin in the car's open window. "What's for dinner, Chum?"

It will be baked chicken with Lawry's Seasoned Salt, Mother's favorite, and we'll eat outdoors to inaugurate the deck my young husband has built. I love him. I love our daughters. I take it all for granted. I'm twenty-eight and my heart does not recognize the perfection of monotony, the power of shared ritual.

And yet the memory of that Mother's Day, and of each family member present remains emblazoned more vividly than anything I can conjure of my new grandson, Gus.

My younger daughter, former Big-Wheel-rider, Becky, lives with her fiancé, Salim, and Baby Gus in California – thousands of miles and thousands of dollars away. Other than one three day visit, all my connections to Baby Gus have come via the computer screen – Skype calls, or videos and photos posted on Facebook, and Salim's Baby Blog. All for an audience of hundreds, including me.

Something is slipping away and I'm having a difficult time naming it.

During the 1970s and 80s, Dad called his short, Saturday morning visits "stopovers." He tapped on the wavy glass of our back door, offered glazed donuts from Machus Bakery and parked himself at the kitchen table with his grand daughters. "What'd you do in school this week? Anyone want help with homework?"

The days of Dad's stopovers and our family dinners are gone, and unless I board a plane, I cannot touch the flesh of anyone who shares my blood, not one person who sat on the deck on Mother's Day 1976. The young deck builder and I stopped loving each other and divorced over twenty years ago. Dad's been dead eighteen years, Mother over five. Becky lives in Los Angeles, Lisa, near Chicago.

My second husband, Don, and I retired from our full-time work in Michigan, to a South Carolina mountainside eight years ago. All four kids, his two and my two, had left the Detroit area for college and to build careers. They've done what we envisioned for them, flown high and far and wide. Thousands of miles from us, they lead complicated lives and seem too busy to breathe. Sadly, I've not mastered the skill of long distance intimacy and am emotionally skewered by my situation. I want to live on this lush mountainside where mammoth tree trunks sprout pastel lichen and granite cliffs glisten in the rain, but I'm isolated from my daughters and their families here.

We planned our retirement home ten years ago when our young adult, childless children were portable and all of us jumped on and off airplanes with ease. Anticipating visits from giggling grandchildren and their parents, we built extra bedrooms and set up a long oak dining table.

I struggle now, to understand what I'm trying to hold onto.

Part of it involves the anxiety of geography, and the flesh of geography. On a recent Sunday, pin oaks shimmered silver against the seamless cobalt sky as I dashed inside to grab the phone. My older daughter, Lisa, and her husband, Ryan, were calling from their car in Illinois on the way to Ryan's parents' house for a cookout. Grandson Luke, fourteen, was fired up over his cross-country training and twelve-year-old Lily chattered about her summer book club.

Ryan's parents live where they raised their family, in Kirkland, Illinois. They've tallied countless stopovers with their four children, who stayed put, like they did. They know their grandchildren's favorite colors and video games, what they like on their pizza, what brands of shoes are cool.

The prospect of knowing my newest grandchild Gus with such intimacy feels daunting. Crossing the country to California is date specific and logistically complicated. And because we're retired now, the expense of airfare, hotels, rental cars and restaurants is suddenly intimidating. Even more difficult is the ordeal of them dragging an infant across the country.

I laughed it off for years, but now believe that proximity may well be the most important factor in human relationships. Humans require physical immediacy to develop intimacy, and the luxury of proximity allows us to form stronger bonds. Memory gets murky when we do not see and touch each other, often.

I remember the sling across Becky's chest the first time I saw Gus, how it cradled him, but what shape were his ears and did they lie flat? I had three days to soak him up and cannot recall. My eyes sting and blink at online photos and videos because as close as the baby seems, just inches away on my desk, the Internet membrane between us is impenetrable. The dimpled hands grasping thin air are out of reach.

Irony hangs heavy these days, forcing me to acknowledge what I hate to admit: That when my parents and children were nearby, warm and touchable, they often weighed me down. In the 1970s and 80s, Mom, Dad and my young family clustered around our dining room table for holidays and all our birthdays. I cringe to recall my snide remarks about those gatherings, "Hallmark Holidays," I said, designed to mine guilt and produce revenue. Now, acutely aware of my age and disappointing geographic realities, I yearn for the weight, the anchor of family members in my life.

Like most women of my generation, pregnancy and motherhood came early as natural functions of youth. I pushed my babies out with pent up vigor, propelling them forward as decades passed, and sure, my girls and I butted heads during their teenage years. I was distracted and working too hard, often didn't decipher what they needed, and when the time came, they were ready to leave home and I was glad to see it. That reality has tipped upside down now. I want my daughters close enough to touch, to see their eyes crinkle with laughter, to relearn their emotional alphabets.

How predictable but uncomfortable, this separation from distant children and dead parents, this winnowing of loved ones. The iPhone photos of my long-distance grandchildren far outnumber the wrinkled snapshots Dad carried with him in his pocket, but it's not the same. Dad was on the scene, clicking his Instamatic, standing in trampled grass by the inflatable pool as little girls splashed his seersucker pants. He witnessed the events portrayed in his photos, lived them in real time.

But it's not just distance that ails me.

When my older daughter Lisa's children, who resemble their brown-eyed, brown-haired father, were born, Dad had been dead only six years. Mother was still alive and we talked about him, how he loved tapioca pudding, Ovaltine, and Ronald Reagan. Dad's face was fresh in my mind's eye and it didn't occur to me that Lisa's children bore no resemblance to him, or to anyone else on our side of the family.

The Skype call from Becky, in California, came early this morning. Baby Gus' brown cheeks and chunky legs fill the computer screen and he blinks his chocolate eyes, flutters his lashes. I smile like a mannequin, swallow the lump in my throat, yearning to squeeze him, fly him through the air playing "babies in space" until he chortles like his mother used to. Gus, however, is digital, untouchable.

So far, Baby Gus does not resemble Becky or anyone in our family who came before her, but he is hers and I want to make him mine too. I'm perplexed and wonder why we examine infants with such scrutiny, explore their tiny faces so intently. Hoping to recognize what? What distance do we hope to bridge?

I miss my parents more, not less, as I age and physical proof that they will live on when I'm not here to remember them would be comforting. I search for their features and mannerisms on my grandchildren, hope to find their hospital-bed-eyes relit and vibrant again above chubby new cheeks. If I lived close enough to tickle Gus' chin or brush his sleeping palms, might I see hints of Dad's high beam grin?

I am embarrassed by this emotional juxtaposition, this faceoff between profound gratitude and derelict desire for genetic immortality. As years slipped by and her first marriage faltered, I was concerned for Beck, who had always wanted a child. Now I'm exhilarated because at age thirty-eight, after a difficult divorce, she has a healthy child with a man she loves. Yet an eerie emptiness persists because I ache to see some sign of her, in her child. Mediating elation and longing is tough.

Last spring, our friend, Fred, sat on the porch with Don and me and we all remarked that we couldn't fathom we'd attained our present ages. Don and I, in our mid-sixties, are well broken-in grandparents, have embraced the role for over a decade. Fred, however, a longtime-divorced guy in his late fifties, was brand new in the role, and wasn't prepared for the emotional earthquake that shook him when his daughter gave birth to a baby boy.

Fred said that although he was uneasy with the milestone of becoming a grandfather, he laid eyes on the boy and broke down because, "He was her all over again." Gazing into his grandson's eyes, he found his own baby daughter's twinkling back at him. He recognized the turned up nose and rosebud mouth on the infant's face, held the tiny thumbs, shaped exactly like his daughter's. He stepped back in time, basking in the glow of his own young fatherhood.

Yes, I yearn to see my tow-headed girls again, to establish their cornflower eyes on their children's faces, but even more, to sense a distillation of past generations of our family. I suppose a primal wish of people my age is that our children and grandchildren will be our future, and that perhaps for now, they will soften the wide empty space our parents left when they died. And, I want my grandchildren to know and remember me.

Salim's mother, Zarintaj, has moved from Houston to Los Angeles to be the full-time caregiver for our grandson, Gus. It is an excellent arrangement. Gus is safe and adored by his Dadima (Daddy's Mama) and Salim and Becky have peace of mind, are able to expedite their powerful careers and manage their new century lives.

Dadima is ever present, radiant in the photos and videos Salim posts online. From Gus' first strained peas to his Pediatric checkups, she is there. I absorb the joy in her actions and try to reconcile my feelings. She murmurs to baby Gus in a language I do not understand and I see that he is listening, concentrating on her face, focusing on the striking dark eyes that match his. The beauty of their connection is excruciating to observe. Gus will remember his Dadima.

I'm upholstered with memories of my Nana, Dad's mother. How her stumpy-heeled oxford clomped the rhythm as she taught me chord sequences for Maple Leaf Rag on the piano. How we sang together, *I've Got Six Pence* and *My Wild Irish Rose*, how her freckled arms hugged me, the way her brow crumpled in astonishment the day she realized I towered over her at age eleven. Nana's eyes, and Dad's, Mother's, Lisa and Becky's all varying shades of sapphire, all here with me this minute if I shut my own.

According to simplified Mendelian genetics, if an individual, like Gus, inherits both a dominant gene, (BB for brown eyes from his father,) and a recessive gene, (bb for blue eyes from his mother,) the dominant gene will prevail in him. The recessive gene remains, hidden, and can be passed on to his offspring. I imagine that maybe Becky's blue eyes, or my father's, or even Nana's, will peek out of the face of Gus' child some day.

I acknowledge that I am afraid, not just that our family's physical traits are lost, but that our traditions have disappeared too. No more stop overs, no Hallmark Holidays, no sleepovers at Nana's when Mom and Dad want a night out. Visiting Lisa and her family in Illinois, easy when we lived in Michigan, is more challenging now, a six-hour drive having become a fourteen-hour one.

Yet Lisa's always had a guest room, and the intimacy of staying under the same roof with her family provides emotional ballast, enables me to face the empty rooms at my house for months at a time. At Lisa's, we wake up down the hall and eat meals around the wormy chestnut table that sat in my dining room for decades. We sweat through indoor swim lessons together and relish roundhouse kicks in Tai Kwan Do. Yes, our memories are compressed into specific time segments but they are profound, sunk deep into memory trenches.

Sadly, there are no memory trenches in California and here's what I fear: that my timidity will turn to regret. I'm a blurt-it-out-woman by nature but am trying to change. I have not told my California daughter that her stepfather and I feel like distant, anemic outsiders. We recognize her overwhelming career demands and are astonished at how she juggles them so adeptly within her sweet, full life with Salim, Gus, and Dadima.

Without thinking it through, I assumed I would share not just ceremonies, but mundane moments of my children's' and grandchildren's lives. That we would savor the innocence and simplicity of unplanned, unplugged time, the way three generations of my family did. However unrealistic, I yearn for Gus' sweaty little hand in mine at the zoo, for casual dinners with Becky and Salim around our table eating squishy meatloaf and those mashed potatoes that stuck to the plate, the ones Dad loved.

I suppose most families remember holiday dinner conversation, and I do too, but what remains more specific in my memory, happened after the meals. How Dad grabbed a droopy old apron from the broom closet, tied it up high under his armpits and clamped it to the placket of his dress shirt with a flat gold tie clasp. I recall how my girls and I trailed him into the kitchen, allegedly to help with the dishes, when what we really wanted was his measured opinions of presidential politics, Tommy Dorsey's big band instrumentation, how Henry Ford built Detroit and then destroyed it. We clustered around

Dad and the porcelain sink of soapsuds, bumping elbows with damp dishtowels dangling from our hands.

If our traditions are lost in the geographic abyss and my family's physical traits are hidden, what remains? How can I cross this gap of generations? Essayist Peter Selgin poses the question: What are memories if not the ruins of experience? Indeed.

If we can't find our children in their children, nor the slightest resemblance to our missing parents, how then do we satisfy this yearning to bridge the space between them? How deep seated is the hope for physical immortality? Very deep, I believe, yet my longing surprises me. Years ago, when a friend expressed her wish to recognize her family in her son's children, I smirked, thought she was shallow.

I am moved by the words of Anthony Doerr's character, Dr. Amnesty, in the novella *Memory Wall*, who says: "Memory builds itself without any clean or objective logic: a dot here, another dot there, and plenty of dark spaces in between. Remember a memory often enough and you can create a new memory, the memory of remembering."

I am remembering the memory of three-week-old Gus as he was, the first and only time I have seen him, over eight months ago. Suspended across Becky's body in a hands-free sling, he slept peacefully when she opened the door. I remember his cue ball head, the wisps of black hair, his full pink lips. But Gus was not Becky all over again. He was not Becky at all. He was perfect, her miracle, and I'd sobbed at news of his birth, overwhelmed that he'd arrived safely and that his mother, my precious girl, was well. But no flood of recognition surged over me when I held him. Gus is Salim all over again. I suppose the years have folded back for his mother.

I was in Michigan recently and drove down the street where I lived with my young family. The giant oak and towering elms have been replaced by disease resistant maples and the new sidewalk is smooth in front of our former yellow clapboard house, which is now covered in vinyl siding and expanded by a two-story addition.

Yet Mother's Day 1976 remains illuminated as time compresses. A day when three generations of my family sat outdoors around the dinner table and focused on each other's faces, simply because we'd been trained to behave that way. A time when none of us clutched small devices to distract us from the momentary present, a time when we sat still and paid attention to what was said at the table, even if we were bored.

It never occurred to me to grasp the hands of those around the table on that day, to feel the flesh of the older and younger people who centered me so precisely in time and in my own life. I assumed there would always be Sunday dinners together and that afternoon sunlight would burst through elm leaves lighting up the faces of those I loved, reflecting in the eyes that matched mine.

Leslie Tucker, a former Detroiter, lives on a Carolina mountainside and refuses to divulge its exact location. She is an avid hiker and zipliner, a dedicated yogi, an ACBL Life Master in Sanctioned Bridge, and enjoys anything that requires a helmet. She holds degrees in business and music. Her work has appeared in The Baltimore Review, So to Speak: A Feminist Journal of Language and Art, Shenandoah Magazine, The Press 53 Awards Anthologies, where her essay "Lies That Behind" won First Prize for Creative Nonfiction, and Fiction Fix, where her essay "Reckless Abandon" was shortlisted for Best of the Net Awards.

Pyromaniacs

By Janel Brubaker

I married at twenty years old; a hollow shell of a woman still unearthing her identity. Still finding in herself barren branches that hadn't yet sprouted leaves or blossoms. I took vows I didn't understand and promised myself to a young man I barely knew. He wasn't a stranger; I had known him almost my whole life. But, looking back, I see that I didn't understand him. How could I when I barely understood myself?

I took for granted the passion and the newness and the flutters. I found in him a solution to the lonely ache I couldn't give a voice to. In hindsight I see that loneliness as a kind of wandering, a searching for the adult I was growing into. I was shedding the skin of a younger me and replacing it with a skin I didn't completely recognize. I felt displaced inside myself, so my solution was to find an anchor in the form of a life partner. The man I married wanted me and that was enough. His arms were open and that was enough.

I know now there should have been much more.

Yesterday he took me to the woods, to a trail we have often hiked that leads to two different waterfalls. I drove us to the trail. It was my idea to go. But I couldn't bring myself to leave the car. My insides were twisted. Knotted and contorted into unnatural shapes. This happens sometimes when I feel that I no longer fit inside of myself, when I question the life I've constructed over the last nine years. In these moments, even the beautiful places around me feel hollow and unwelcoming.

My husband said the trees wanted me to touch them, wanted me to wrap myself in their bark and carry their leaves in my hair. It was the encouragement I needed and he knew it. I can always be prevailed upon with trees. I smiled and climbed from the car. We walked the downhill path to the southernmost waterfall; along the way I slid my fingertips on the edges of many trunks, sucking in the breath of leaves, my husband's words ringing in my ears. My insides felt less twisted not only because he had said what I needed to hear, but also because he had known what to say. In that moment the world constructed around me felt less hollow. In that moment I felt that, perhaps, he knew me better than I gave him credit for.

As a young couple newly married, I romanticized our relationship, scribbled sonnets and love letters, sewed a whirlwind romance out of what had merely been a discovery of sexual pleasure. It was too new, too intoxicating to be anything other than pure, unadulterated love, I thought. I was taught next to nothing about love or marriage. The adults in my life were too preoccupied emphasizing the importance of purity and abstinence to recognize the gaping holes in their lessons. Maybe they assumed I would learn about love and marriage as I matured into adulthood. Maybe they thought it best for me to learn how to be married after I was already a wife.

If so, then I hope they are ashamed. Love can wreck a life. Learning about marriage through the process of trial and error almost guarantees failure. An early divorce. A broken view of commitment. I was told, "So long as divorce isn't an option, there isn't a single marital issue that can't be solved."

It was the only advice I was given and it was to be the phrase that often paved the path to the almost-graveyard of my marriage.

I learned early that simply avoiding the word "divorce" wouldn't make either my husband or myself less selfish people. It wouldn't help me express my needs and my expectations in healthy ways, and it certainly wouldn't create in me a heart filled with compassion and understanding. Only time allowed for these things to flourish, time and an almost endless repeating of my mistakes. Perhaps if we had been raised to value a healthy romantic relationship over the appearance of sexual purity, these lessons would have been easier to grasp. Instead, we rushed into a marriage neither of us was ready for to avoid the consternation of parents and family members, only to find that we were utterly unprepared to build a life together.

We walked to the waterfall and her collection pond that fed the river. The sky was bright with sun and the forest so illuminated that the pond glowed with emerald. I walked to the edge of the water and slid my fingers in the shallows. The last remnants of winter lived there. I climbed over logs and large stones to get to the cavern behind the falls. I wanted to be carried into the water; wanted to sink beneath the surface and feel the rage of the falls against my body. I can also be prevailed upon with bodies of water. I think I am made half of water and half of forest; I am both a dryad and a nymph. My soul is made of waves and branches.

Finding reflections of myself in nature is one way I make sense of this person I've constructed, this woman filled with loss and grief and a fading sense of hope. I am still shedding old skin and, much like when I chose to get married, now find myself hovering between two selves. With each shell of skin cast off, a piece of me is changed. But instead of trying to ground myself in a person, I lay anchor in the trees and the rivers and the ocean. I immerse myself in the natural world because it's the strongest thing I understand about myself.

I am now almost thirty and I have often mourned the death of a marriage that is still alive. I have sometimes worn black to signify its end, even though we are not divorced. We are not even separated and have no plans to be. I have seen the end on the horizon many times; each time we inch closer to it only to shrink away. We frequently set fire to this relationship, making kindling out of words and raised voices, but never seem to let it burn for long. We save it, dousing the flames with water and blankets time and time again only to reignite the flames with kerosene and lit matches. Then we watch the flames dance in the darkness.

I have learned to make ink from the ashes.

In the cool shade of the cavern behind the falls, I felt I could split in two and dedicate each half of me to the earth; one would be given to the trees and the other would be given to the falls. I would live on in the leaves and the bark and the roots that cling to the heart of the earth; my essence would pass over the falls into the pond, would flow down river, would bring life to the surrounding wilderness.

I am a spirit-woman. I immerse myself in places and people. I dive in without considering who and what I will leave behind. I dive in, shedding a bit of myself in the process. That's why I often see my reflection but don't recognize the woman staring back. I know her face, her blue eyes, her olive skin, but they are just the outer shell of someone who married too young. Someone whose identity has been constantly rooted in other people and who has now been forged in the fires of her marriage. This marriage that has split her in two: the one who wants the relationship to last, and the one who wants to watch it burn.

Janel Brubaker graduated from Clackamas Community College with her associates in English and Creative Writing. She also graduated from Marylhurst University with a Bachelor of Arts in English Literature and Writing. Her essays have been published in Bookends Review, The Bella Online Review, Crab Fat Magazine, Linden Avenue Literary Journal, Phenomenal Literature, Adelaide Literary Magazine, Sheepshead Review, DoveTales Journal, LEVITATE Magazine, and Timberline Review.

The Time I Got Naked in Front of a Female Student and It Wasn't a #metoo Moment

By Ray Savoie

Perhaps I volunteered to be a nude model for a collegiate art class. As a male professor teaching at the same college I can see how that might be *creepy*, but give me the benefit of the doubt and consider that I'm just comfortable with my body and believe in the free expression needed for good art. Maybe you agree that modeling shouldn't be the sole purview of the young and sculpted, feeling that ethical quiver you get when you see a plus-sized bikini model smiling among the pap of the checkout aisle. Imagine me a white middle-aged professor in a plush white robe entering an enormous studio painted entirely in black. The studio smells faintly of toxic chemicals, not enough to curl your nose hairs but certainly enough to pollute a good cocktail. In the middle is a vinyl red divan on a circular stage that's lit up like the sun. Orbiting it is a circle of wooden easels abused by semesters of paint, from behind which various young heads bob in and out. As I ascend the stage my head is welded to my neck, my eyes are made of glass, and I'm realizing this won't be the existentially liberating experience I bullshitted myself into believing. But I'm already there, *committed*, so I might as well go through with it.

I disrobe and position my body on the divan in a pose choreographed by the art professor. This professor is a friend whom I suspect concocted this position using a *Twister* wheel as revenge for goading him into too many shots last Friday. My right arm is a mic stand planted behind my back and my left leg is crossed over my right knee, leaving my foot dangling in a way that'd make a fetishist squirm with delight. This art professor is also white, male, heterosexual, middle-aged, and we have a few beers together at a pub once a month where the alcohol and privacy encourages us to speak openly about female colleagues and the occasional student crush. This is when the bastard talked me into being a nude model.

The following minutes feel like an endless extension of the first time you saw nudity in a movie with your parents, which I'm fairly certain was Sarte's backup plan for *No Exit*.

As I finally accept the exposure my right trapezoid begins cramping and my dangling foot goes numb. I maintain focus by counting down to a promised five minute break.

That's when I hazard a look out at the easels and meet eyes with a female student from my ENG 101 class.

We'll call her L-. There are several problems with this scenario, the worst of which is that L- is really attractive. If you tell me this shouldn't matter I will agree with you and explain that I'm an android from the future who used a time machine to escape the murderous blade runner hot on my trail. But even then, even with manufactured neurons and a synthetic heart and a robo-penis, it would still matter that women like L- are the reason *callipygian* is cherished by word dorks like me.

L-'s wavy blond hair is a strange yet appealing throwback to Veronica Lake, her blue eyes are full of wonder and honesty unbroken by time, and she possesses the type of body you'd expect of a nineteen year old obsessed with yoga and who has studied enough Wing Chun to participate in ritualistic sparring matches *with real knives.*

Worse: she's a self-professed "front row geek," one who smashes every other student's papers to shame with her maturity, style, and intellectual depth. Only once did I witness a male student attempt conversation. She was polite, but also so unmoved that I couldn't decide if she was that far beyond her peers, or just a lipstick lesbian. I told myself the later out of self-preservation.

I am constantly looking at her by painfully cataloging the frequency with which I actually look at her, self-conscious of when I yield the floor to her in discussion, the number of times I glance her way when sweeping the room to gauge class engagement, all while not wanting to give myself away by completely ignoring her, which could inhibit her learning because she thinks her professor hates her. In sum, I have to *force myself* to treat her like any other student, which I manage to do with a shit ton of effort. (Here is where I pat myself on the back.) This is the young woman who is peeking out from her easel with full license to study every inch of my naked body as she records, to the best of her ability, my back, chest, arms, ass, numb foot, and what I suddenly hope is a flaccid penis and but then remember I'm a grower not a shower so kinda hope gets halfway erect without going full porno.

All of which may be repugnant and/or traumatic for the young woman, or maybe, let's be honest here, kind of appealing. It depends on how you imagine my personality, looks, and moral compass.

Now hear me out.

Women, think back to that overweight hairy middle-aged professor whose gaze lingered a bit too long on the pretty girls, which regardless if you were a target made you cringe every time and turned that class into an irritant if not an outright emotional sinkhole. Now recall that fit middle-aged professor who was stylish and personable, sensitive yet commanding, whom you secretly fell in love with but were ethical enough to never voice and so instead settled for imagining that one day, when you reached his age, you'd be married to someone like him. See what I mean? It's either the stuff of nightmares or material for a removable shower head.

The truth is I'm neither of these men. (I think.)

The further truth is that while a $15 modeling fee is appealing (that's three pints of Guinness at a dive bar), I have never modeled for an art class and never would. Not because I'm ashamed of my body or don't believe in the creative process, but because of the nightmare scenario described above.

The further-further truth is that the description of L- and our classroom dynamic is dead accurate.

The even further truth is that *she* was the one who tricked *me* into getting naked in front of her.

Did I mention I'm married?

I met L- while teaching at a campus three towns away, a familiar act to adjunct professors burning tanks of gas they can't afford to shuttle around a fifty mile radius.

When the last day of the semester came and her class said their goodbyes and thank-yous and stony quiet fuck-yous, L- told me she drives to my hometown a few times a week (*oh no*) because her boyfriend lives there (*picture an umpire bending over home plate screaming "SAFE!"*). I'm the one who suggests we get coffee. She agrees, but laughs when I admit that I hate cellphones so we can't coordinate via text.[1] She doesn't really

---

[1] I've since been dragged into the twenty-first century, leaving a trail of bloody claw marks behind. I held out for as long as possible because I knew,

do social media though, so despite adding each other on Facebook[2], we decided to coordinate over email.

How quaint.

That summer we meet an average of twice a week. When late May hit the mid-80s, she brought me to a secluded spot in a state park where people jump off a fifty foot cliff into the town reservoir. Being the type of lunatic who laugh-orgasms on 88mph rollercoasters, I absolutely loved this and insisted we go as often as possible. So twice a week I screamed my middle-aged masculinity over fifty feet of air, then swam over to where L- was laying in a black bikini reading Goethe, orbited by a rough circle of anxious young men struggling not to notice. We spent hours and hours together in this socially acceptable state of undress.

Did I mention her bikini was black?

Did I mention that all my friends and acquaintances knew her bikini was black?

My wife too?

This was because we took a couple selfies (duh, she's a *millennial*) and a few ended up on Facebook among the ones of me hanging fifty feet in the air making Ozzy Osbourne devil horns or hand-in-the-armpit farting gestures or cross-armed Kazotsky kicks in L-'s laughing direction.

Facebook's reactions were much as you'd expect.

Let's play the Facebook Feud!

Name a male response to a picture of a married man cliff jumping with an attractive young woman.

Top six answers are on the board. Survey says!

---

in the words of Dave Chappelle, that it could cripple my ability to do the Care Bear Share.

[2] This was before armies of Russian agents and American grandmothers executed Order 66 on Mark Zuckerberg.

1. Wow. You're crazy!
    Awesome jump, right!
2. Are you insane? Why the hell are you posting that on Facebook?
    Why not?
3. Holy hell, who is **that**?
    A friend.
4. Solid 9, you lucky bastard.
    [*no response*]
5. I should have been a college professor.
    [*no response*]
6. Awesome cliff jump. Where were you?
    [*name of the place*]

Bonus round!
Name a female response to a picture of a married man cliff jumping with an attractive young woman.

Top six answers are on the board. Survey says!
1. You're crazy!
    Awesome jump, right!
    Does [my wife] know about this?
    Yes.
2. What does [my wife] think of this?
    She doesn't care.
3. Is that a student?
    Ex-student, but yes.
4. Are you serious? What the hell are you thinking?
    Cliff jumping is awesome.
5. -shock emoji-
    -turd emoji-
6. OMG that place is beautiful. Where were you?
    [*name of the place*]

All of which told me that at least half my Facebook friends suspected or assumed I was having sex with L-, and four out of six women expressed *concern* and *suspicion.* Just look! She's young and attractive and I'm an older guy who isn't utterly repulsive! Of course we're having sex!

I removed all pics of L- the next day.

My friends' responses made me wonder a few things. What does this say about what we think about men? What does this say about how we see male college professors? What does this say about how we perceive marriage in America? What does this say about me?

It's a common misconception that the divorce rate has risen in the past three decades. We hear it all the time. Families are falling apart! We've grown so selfish! It's technology's fault! It's Hollywood's fault! It's the gays' fault! On and on. Have you seen ashleymadison.com? But according to Steven Ruggles, Regent Professor of History and Population Studies at the Institute for Social Research and Data Innovation at the University of Minnesota (try saying that three times), divorce has actually *declined* in recent years after a massive spike between 1940 and 1960, when "male breadwinner" families were slowly slipping away (Rosie the Riveter, *holla!*) As economic equally increased, the divorce rate continued to spike *among women over forty*, but after 1980 it *only* increased in couples over 40. More and more younger couples were staying together.

Why? Why have divorce rates continued to plummet? Could it be that boys born into homes where both mom and dad contributed fairly equal income taught us *how treat our wives as equal partners*, or as Ruggles put it, "undermined the economic logic of patriarchy"? Could it be that starting with my generation (GenX), more and more boys learned how to not be dicks?

It's notable that the eruption of #metoo started in Hollywood, a notorious haven of patriarchy where sleazy men drunk on power do whatever they want, including sexual harassment on the droves of beautiful young women and men who arrive daily at LAX looking every bit as stupendous as Naomi Watts in *Mulholland Drive*. Is it any wonder that, as writer Laura Kipnis noted, the Harvey Weinsteins and Donald Trumps of the world are "not the most attractive specimens on the block: bulbous, jowly men; fat men who told women they needed to lose weight; ugly men," then asked them, "When you look in the mirror, is it a great white hunter you see staring back, with women as your game of choice?" [3]

Which is what I'd like to shout at every creepy middle-aged (and older) professor who fits my first description above. Stop making us look bad, you dicks.

However, I am not a saint.

L- and I definitely slipped into the danger zone.

I know, right? Who could have seen that coming.

Sure, I thought it *might* happen, but if it did I figured we'd sit cross-legged before each other and have a nice long adult conversation about loss and sacrifice and the need for boundaries and then we'd collapse into a frenzied sex session and feel guilty in the aftershock and never see each other again, and then I'd have to tell my wife and she'd leave me and I'd never see her or my son again, and one day you'd pass me on the sidewalk on your way to Starbucks and do your best to endure the ammonia assault of my urine-drenched body as I implore you for charity with evocations of the same deity my finely honed schizophrenia had long blamed for this entire mess.

Which of course didn't happen. What happened is L- and I discussed our feelings in email because we intuited the bloodless arena of cyberspace was a good cage to poke at the beast.

---

[3] "Kick Against the Pricks." in the December 21, 2017 issue of the *New York Review of Books*

Our thing was colored text. Replies grew confusing in our 20+ ping pong exchanges, so we colored our responses to keep track. It was oddly endearing.

I was first to crack the egg -

"We're kinda into each other, aren't we?"

"Yes."

"It's really bad isn't it?"

"Yes."

"We should probably just admit it and agree not to act on it and promise to just be friends."

"If you want."

"God damn it, L-, that's not the answer I needed. Talk me off the ledge here."

"Ha. Ok, yes, friends only. Promise."

"Thank god. I'm a weak man. I can't do this alone."

"Ha. See, this is why I adore you."

"WHAT DID I JUST SAY?"

"Sorry, this is why I put up with your pathetic drivel."

"Better."

I introduced her to my wife. I introduced her to my son. We remained close friends for another year until she graduated *magna cum laude* with a BA in art history, which she promptly threw in a cardboard box. Then she spent the summer in India doing the millennial-white-girl-finds-peace-and-instagram-authenticity-among-impoverished-brown-people thing.

Just kidding. L- is better than that.

She actually spent the summer training her limbs to be rubber bands at a remote ashram. They gave her a certificate that was super impressive to yoga studios back home, which she promptly threw in the same cardboard box as her BA.

Eight months later I received a surprising email. It was our first contact since she had returned from India and it was in plain black text. I was one of five recipients.

L- had enrolled in massage school and needed a test dummy for her first massage on a real person. "It's going to be monitored by my teacher," she wrote, noting that it was also "a test." Would anyone like a free massage?

Two things made me reply *yes.*

1. It was midterms, which every college professor un-blessed with TAs knows is when mental exhaustion sets in and your shoulders start to cramp.

2. The teacher in me felt bad. She needed someone for a test. What if no one responded?

3. The thought of L- rubbing down my shoulders in a safe environment was not unpleasant.[4]

The massage school was in an ancient stone building with a manicured lawn that ran like a golf course down to a long clear lake. It was once a private Catholic school used by rich people to launch their kids into the Ivy League, but then a couple priests played hide-the-confession with some students and the Vatican used a giant God-powered eraser to wipe the place clean. Now it was a massage school. Note the sick irony if you must.

L- met me at the entrance. She looked much the same as those bikini days, insanely fit, big blue eyes, long blond hair wrapped in a top knot. She was wearing the kind of soft cotton muscle shirt you see draped over Vinyasa enthusiasts, and a pair of sleek black yoga pants.[5]

We waited in line to report to the dean or head teacher or whomever was running the show from behind a lectern. When it was our turn to report, the massage school *maitre d* smiled

---

[4] I know I said only two things made me say *yes*, but the third one doesn't really exist, nope, pinky swear and denial on my deathbed.

[5] Callipygian.

one of those unnervingly calm smiles that only spiritually-secular white people make, took our names, then waved at the double doors behind her.

"Ok, go ahead and join all the naked people," she said. *Naked people?*

As with many social movements riding their moment, #metoo zeroed in on one specific micro-issue, creepy old male predators, while ignoring the wider issue of sexual predation. I'm not pointing this out by way of chipping away at #metoo's legitimacy. I fully support castrating the big swollen phallus of Hollywood and Washington. The problem is that #metoo's narrow scope has inadvertently reinforced the gender roles that have long been the bane of men victimized by female predators. (Yes, female sexual predators is a thing.) Gender roles assign sexual predation to men because we're supposed to be more aggressive and physical and just down right hornier than *the fairer sex*. As feminist Laura Stemple and LGBT advocate Ilan H. Meyer noted in their 2014 study of male victimization [6] -

We identified factors that perpetuate misperceptions about men's sexual victimization: reliance on traditional gender stereotypes, outdated and inconsistent definitions, and methodological sampling biases...

If numerous sex crimes against women go unreported, imagine how many more go unreported by a gender that's defined by strength, toughness, physical violence, and sexual aggressiveness. Men themselves snicker at the thought of a twenty-seven year old female teacher having sex with a fifteen year old male student. Who wouldn't want to bang that young hot art teacher you had in high school?

---

[6] "The Sexual Victimization of Men in America: New Data Challenge Old Assumptions," published in the *American Journal of Public Health*.

When a young female teacher is accused of sexual misconduct, a picture of an attractive smiling blond splashes across the news as delectable scandal. Google "Sarah Fowlkes" and you'll be tickled by dozens of images of a pretty young blond smiling her sugar and spice and everything nice. The homier, the more tantalizing. But if you google "male teacher sex with female student" the first fifty images will only show two men accused of sexual misconduct. *Two in fifty!* The rest are images of women, and two of the top three links are about female teachers sleeping with male students.

Why?

I'm not suggesting that male teachers don't victimize female students. Of course they do. However, nobody but the worst sorts of people ever claim that the female students *wanted it*. It's almost always framed in the narrative of men abusing a power imbalance. Yet *wanting it* is the near universal assumption about victimized males. A vast majority of those fifty images show attractive young women, the type of women that a young teenage boy *would love to fuck*, has thought about fucking, has locked away in his mental spank bank, all of which reinforces the idea that men and boys always want it. Maybe we shouldn't dress so provocatively? Maybe ditch the sleeveless shirts and bulging gray sweatpants (i.e. the male version of black yoga pants)?

Or maybe men suffer from a gender role that assigns them an aggressive sexuality, one that prevents them from being sexual victims *except from other men*. Did #metoo reinforce this? After all, a few male victims did come forward in the initial thrust of #metoo, including an incredibly courageous and heartbreaking account by actor Brendan Frazier. But all of those men were victims of other men.

Men, men, men.

Perhaps female sexual predators are tougher to identify. After all, they tend to expose *intimacy* rather than leverage overt power, establishing a base of appropriate contact rather than flatly demanding a blowjob in their office. Common female perps are nurses, teachers, therapists, councilors – all fields that involve a trusting, intimate contact with their victims. A 2012 Department of Justice report found that males in juvenile facilities were twice as likely to be sexual victims than females, and a whopping 89% of them were victimized by female staff members.[7] The numbers are so shocking you almost suspect data manipulation. But perhaps this is because even in the twenty-first century gender roles make it vastly more difficult for male victims to be believed. The FBI didn't even consider rape possible on a male body until 2012. Before then rape necessitated "carnal knowledge of a female."[8]

2012.

Even though L-'s email and follow-up texts didn't say anything about getting naked, I don't consider L- a sexual predator. She continues to occupy a special place in my heart. Our story is a comedy, a comedy prompting a broader meditation, but still a comedy. Her intentions were clear: she was a massage student in a bind. There was little if anything sexual about our encounter, just a lot of awkwardness that on reflection was really, really funny.

But if something creepy had happened, say if her hand had slipped down under the white towel covering my hips and her fingers lingered there, sliding around in slow circles, what could I have done? Screamed like a girl? Ran to the authorities with a face full of tears?

Look at her.

---

[7] "Sexual Victimization in Juvenile Facilities Reported by Youth, 2012 (National Survey of Youth in Custody)."

[8] "Crime in the United States: forcible rape" (via Stemple and Meyer).

Look at me.

Look at the history of our relationship.

What do you think would have happened?

Mock care by the police? Sighs? Groans over the necessary paperwork? Old male cops staring longingly at a picture of L- and wondering if I'm gay and snickering and confessing that they'd let her finger them all she wanted? Female cops scowling because of course I had wanted it, the more ardent ones hypothesizing that I was seeking revenge because she'd actually *refused to have sex with me* and there's no way we're letting this scumbag ruin this poor girl's life?

I don't know if any of that would be true, but it's what I'd expect.

It's what any male victim would expect.

L- wasn't guilty of anything except not telling me that I'd be getting naked.

Considering the circumstances, I understand.

Would you agree to a student massage if you knew you'd be getting naked in a room full of naked people? What is this, some kind of a veiled invitation to an orgy? How about the stress of doing the full monty before of a gorgeous ex-student with whom you once shared a very ethically distanced mutual attraction? What if I get an erection in front of twenty other naked people, sleek young women with exposed breasts, hairy old men with shrunken dongs, glabrous young guys with the naked nonchalance of a man who lifts weights six times a week. Oh my god, what if *they* gave me an erection? I'm a middle-aged married man! I can't have a sexual crisis!

The long room we entered reminded me of a perspective exercise I drew in seventh grade. Two rows of massage tables flanked a wide central aisle. I followed L- to her table in the middle of the left row. There we stood facing each other. Most of the other subjects were already naked on their tables with a small white towel covering their naughty bits. We looked at each other. She looked away, perhaps with guilt, perhaps with embarrassment, perhaps with both.

"Um, do I have to get naked?" I asked.

She became really nervous, hands fidgeting with the tail of her shirt.

"It makes it easier and more effective," she muttered, "but you don't have to."

I noticed the creepy-calm *maitre d* patrolling the center aisle with a clipboard.

Damn it.

So I did what I needed to do. I was already there, *committed*, so I might as well go through with it. I stripped off my clothes and showed L- the full monty, then jumped up on her table and surrendered my body to her fingers to rub and kneed and grind as I tried to relax as much as possible to help her pass the test.

Which she did.

Later I sat down with my wife and told her what happened.

She laughed her ass off.

Which is one of many reasons why I love my wife.

R.C. Savoie is a graduate of both Binghamton University and CalArts. He lives in Ithaca, NY.

Covenant

By Steven Sherwood

The residents of Turkey Heights disliked weeds, Democrats, trespassers, rotting fences, and other people's children—anything that might send property values plummeting.

Into this gated neighborhood on the suburban fringe of Fort Worth, Texas, whose residents were mostly well into retirement, my fiancée Jill and I, both Democrats, had moved her two daughters and my two sons. We had found there an almost-affordable five-bedroom house in which to blend our families. A justice of the peace married us in our living room, with our kids standing up as our bridesmaids and groomsmen. In the rush to sell our previous homes, each too small for our current needs, we closed on the new place with little more than a glance at the 60 pages of covenants that governed life in Turkey Heights. Two days later, an officer of the homeowners association—tall, lanky, in his early sixties—dropped by to educate us.

He introduced himself as Hank, our next-door neighbor and chair of the Turkey Heights Architectural Control and Compliance Committee. "I notice you have a portable basketball goal in your driveway." His face twisted as if in pain. "I hate to tell you this, but it violates the covenants."

I stared at him. "Why is a basketball goal a problem?"

Hank pointed to Article 8.17, on page forty-six of the covenants, which governed the type and placement of recreational equipment, such as swing sets and basketball goals. Residents had to place playground equipment in the backyard, invisible from the street. They could install a basketball hoop with a clear, acrylic backboard above a garage door or along a driveway, but the covenants prohibited the sort of goal, with a weighted base and a solid metal backboard, I had bought for my boys the previous Christmas.

My eldest, Evan, was trying out for his high school basketball team in a few weeks and, freshly house poor, we could not afford to replace the existing goal with an acrylic one. Our new home occupied the end of a cul-de-sac, and our driveway curved around to the garage, out of our neighbors' view. I told Hank we would keep the goal next to the garage.

His face twisted again. "That would solve the eyesore problem, but not the noise issue." He pointed to Article 7.42, which prohibited anything deemed a nuisance, including "any noxious or offensive activity." Apparently our neighbors deemed as noxious the sound of a basketball being dribbled. This sentiment struck me as contradictory since the covenants permitted basketball goals and, by extension, the dribbling of a basketball.

After a short debate, Hank agreed to let us park our goal beside the garage, but he insisted we limit our dribbling to the early evening hours (before the old folks went to bed).

My small victory emboldened me. For our first four years in the neighborhood, I defied the HOA whenever neighbors complained about weeds in our yard, the color of our front door (red), our delay in replacing a window screen destroyed by a gust of wind, and my youngest son Scott's strumming of his guitar on our back patio—all violations of the covenants. The HOA also prohibited yard signs, including political ones, but during the 2008 presidential campaign McCain-Palin signs had sprouted like weeds on our neighbors' lawns. We responded with an Obama-Biden sign. No one, including Hank, confronted us about the sign, but it vanished one night, and neighbors who once waved when we passed by glared or glanced away.

Because we violated so many covenants, I got to know Hank well. A reasonable man, and a good neighbor, he said over drinks on the deck of his pool one evening, "I despise half the rules I have to enforce as ACC chair, so I tend to take a soft touch."

I raised my glass. "And I appreciate your attitude."

During our fifth year in Turkey Heights, Jill and I broke still another rule when we failed to pay our $400 annual HOA dues by the February 1 deadline. Christmas shopping and Evan's freshman year in college had depleted our savings. On Valentine's Day, with a hundred bucks in seed money, we tried our luck at the WinStar casino just over the Oklahoma line. On the casino floor, though, gamblers had claimed every last slot machine. We were ready to give up and go home when a woman vacated a dollar machine. I took her still-warm seat, and Jill stood at my shoulder to watch as I lost a dollar on each of my first five spins. On the sixth spin, I won fifteen dollars. On the seventh, I won three hundred. Over my objections—I was on a roll—Jill punched the cash-out button and said, "We're leaving." The next day, we used our winnings, plus the seed money, to pay our homeowner's dues.

Later that same week, the new president of Turkey Heights, a retired rear-admiral named Tyler, knocked on our red door. Tyler looked like a natural leader—trim and gray, with a stern but calm demeanor.

I braced myself for a complaint about our late dues, untrimmed hedges, or other violations. Instead, in a gentle voice laced with the iron of command, he said, "Hank's stepping down from the ACC chair, and I want you to take his place."

Surprise muted me. Finally, I said, "You don't want me for your ACC chair. I disagree with most of the covenants, including the one prohibiting parking on the streets. The rule may give the neighborhood curb appeal, and we probably shouldn't park our cars on the street overnight, but what can people do if they host a party or a family gathering?"

"Well," Tyler said, "I'm not looking for a yes man. Some of the covenants are too strict, which is one of the issues I want to address as president."

Like Hank, Tyler struck me as a good, reasonable man, especially for a former rear admiral. "Can I think it over for a couple of days?"

"Of course," he said and shook my hand.

I told Jill about Tyler's invitation, half expecting her to laugh.

"Most of the directors are Tea Partiers, aren't they?" she asked. "Are you sure you want to associate with Tea Partiers?"

"No," I acknowledged.

But in spite of political misgivings, I figured as ACC chair I could subvert or soften the worst covenants and have a positive impact on the neighborhood. When I called to accept the appointment, I told Tyler I knew next to nothing about the workings of the HOA or its ACC committee.

"Don't worry," he said. "We seldom have problems you'll need to deal with, and if issues do come up, the other directors and I will walk you through them."

As a board member, I planned to do little more than attend the monthly meetings and fight any attempts to strengthen the covenants. My complacency lasted for one month. Then Tyler asked me to visit a Mr. Caruthers, on Snood Drive, whose backyard shed protruded above the six-foot-high brick wall surrounding the neighborhood. To resolve this violation of the covenants, Tyler said, Mr. Caruthers could put up a screen of plants, lower the shed so that its roof did not show above the wall, or have it hauled away.

When I inspected the shed the next week, Mr. Caruthers, a retired professor with a sonorous voice, explained that a wooden frame, covered with vines, had once screened the shed. "It rotted and fell apart last week," he said, "and I guess someone filed a complaint."

As we talked, his son arrived. "This whole thing is bullshit," the son shouted. "I'm an attorney and we're seriously considering suing the HOA."

"Let's not get ahead of ourselves," Mr. Caruthers said. "This gentleman's here to see if we can find a solution, and so far he's been polite."

Yeah, so far, I thought. "Why not put up another frame to hide the shed? Wouldn't that be the cheapest solution?"

He looked doubtful. The son swore again, and Mr. Caruthers told him to wait inside. Without his attorney present, he said, "Even if we rebuild the frame, the vines will take time to grow and the wood will only rot again. And then the neighbors will complain."

"I'm sure the rest of the board will understand. I'll recommend a delay long enough to let the vines grow back."

His shoulders sagged. "Maybe I'll get rid of the damned thing."

I studied his face. "I'm not suggesting that. There are other good ways to go."

He gazed at the shed as if already mourning its loss. In the end, with his son glowering from the house, Mr. Caruthers decided to have his shed hauled away.

At the next board meeting, Tyler and the other directors congratulated me on my first victory as ACC chair. I smiled uneasily. Pressuring an old man into surrendering his garden shed had cost me some sleep. Now Tyler asked me to tackle a far more difficult issue: a property-line dispute between two neighbors—an elderly couple, Mr. and Mrs. Fielding, and a local realtor named Rita Ringler.

Ms. Ringler had served on the HOA board, and Tyler's attitude suggested he believed the fault lay with the Fieldings. When I met with the couple, though, they told a tale of long-term harassment that had nearly driven them from their beloved home. The Fieldings struck me as inoffensive, baffled by their neighbor's behavior. The feud started, they said, when they pruned some of Ms. Ringler's trees, whose branches overhung their fence. The trees dropped bushels of leaves into their backyard each fall. They had a legal right to prune any branches on their side of the fence, so they had not anticipated her reaction.

"When we realized Rita was upset," Mrs. Fielding said, "we apologized, but she just stood there, staring."

Garbage and dog droppings appeared each morning in their backyard, and most weeks they found the contents of their recycling bin on their front lawn. Their stone-lined front flower bed ran to Ms. Ringer's property line, and in the past Mr. Fielding had pushed his mower through her yard to reach an otherwise inaccessible strip of grass beside his house. After the pruning incident, she stood at their property line with her arms folded whenever he mowed. As the grass grew shaggy in the side yard, Mr. Fielding grew frantic enough that, one evening, when Ms. Ringler stepped in his way, he pushed her aside and mowed the neglected grass. The same night, she filed trespass and assault charges against him.

"I'm a retired CPA," Mr. Fielding said. "I've never had trouble with the law."

"Well, I'll talk to Ms. Ringler, see what we can work out," I said. "Meanwhile, please don't try to mow your side yard."

After a calming breath, I rang Ms. Ringler's doorbell. A moment later, a stern and weathered blonde regarded me through a crack in the door. As I stammered out an explanation for my visit, she said, "Get off my property. I won't speak to anyone but Tyler."

I got off her property. A week later, Tyler passed along her conditions: she would drop the charges if Mr. Fielding promised never again to trim her trees or enter her yard without permission.

The next day, I delivered the news to the Fieldings. "Maybe you could reach the side yard through your flower bed and use a weed whip instead of a mower. Better yet, why don't you move the flower bed a few feet away from the property line—enough to make room for your mower?"

Both Fieldings made a face, as if imagining the damage to their front yard. "Well," Mrs. Fielding said, "I suppose we could do that if it would keep the peace."

Problem solved, I thought, but Ms. Ringler insisted Tyler and I measure the width of the Fieldings' mower against the distance between her property line and the revised flower bed. With her standing over us on her side of the boundary and the Fieldings on the other, we confirmed Mr. Fielding could now mow the side yard without trespassing.

Iron firmed the edges of Tyler's voice as he said, "This matter ends here, Rita. I don't want to hear any more about it."

Months passed without another major controversy. Having learned to respect the HOA directors, who did the difficult job of running the neighborhood, I embraced my own role as ACC chair. As I discovered, a lot of our new neighbors had, like Jill and me, ignored the covenants when they closed on their homes and now saw them as nasty surprises. Even so, I had to enforce the rules, including those requiring residents to use HOA-approved paint and shingle colors on their homes, to replace dead trees with new ones of requisite size, and to avoid parking on the streets overnight. When my neighbors defied me—as I had defied Hank—I complained about their obnoxious behavior.

Jill met one such complaint with a sardonic expression. "Maybe they think they actually own the home they're paying for."

I wondered whose side she was on. "Well, of course they do, but we all signed the covenants and we have to obey them."

A few days later, I found myself lecturing her about leaving her car parked on the street all night. "Can't you see the position you're putting me in? Here I am, telling everyone else about the no-parking rule and my own wife is breaking it."

The look Jill gave me conveyed no traces of amusement. "You're really part of the club now, aren't you? Will you start voting Republican now?"

I sputtered before saying, "All right, honey, I see the irony."

"You mean the hypocrisy?"

As she walked away, I said, "Just please stop leaving your car out."

An awareness of a gap between my principles and my duties as ACC chair grew at the next board meeting, when one of the directors complained about a decaying fence along Fantail Lane, one of Turkey Heights's main roads. The fence, which enclosed a family's backyard, had become an eyesore that threatened the neighborhood aesthetic. Tyler asked me to confront the family about replacing their fence.

"Wait a minute," I said. "Don't homeowners have the right to decide when to replace their own fence?"

The other board members smiled and shook their heads. Tyler pointed to Article 6.54 in the Turkey Heights Covenants, which said that a homeowner must "replace or repair any fence that is out of repair or out of harmony with fencing on the adjacent property." Failure to comply activated a clause that allowed the HOA to hire a contractor to replace the fence, demand reimbursement, and after ten days put a lien on the offender's property for the cost of repairs, plus interest and attorney's fees.

"Of course," Tyler added, "we'd prefer they do the right thing."

"What if they don't have the money?"

Another director, a recently retired bank executive who lived with her sister, scoffed. "The husband's an attorney."

Wonderful, another attorney, I thought. "Okay, I'll give him a call."

I procrastinated for three weeks before phoning the homeowner at his law office. When I conveyed the HOA's demand to fix or replace his fence, he said, "Well, you bastards really know how to pile on when someone's down, don't you?"

"What do you mean?"

"My practice is in the shitter, my wife may be terminally ill, and you want me to cough up two thousand bucks to replace a fence. Are you trying to push me over the edge?"

I took a breath. "I'm sorry to hear about your wife. I doubt the board members have any idea what you're going through, but I'll tell them. Maybe—"

The dial tone cut off my words. I sat there, heartsick at having bothered him about something so trivial when he and his family were facing a crisis. At the next meeting, I reported my findings and advised the board to grant the family some breathing room before pursuing the fence issue.

The retired bank executive asked, "What sort of terminal illness?"

"I don't know. He only said she might be terminal."

She rolled her eyes. "What do you bet the wife's just fine?"

All around the table, the board members smirked. Then the chair of the neighborhood welcome wagon, a sharp-featured older woman, piped up: "If people can't afford to pay their dues or properly maintain their property, they should move."

I studied the faces around the table to see if anyone else found this statement outrageous. "You know something? Not everyone in Turkey Heights is wealthy. A lot of our neighbors are on fixed incomes and the rest of us sometimes struggle. Hell, to pay our dues last year, Jill and I had to gamble in an Oklahoma casino. Luckily, we hit a jackpot playing the slots."

The other board members, Tyler included, transferred their disapproval from the attorney with the rotten fence to me, clearly seeing their ACC chair as an unexpected threat to the neighborhood's financial and aesthetic integrity.

"I'm only saying we don't know everyone's situation, so we shouldn't be so quick to judge."

Moments of silence passed. Finally, Tyler nodded. "Okay, we'll revisit this issue next month. Meanwhile, some of us have been discussing the need to keep a closer eye on covenant violations. The Drakes on Rafter Drive, for instance, are parking a trailer in their driveway. That's not allowed. We'd like you to patrol the neighborhood more often—take on a more active policing role."

Having already shocked the directors by revealing my family's shaky finances, I shocked them again. "I'm sorry, but I won't do that. The ACC chair needs to be someone who cares about the covenants and doesn't feel like a hypocrite for confronting people about their own homes. That's not me."

Tyler released a long sigh. "So you're resigning?"

I nodded, already picturing Jill's smile when I told her the news.

But Tyler was not done with me. "You teach college English, right?"

I frowned at him. "Yeah."

"As you know, we lost our secretary a few months ago. I'll start looking for a new ACC chair if you'll agree to stay on the board and take minutes. The secretary job's a perfect fit for you, right?"

I felt the gaze of the entire HOA board. "Can I take a few days to think it over?"

Tyler smiled and reached over to shake my hand. "Of course you can, Mister Secretary."

Steve Sherwood has published fiction or creative nonfiction in *Talking River Review, Red Rock Review, Northern Lights, descant, Adelaide Literary Review,* and other journals. A collection of his stories and personal essays, *Field Guide: Essays and Stories* (Angelina River Press), appeared in 2014. Later that year, the Texas Review Press published his second novel, *No Asylum,* a mystery set on the high plains of Kansas. His first novel, *Hardwater,* won the George Garrett Fiction Prize and was published by the Texas Review Press in 2005. Currently the director of the William L. Adams Center for Writing at Texas Christian University, Sherwood has taught writing and literature courses there since 1988.

Chesterfield Road

By Jason James

The times I would see headlight glare strobe across my bedroom ceiling, I would take to waiting for its departure, often late and long after I was tucked in to bed. I studied what I could see in the dark without my glasses on, the tempo of flickers that faded and always gone with a whoosh of some car going by, each night, until all light dimmed deep blue or to black, until morning. Once though when I was eight or nine or ten and not quite asleep, the lights returned, and this once, they lingered. They danced and rolled along the walls before reaching like fingers to the ceiling. They stayed far longer, before finally disappearing, all without a sound. The lights, they never acted that way with me before or since. I wondered then where the car went, or that maybe it hadn't been a car at all. It had to be, and I wrestled that into my head, then settled in. That is, until I considered whether our house, somehow, maybe, had been haunted.

For so long, I recalled the dancing lights, what I finally resigned to be driving cars and my overthinking thoughts. This was the house my father built and on the last parts of our family's land, the only house I'd ever known through all my childhood. Our house was warm, and only ours, and after all, seeing those silent lights on the walls and ceiling would have been more that twenty-years before I found out what actually happened there. And having learned about our family and its history on that land, being haunted, I'm surprised now our house hadn't been.

I spent a lot of time as a teenager, touring the shoreline roads in the south end of town I wanted to, but knew I never would get to live in. I longed for the foot-busy bustle of cul-de-sacs and side streets — to wander and ride bikes, to mischief and collect at the corner voltage box for impromptu tag and backyard football with the lopsided teams, bigs versus littles. I found myself drawn most to the neighborhoods by the shore. There, the ocean sat stifled by Long Island Sound, lapping gently along pebbly sands. Small beach crests, quiet and private, held their staid identities — Saunders Point, Oak Grove, Giants Neck, Crescent Beach — their sandy paths and sidewalks connecting seasonal cottages that one by one pulsed alive as full-time homes. Further south and past a swing gate and summertime guard, prim, spiffy girls I never saw during the school year inhabited some of the big houses in Old Black Point, with placid familiarity if not a bored indifference. On their saunters to and from their neighborhood clay courts for tennis, or past their permanent field for playing croquet, I roused as much attention on my bicycle riding by as it seemed they gave the carpenters and gardeners, a passing glance, if that at all.

Our town wasn't quite divided into an us and a them, but in the spectrum, the monied Old Black Point was on one end, and eight miles away and north from the ocean, I was on the other. Names in town sometimes carried weight, some for better or worse. There were the institutions of sports name families that seemed to churn out son after son that lettered in three sports. Other names were well-to-do, the flip collar Izod and smarty-pants preps whose fathers worked in New

Haven, Providence or Hartford. And mine? My dad grew up in town then became a Connecticut State Trooper. At school, my brother and I were always well-mannered, shy and quiet — a class act, a girl I knew since grade school said in passing, sometime last year. Our father's drilled-in warnings must have worked. As unassuming as we were, he still was strict, and with us made one thing clear: If you embarrass me, I'll embarrass you.

The north end woods where I grew up was a far different place from the shore and the rest of town, and my house, specifically, existed with a tarnish that I came to find stained deeply. At differing times there had been three houses that belonged to my family along a single stretch of the same land. One beheld a cramped, farmhouse squalor, and with it, beatings, a murder and suicide. The second, at some point, had been reclaimed for an escape — or at least the hopes to — from the first family house. And the third, where I grew up, unbeknownst to me, was the rampart and battle line, the standing ground my father decided on us holding, for sake of himself and us and the family name. My childhood of tree fort building, ball and glove passes and wood line walks with the dog was our soldiering, where we dug in, rather than yield, take shame or simply move away. The houses were each just driveways apart, one after the other, along a break in the winding, thicketed stretches of Chesterfield Road. And all my life living there, I knew nothing of their twined connection in those bold and sinister ways.

By the time I was eight and nine and ten, Dad had been curating an edited history on hikes for my twin brother and me, through a vast excavation on the other side of Latimer Brook, behind our house. This, he explained, had been our family's farmland. Past a nearby hay lot, the steep slope we sometimes traversed marked how far down the bucket loaders dug, stripping the soil to bare sand. Silt and gravel piled like mountains overtook the clues of where the farmhouse and barn once stood. Dad pointed out the only discerning remains, an open well head he causally warned us not to step by because, otherwise, we'd fall in and altogether disappear. This was House One, where my father grew up and was terrorized by his father, and with difficulty, finally left from. He never lingered past this place, trudging on instead, up paths into the ledge land too rough and rock laden for the excavators to rape usable soil from. He used that word, rape, under his breath and full of its meaning, for the land beyond our backyard and no longer his, scraped to a lifeless, chalky moon I knew in no other way.

A row of large ledge rocks fringed one side of our yard along Chesterfield Road that I scaled by hand and with ropes with my brother, with backpacks and green plastic M-16s shoelace strapped to our backs on our journeys, in view of our neighbor's yard. Once, I happened on a green glass 7-Up soda bottle intact at the bottom, a painted label treasure from twenty or more years before, protected under crisp, colorless leaves, a relic perhaps from when Dad was just as old as my brother and me. We wandered and searched and fanned out and spied, reporting back and forth in choppy walkie-talkie words, minute to minute, most often on next door. There, a bald man with a knit yellow hat and blue cover-alls drifted be-tween his house and his machinery, the tall cranes and trucks he kept there for his ocean and river salvage jobs. His dogs — Roger, then Duke — roved our yard regularly, uninvited guests on walks most days, down the hill to the grass lot behind our house and across a footbridge to the hay lot, in company of whichever dog of ours, Bertha, Jane, or Big Bert. I never met him, our neighbor, Mr. Rogers. My father left him fixed in his glare, without words, with encounters ending each time in a silent turn of shoulder. Dad froze him out, the man who always lived next door on our lonely road. This was House Two, and I was well in my thirties and gone before I realized Dad had lived there for a time, if briefly.

There are things still a mystery about my father. Like, day to day, what he did after his father murdered his mother then killed himself at House One on Chesterfield Road. It occurred to me that after that, Dad simply left, and lived in his car and at the volunteer firehouse in Flanders. He was homeless, for a time he was, riding it out alone, perhaps until he would no longer be forced into foster care. But then there was House Two, and the unraveling family secrets Dad and Mom and all my aunts and uncles held from my brother, all my cousins and me, well into our adulthood.

There always was the conspicuous absence of Dad's parents. In my childhood they never existed, except for her, Dad's mom, in a single portrait on the wall in the dining room. She was full body stout, and for the sitting she was neatly dressed, a formal picture-frame stranger overseeing holiday dinners too special to be eaten in the kitchen, captive in monochrome and a metallic patina. And under a disconcerting closer study, I recognized her eyes were dented in and marked by the head of a ballpoint pen. She was Pauline and I never knew to miss her. In earnest, what first most troubled me was the backlog of presents from Christmases and birthdays gone by from just one set of grandparents. I had gotten by with half of what everyone else did in my elementary school, and that was my quandary when I was bold and naive enough to ask when I was nine or ten, what Dad replied so tersely and a bit flippantly — that his parents were playing with guns, and they were dead. I couldn't conceive then on how tender a ground I treaded, nor how plainly I was tripping alarms and zeroing in. Just a generation back. A tortured past. What sullied our family and sent it whirling in tailspins.

The newspaper story was precariously descriptive from that night, in November in 1961. Names, locations, the time of night, where the shots were fired, the places on her body she was shot, and which car he went into to finally end it for himself. One uncle was in Okinawa, staged for Vietnam. My father was out someplace. He was sixteen. The rest of them were there, five of seven of my future uncles and aunts, there as witnesses and victims with fresh scarred psyches, all when they were twenty-five and twenty-two and eighteen and thirteen and nine. They were there at House One, with their grandmother and mother when he showed up, their father, and when he brought his pistol with him. By then, none of them called him that. He was referred to as "the father" by each one, which I'm sure he mistook as reverence for him. They meant it instead to hold him apart from them, his children, as far as they could, even by reference and name. To them, he wasn't their father, just the father, a place holder for the monster among them. His name was Stephen and even now I've never considered him my grandfather.

The father, as his children called him, was an out of work printer and bus driver, and quite the clarinetist, as good talk goes. He was smart and charming and easily bored, often caught reading between two and three books at a time. Ruddy pockmarks dotted his cheeks and leathery jaw. His hair was a wiry, balding crown. His face beheld a flat, tight lipped smirk that he adorned with a stylish, Clark Gable mustache. People who really knew him, knew what he doled out at home. Within his family, there were whispers he was tied to Russian mafia from his years in New York on the Lower East Side, though his family was all Ukrainian. He parlayed household money into rounds of drinks and he liked fancy cars — he wanted a Cadillac but drove a Lincoln. He also kept a gun. State Police arrested him for that a year before, for beating his wife and threatening, too, to kill her. To most people though, he was a man about town, a frustrated savant and a bit of a cad. He was a well liked man, a man about town, and at home he was horrifyingly abusive, to his wife, his sons and his daughters.

There are tiny, scattered details about the family from then that make no sense, while some ring crystal clear. Like as kids, some of Dad's siblings remembered seeing little, silver skull faces hanging from the trees like tinsel, by House One, and that they reminded them of the skull head ring the father sometimes used to wear. There were the fights with rocks the brothers had, and my father had to lay low in the barn for days until the swelling went down — or else they'd all get beaten — and that no one noticed he wasn't there. There was the murder and the suicide, and after, the squabbles about the gun the father had — the pointing fingers, who knew he had it, and what who did and didn't do to let this torrent hail and thunder to its fury. Anger boiled. For my father, he didn't cry hearing word his mother died and he didn't at her funeral. The walled-off father with numbed emotions I was raised by had soothed himself in just that way, since his beatings started as a child. His siblings, though, clawed and lashed, they pinpointed rage on him, the brother who didn't cry at all, and not for their murdered mother.

There was talk of a wicked sister who brewed dissent between the older siblings and younger ones who didn't know better, when they tried to hold the family together in House Two, after the murder and suicide. In that festered fracas, the family fractured, parted paths, just split, all of them — twenty-somethings, teens, and a little sister still in grade school. The youngest was just nine and promised a valuable violin the family somehow had — that vanished when she was passed from house to house around in foster care after the arrangement living together in House Two collapsed. Then there were the fights my father and his brothers were known in town for, sometimes with each other, or to stand up for their sickly north end friend, or in parking lots and side alleys, sometimes for little cause at all and after the slightest agitation. These were the twists in my family's spiral down, a life endured brutally and what their mother's murder made them. The closed door demons leached out, nearby and far past New London, in newscasts, headlines and gossip. Our die then was being cast. What was it our name would long hold for us — wild, lowlife townies from that dirty north end farm on Chesterfield Road? I've heard versions of that before.

If there was a manifesto of mine to my family, it would start when I was nine and ten, about the clouds of shouting, the bombast on Thanksgivings and Christmases, after wine and cans of beer, between my uncles and aunts and my father. The eruption from the table. The stale end to a once wondrous day. My cousins, my brother and me, we all were left disbursing early from the Monopoly board we had circled around with bowls of chips and popcorn in the living room for the long haul after dinner. The retched tentacles of our family past outstretched and whirled and reached for us, the generation next, and at some point after, unceremoniously, we stopped having family Christmases altogether.

I wondered often what pushed my father into police work, especially, all along, since he warned me not to ever do the job at all. After he died, I did, so I know firsthand why he waved those warning flags. The work numbs and is unyielding, it sours your soul, over nights and weekends, year building on year, the dealing with death, and living night to night in everyone else's horror. But Dad's life growing up had already been that way, in horror, and for him, becoming the police was one clear way to stand up from it. But having become any kind of cop wouldn't have been enough. In Connecticut, especially in the 1970s and 1980s, the State Police beheld mystique and awe and induced, too, a nauseating fear. They rode patrols like hungered wolves that covered miles of highway and towns, alone. If there was more than one somewhere, hell there was going on. They rivaled the FBI and guarded the governor. They took charge and took control and took no shit at all. And my father was one of them, the last of the hard, old-time road troopers. And with it, he reset our roots on land with a tainted name, where all too many had made up their minds, turned up their noses, fanned the flames and whispered. He wrote our new narrative, unexpectedly, and just stayed. He looked everyone in the eyes and stifled their balking talk. And moreover, for everyone in town, he had become the one sent to pull them all from the worst of all their moments. With that, he didn't simply stay. He unquestionably had become the good. He restored the peace, brought the calm, and he was unavoidable.

With years passed and us grown up and gone, the house now finally has sold. If Dad intended to live his whole life there, he fulfilled his wish. He died in the driveway from a heart attack when he was fifty-three. Mom since downsized to a condo near the boardwalk, toward the shore. My brother is gone from town now and I left the state for what's been years. I thought of flying out to help sort through the lifetime of boxed and stacked up memories. I didn't go further than that though, just the thought, as I reconciled the facts and fables I had gathered over years. The house I longed to leave for ocean views and all the places someplace else, I've left, been gone, and now the house is too, from us, forever, except what's in my head.

What I see most clear is my wonderment from when I was four and five and six and wide-eyed at the window. Dad is driving a dented, chalk blue pickup truck through the yard. Our dog Bertha trots alongside with the neighbor dog we called Roger, before they race off in the woods together. He's been chainsawing trees and slashing brush with a machete, carving the truck path further down through the thickets, to the banks of the brook below, and he hasn't told Mom it will work as a go-cart path as well. Up by the ledge rock out-crops, our tree fort hugs a cluster of well-aged maples in good surveying view of our neighbor's yard. Boulders that bulged amid the lawn he's pried with shovels, picks and iron rods, he's breaking them down to build stone walls, like the moss-grown ones we found up from the ledges of the sandlot. He put us out there too, picking stones imbedded in our grass lot from the big-time, summer flood. After lunch, we toted the buckets of stones to the banks of the brook and hit them over, one by one, into trees toward the sandlot, for batting practice, and to give them back. These sights and moments flood back to me, and I see the lights that come and go across my ceiling, they're just lights from cars that come and have gone by. Our house on Chesterfield Road, the one I replay and I still see, is warm and always ours. It never has been haunted, without a trace of taint, doing my father's will in giving our family back its name.

Jason James primarily writes literary nonfiction. As an award winning investigative journalist in Connecticut, he published under the name Jason Barry. He has been a staff writer for the Hartford Courant, New Britain Herald and the Record-Journal. Jason later served as a uniformed police officer, then a Special Agent for the U.S. Drug Enforcement Administration.

For his writing, Jason was named a Shortlist Winner Nominee by Adelaide Magazine in 2017 for the essay "SAT Saturday" about teen depression and the suicide death of a Torrey Pines High School student. This writing inspired de-velopment of the teen blog site prattlon.com, where his essays on teen life have been featured.

Currently, Jason is building a catalogue of essays reflecting on adolescence, as well as co-writing with a female martial arts champion about life endurance and inner ferocity, and is chronicling the trauma endured by an Afghanistan war veteran.

In his off-hours, Jason restores antique cars, studies Muay Thai and Brazilian Jiu Jitsu, frolics with his bulldog Lulu, and procrastinates his next writing project. He lives with his family in Southern California.

Queen Street Misfits

By Marilyn Duarte

The summer I was fourteen I began itching for some adventure. I was a shy, quiet teenager who, outside of school, spent several hours each week taking ballet lessons, but after a dance injury prevented me from training for a few months, I became desperate to have some fun in my spare time.

This didn't bode well with my Portuguese single-mother whose strict rules kept me under her watchful eye. We lived amongst other Portuguese immigrants in a neighborhood of Victorian row houses in downtown Toronto, and my mother constantly reminded me that we needed to appear respectable in front of them. It was bad enough, she'd said, that they criticized her for being divorced. Portuguese women were expected to stay married at all costs, even if their husbands were abusive, absent or adulterers. It didn't matter that my father had been all three. In order to keep a low profile, I wasn't allowed out at night, and I had to have her stamp of approval on everything I wanted to do. She might as well have said that we were to be as invisible as possible.

One afternoon in mid-August, after being granted a tidbit of freedom, I ventured downtown, stopping at a record store to buy "Courage," the latest National Velvet album, then continued further south to the trendy Queen Street West strip. I walked past its quaint coffee shops, vintage stores, one of them a clothing store with used blue jeans flapping wildly in the wind out in front, and stopped outside of a head shop, daring myself to go in and buy a fake I.D., so that I could get into clubs to listen to the local indie bands I loved.

"What record did you get?" A male voice asked me.

I turned to see a guy sitting on a red milk crate, next to the head shop, and in front of a large graffiti mural. I later learned that a few street kids slept behind this mural, and had dubbed it the "Cardboard Condominium." For now, I examined this stranger that stood in front of me: his jet-black hair was to his shoulders, and he wore silver earrings that dangled with the slightest movement of his head. Despite it being the middle of a hot summer afternoon, he wore a black leather jacket and black boots laced up to his knees.

"National Velvet," I replied.

"No way! I met the lead singer, Maria Del Mar, the other day." He started unfastening his belt buckle. In an instant, his faded black jeans hung over his tall boots, scrunched down at his ankles, leaving his grey boxer shorts fully exposed. "Look. She autographed my underwear," he said turning around so I could get a better look.

Sure enough, Maria Del Mar's signature was planted on the butt cheek of his underpants.

"My name's Shaggy," he said, pulling his pants back up. "From the Scooby-Doo comic. See?" he slid off the leather sleeve of his right arm to show me a tattoo of Shaggy.

"Why are you named after a cartoon?" I hoped that this question wouldn't prompt him to remove even more clothing.

Loud swearing interrupted us, preventing me from hearing his response. Slightly down the block was a group of people, some with pink hair, others with Mohawks, some with shaved heads. Most were accessorized with chains. All were loud, rowdy, noticeable. All the things I wasn't allowed to be.

"Want to meet my friends?" Shaggy asked.

"You bet I do."

As often as I could, I would lie my way out of the house, often telling my mom that I was meeting a female friend from school, and then head down to Queen Street to meet my new friends.

Shaggy knew many of the musicians around town, and even though I wasn't legally allowed in clubs, he managed to get me in to see their concerts. He was always up for anything, and there was also an air of mystery surrounding him that I found intriguing. Once someone asked him where he was living and he answered, "Everywhere."

Eventually, I discovered that most of the kids who hung out on Queen Street were there because they had nowhere else to go. They had dropped out of school, run away from home or had been kicked out. The only one with a job and a fixed address was Jon, a seventeen year old runaway. Someone from the group had mentioned that he worked as a bike courier and lived in an apartment above the Black Bull, a tavern type bar on Queen Street frequented by burly bikers. Although I had occasionally seen him around, we hadn't spoken. He had dark brown hair that had been transformed into dreadlocks, which he kept pulled back with a red bandana, and often wore ripped blue jeans and combat boots. As if a reason was needed to clarify Jon's medium brown skin, someone had pointed out that Jon's dad was from Trinidad, while his mother was from Greece.

"That's why he looks like a mutt," one had said.

"I think he's kind of cute," I had replied.

"If you like brown," another said.

Jon stood in the center of the group as I approached one night.

"Hey, have you seen Shaggy?" I asked. Even though I was friends with some of them, Shaggy remained my main connection to the group. I didn't feel entirely comfortable hanging out with the others on my own.

"Why does Shaggy always get the good ones?" someone snickered.

"Because he's twenty-seven and women like older men," someone else answered.

"Shaggy's twenty-seven?" I asked. Despite having shown me his underwear on the first day we met, he hadn't told me any relevant details about himself, like the fact that he was thirteen years older than me.

Jon looked at me, thoughtfully. "I don't know where Shaggy is. Want to hang with us?"

"Thanks, but I should get home before my mom freaks out."

I left Jon and the others, and headed home.

A few days later, on the last Sunday of the summer, in order to avoid the staleness of Sunday afternoons following church service, I told my mom another believable lie and headed to Queen Street. Once there, I wandered into a coffee shop. It was unbearably hot inside, despite the air conditioner being turned on full-blast. My legs stuck to the brown leather of the chairs as I sipped my double-double coffee which tasted like sweet warm water.

Jon entered, gave me a nod and took a seat at the table behind me. I felt his stare and turned around.

"No Shaggy today?" he asked.

"No."

"You should really stay away from him."

"I haven't even seen him lately."

"But aren't you two an item?"

"No. Not really." *Not at all,* I could have said.

"That guy is bad news. Did you hear that he hurt Laura?"

Laura was a runaway.

"Hurt her how?"

"She said she went home with him and that he beat her up while they were…you know. She's black and blue."

"Jesus!" I said.

"Did he ever do that to you?" he asked.

"No. Shaggy and I never…you know…is she going to the police?" I asked.

"No one goes to the police," he said.

The waitress delivered him a cup of coffee and an egg salad sandwich.

"Want some?" he asked.

With the start of a new school year, I became an even better liar. I could see Jon if I tacked on a pretend after-school activity. As far as my mother knew, I hadn't given her any reason not to trust me, so when I turned fifteen that fall, she began loosening her grip. She allowed me to wear Doc Martens, and didn't object when I wore deep red lipstick, her only critique being that it contrasted too much with my pale white skin. I should try and get some color. At least take more vitamins. Or eat a steak.

Jon and I developed a comfortable rhythm. Often, during the week, he would pick me up from school, take me for greasy

Chinese food in Chinatown, then walk me home, dropping me off at the corner of my street, a safe distance away so no one would see us. On the weekends, he'd take me to bars, or sometimes we'd watch the *Rocky Horror Picture Show* one too many times, and intake an excessive amount of coffee and cigarettes late into the night. He gave me the keys to his apartment. When we went to restaurants, he always made sure I sat away from drafts, and insisted I take a cab and paid for the fare when he couldn't walk me home. In the midst of looking for fun and adventure, I had gravitated to the most constant, responsible person in the group. Together, we created a quasi-normal existence. While to the world we might have looked like a young couple, the reality was that we were like brother and sister.

The more Jon and I hung out, the less we saw of the others. When I had first encountered the people in this group, I had wanted to dive in and participate fully in their adventures. As I spent more and more time with them, I realized that I would never be able to completely do what they did: I had to go home every night. I had to show up to school each day. I could stretch the boundaries a little bit by breaking curfew and skipping class once in a while, but ultimately I knew I would not abandon my life completely; I didn't need to and I didn't want to. Besides, I had plans for myself. Once my dance injury healed, I planned on returning to my training. I wouldn't have time to hang out with them. I had also realized that they weren't fun most of the time. They spent their days sitting on street corners, aimlessly watching life go by, and complaining about how unfair things were. I also knew that I wasn't interested in wrecking my mind and body by taking all the drugs that many of them took. Aside from my mother's voice echoing in the back of my mind, warning me not to venture down that rabbit hole, I knew I wanted better for myself than to hang out in alleyways with pretend-friends, and walk around with red, bloodshot eyes. I did not want to start something I'd spend the rest of my life battling to get away from. I needed to be healthy, and hanging out on Queen Street with anyone other than Jon wasn't good for me.

Promising to be back home by 6:00 p.m. for Christmas Eve dinner, I headed to the Black Bull, where Jon and I had arranged to meet. Even though I was four years too young to be legally allowed inside, the bouncers let me in since they recognized me. Once inside, we spotted each other.

"Shall we?" he asked, grabbing a cue stick.

"You know I'm terrible at this," I said, taking the cue stick from him.

He racked the pool balls, aimed his cue stick at the triangle then forcefully broke them apart. "Any special plans for later? It is Christmas Eve." We watched the balls disperse in different directions on the green felt of the billiard table.

"Family stuff. You know, boring things."

"Looks like I'm stripes, you're solids," he said. He took a shot; the red and white ball spun until it dropped into a corner pocket.

"I have to be back in a couple of hours for dinner."

"Lucky you." He took another shot but missed.

"Me? Lucky? My mom is super strict. It's so annoying." I walked slowly around the pool table, not knowing how best to proceed.

"She can't be that strict. You're down here all the time."

"I guess. But that's because I'm sneaky."

"You are that," he said, chuckling. "I kind of miss having my parents boss me around."

"You do?"

"I do. I hated it when I was living at home, but being on my own like this isn't always that great either. Trust me, you're lucky."

Did he think I was spoiled? Was I?

"Will you be having lots of food?"

"We always do," I said, still studying the table.

"If you hold your stick here and aim to hit this green solid one on its right side, it should go in over here," he said, showing me how he saw the game unfold.

I set up my cue stick and peered over it.

"I love Portuguese food," he said. "Do you eat those shrimp patties, what are they called?"

"Pasteis de camarao."

"Ah, yes, pasteis de camarao," he repeated. "So good. I knew a Portuguese guy once. He said his family eats a ton of seafood for dinner on Christmas Eve, and then everyone stays up until midnight to open presents. Do you do that too?"

"Yup. My mom makes this amazing shrimp soup, and buys cod patties from the bakery. After dinner, we make fil-hóses, which is this doughy dessert sprinkled with sugar and cinnamon. Those are my favorite." I took my shot and watched in slight disappointment as the green ball hit the side of the pool table, then slowly come to a stop in the center. "Ugh, I missed!"

"That sounds amazing."

When I looked up at Jon, he was looking at me, a serious, hopeful expression on his face. We remained looking at each other for a few seconds. I knew he wanted to be invited, but I was afraid of my mother's reaction. I didn't see how I could show up with a seventeen year old high school dropout, who lived above a bar. How would I tell her we met? What would our nosy, judgmental neighbors say? If he asked to be invited, I'd have to say no, hurt his feelings, and risk damaging our friendship. I hoped desperately that the moment would pass and that things between us would go back to normal.

"What are you doing for Christmas?"

"I guess I'll stick around here." He narrowed his focus on the pool table.

"That's great," I lied.

"Yup." Jon took his shot. We watched the yellow striped ball hit the green solid one. They both spun in opposite directions, until the striped one took refuge in a pocket.

Shortly after the Christmas frenzy, I went by the Black Bull once again. I walked up the beer-stained and sticky steps, and opened the door at the top of the stairwell. The hallway light flickered on and off. I took out my keys and walked down the hallway to Jon's apartment. As I approached, I could see that the door was already open. I stood in the threshold and registered my shock. The room looked a lot smaller now that all its contents were gone. Only an unplugged beige phone lay discarded near the window. I stepped inside and stood in the middle of the room. I asked myself where Jon could have gone and why, but deep down I knew the answers.

I turned from the room and walked slowly down the hallway. Once I reached the door at the top of the staircase, I looked back again. Had I imagined him? Had we ever been friends? The realization that I had placed more importance on him than he had placed on me, made me feel ashamed. Why hadn't I seen it? What else had I missed?

I opened the door and made my way down the sticky stairs, for what I knew would be the last time, and stood outside absorbing Queen Street's loud traffic noise. My eyes focused on the traffic lights at the nearby intersection. Red, green, yellow. They'd continue changing, traffic would keep on moving. I cut through the abandoned parking lot on the corner, and walked home.

Eleven Christmases passed. On the twelfth Christmas Eve, I rushed uptown to buy a last-minute present at Yorkdale, an up-scale mall in Toronto's north end. As usual, I was frazzled. My life had become a series of adult responsibilities, and this night was no different. I needed to be home by 6:00 p.m. to begin my family's traditions and I still had a turkey dinner to orga-nize, and stocking stuffers to distribute. I navigated through the crowd of last-minute shoppers as quickly as possible.

And just like Christmas Eve over a decade earlier, I spotted Jon in a crowd of people. He was power walking through the hectic mall, wearing adulthood. Decorative shopping bags lined his arms, a small belly protruded from him, and his hair was cut short leaving no evidence of his dreadlocks. As he walked past me, he did a double take, then stopped. He remained standing a few feet away from me and smiled. I smiled back. Suddenly, I was fifteen years old again. My shock and hurt over having lost my friend crept up over me. I could have asked him for an explanation. Even demanded one, but I didn't.

In that moment, as a grown woman, I made peace with his betrayal, and with mine. Perhaps he also made peace with my betrayal of excluding him when he needed a friend, yearned for a family. I hoped that he'd made peace with himself too. Apologies weren't needed. It only mattered that we had, in fact, abandoned each other. What had been left unsaid, would remain that way.

I didn't move any closer to him and he didn't move any closer to me. The space between us became filled by the constant stream of people who kept walking between us, swelling into a full-blown crowd, nudging us further apart, until my view of him was fully obstructed, and I could no longer see him.

Marilyn Duarte is a writer from Toronto, Canada. She is currently an MFA Candidate in creative writing at the University of Tampa. Her work has appeared in or is forthcoming in The Tishman Review, Junto Magazine, and Assay.

Left Over from Eden

By Tara Shepersky

A loose and floating day, the end of summer-green. Breeze all afternoon, white cumulus on the move. Clouds recall the geese I heard this morning: stroking purpose-filled into the sunrise. Air carries the half-playful hint of chill, like the water in the river down the road.

Where I live, intrusive sound is epidemic. My concrete pad sits 30 feet from the road, poured between tree and townhome. I take a long breath when chance and city planning contrive a break in the growl and shout of friction and the commerce of convenience. For five delicious seconds, the rattle and hiss of maple leaves rises like a prayer.

Which is exactly its nature. More than any of my daydreams, quiet is the desire that resurfaces daily. The natural silence of wind and water, birdcall and humansong. The wind in Ponderosa pines sings too, differently than through the Douglas firs that shade me now. It's distinctive in redwoods, or in maples of varying leaves. Where I lived so long in Southern California, it clatters in the great fan palms, and rustles the skirts of the silver-glinting queens. I pray to hear the wind.

The image that comes, sometimes when I ask this, is a blasted land, humanity fled and trees dying of thirst. The wind still wanders, touching the broken earth and crying. Shaking it in what seems to me like fury, or maybe like grief.

We live in a time of increasing information, and desperate refusal to see. We know that our planet's climate is destabilizing, our seas rising faster than we truly understand. We know our human population is crashingly high. Our technology snags between politics and profit, under-harnessed to save our lives and hope. Our philosophies are weak, unpracticed things.

As long as others count the immediate costs, a critical mass of us can shrug off a few more wildfires each year in the mountains, a bit less rain in a gathering drought or a great deal more at once than the land can channel. We can ignore a widening swath of pines in far-distant mountains, dead by the gnawing mouths of beetles who will not die back themselves without a winter cold enough.

It's a hell of an answer to prayer, this vision. I can't decide whether to chase it back or stand inside it and allow myself to mourn.

Do I have hope? I have, for the moment, inertia on my side. False comfort, perhaps, in anything but that moment. The moment matters, though: take action, take comfort, take courage. Change is inevitable, and we have survived it before. Will the magnitude of this one, and the fact that we ourselves have caused it suddenly, break that? No one knows the answer, but sooner or later, all of us will. I find myself recalling Pascal's wager.

This year (this decade, century? this moment), the wind greets me in a green and pleasant land. By the river in my town, a monument to our native poet stands in scattered columns with bits of verse engraved. "Oregon is insanely green. It is the thin light left over from Eden." I have something like love for this land -- though perhaps not yet William Stafford's long practice of devotion; something to aspire to -- and I do not want to watch it shrivel and ungreen. So I hope with active hands: by shaping words; by reading, giving, voting, driving less.

And in my smug suburban life, I hope the other way as well: by ignoring the rising water bill, and pushing the vision away.

I imagine, instead, quiet of a less drastic sort. Broken, I'm sure, by the whir of bicycles passing, by children's playing and families' backyard laughter. Around all that, I'll listen in on the squirrels in the afternoon shade and raccoons by night, and the intrigues of the birds who visit the small patch we share. I'll notice the rain tapping leaves, one by one by one, as it begins.

And the wind. Always, I'll be listening to the wind.

I don't know if this is pipe dream. By the bonds of both economy and the heart, imposed and freely woven, I am un-likely soon to leave this home of mine, this small and noisy patio in the beating heart of my town. If I did, I would miss it: my arched and spreading maple tree, heavy with seed in this season, my sheltering Douglas firs, the local ospreys claiming my patch of sunset sky. The river close enough to walk in five minutes, dip my toes and sing praise.

Home is the process of loving a package deal, including the fiddly bits and the awkward corners. Including the traffic roar I pretend without success is a waterfall. Including the reason for the water bills, and the maddening difficulty of con-certed right action in a world of stubbornly individual paths.

There's comfort in this, of a sort that grows from famil-iarity. You might also say it's our shifting baseline: our human tendency to adjust to the new normal, and to tell ourselves the necessity is the virtue.

False comfort. In this case, I'll also name it love. I'll stay here on my patio, listening for the wind. I'll write, and con-verse, and give and read and vote, and pray the river never rises more than we can bear.

If hope is the comfort you take when you have already done all you can, then I don't have hope.

I have work to do.

Tara K. Shepersky (she/her) is an Oregon-based taxonomist, poet, essayist, and landscape enthusiast, with tangled roots in half-a-dozen soils of America's West. Her work has appeared in Cascadia Rising Review, Empty Mirror, Mojave Heart Review, and Sky Island Journal, among others. Find her on the trail, at pdxpersky.com, or on Twitter @pdxpersky.

Big Mama's Porch

By Mattie Ward

Big Mama (Lula) and Big Poppa (James) were the matriarch and patriarch of the Wright Family which included seven daughters, six sons and thirty grandchildren. They were born, raised, worked the fields and married at an early age on the Smith's Plantation in Tunica, MS. After the death of their parents, they moved twenty-five miles from Smith's Plantation to Robinsonville, MS; and this is where they started their family. The house was a four room shanty shack with splinter floors, kerosene lamps, woodstove, an outdoor pump and an outhouse. But the front porch of the house is where I learned the fundamentals of life and survival. This house emitted love, happiness and a sense of well being to all who had the privilege of being there.

Big Mama's first ten grandchildren were all born in her home or two houses down the road. My name is Ana Bell, and my mother Georgia Mae was the middle child born to Big Mama and Big Poppa. Big Mama got up at 6:00 every morning to make breakfast for the adults who dropped their children off each day for her to care for, before going to work. Once breakfast was served and things calmed down, Big Mama would load us in her wagon and pulled us to her garden. While there, she picked the vegetables to be cooked and eaten at dinner.

Although we had a frugal life, never in my wildest dreams would I have thought we were poor. We were never hungry because Big Poppa raised all kinds of livestock, including chickens and cows. He also grew many types of fruit trees and as a supplement to these delicacies; he would go hunting and fishing. In addition the items he grew independently, Big Poppa was also a share cropper.

Not a day went by without a lesson from Big Mama. After working in her garden, she would sit in her rocking chair and while holding whomever happened to be the baby at that time she would sing old spirituals like 'Amazing Grace or Twelve Gates to the City' to all of us who surrounded her in a semi-circle on the porch. Her melodic voice covered us like a security blanket and we would soon all be asleep; perhaps dreaming of angels, and streets paved with gold, which were often the subjects of her songs. When she wasn't rocking and singing, my Big Mama read to us from her Bible, or entertained us with family stories, i.e. how she met Big Poppa when his family moved to the Smith's Plantation. Although we did not realize it at that time, these stories were our way of learning family history.

Sunday mornings were different. On Sunday morning, Big Mama would take all of her grandchildren to church. We were dressed in our best clothes and she wore her favorite blue suit and wide brim hat. Although she was a grandmother, her Hershey smooth skin was flawless. We entered the church like a mother duck and her ducklings, and all eyes were on us. At every Sunday service, the pastor preached a dynamic sermon which had people shouting, jumping and running up and down the aisles.

After the sermon we returned home to devour the dinner that Big Mama had prepared before leaving for church. I can still taste the biscuits, fried chicken, greens and chocolate cake that made our eyes water and filled our bellies.

When I turned five years old my father was transferred to the Navy Military Base in Colts, N.J. and our family moved to Princeton, N. J. On the day of the move, my father called out to me "Ana Bell it's time to go, come and get into the car." I cried out "no, I don't want to go to no old New Jersey!" I wanted to stay with Big Mama: to pick vegetables, help feed the animals, run the rocky roads but most of all I wanted to sit near her on the front porch while she rocked and talked about her family. When my father came to get me, I ran to Big Mama and as he took me in his arms, as I kicked and screamed, "Let me go, Big Mama help me." Those words were the last I remembered prior to crying myself to sleep.

The city had streets but no yards; there were no houses like Big Mama's house only buildings like the one we had moved to - my mother called it an apartment. My parents had enrolled me in school, and I was in the kindergarten. While in Mississippi, my cousins and I spent the day with Big Mama, we made up games to play, even after work and on week-ends. Big Mama's house was filled with family to share love, joy and have fun.

However, while in the city school, I didn't talk or play with the other children because they laughed at the way I talked and at my happy nappy hair. I cried or wetted my pants daily so I could go home but this would upset my mother because she had to leave work in order to pick me up. Here in the city learning to trust strangers proved difficult and soon I knew the meaning of "homesick." I regretted the fact that I could no longer see my grandparents and cousins on a daily basis and felt like a caged bird, but whenever I was told that a trip to Mississippi had been planned, I became a free bird.

I was seven years old when I took my first solo flight to see Big Mama. My aunt and uncle were picking me up from the airport. Once the plane landed, the stewardess had to grab my hand to stop me from taking off like a late freight train. I ran and jumped into Aunt Flora Mae's arms. Uncle John was waiting for us in the car. Thinking like the youngster that I was, I simply assumed we were driving back to New Jersey – but when I saw the "Welcome to Mississippi" Sign, I slid from one side of the back to seat the other side so many times; Aunt Flora Mae said "Ana Bell be still and sat in one place." When Uncle John turned down the gravel road; I had my hand on the handle; and before the car came to a complete stop I jumped out ran up on the porch and hugged Big Mama.

It was one day during that visit, as we sat on the porch, Big Mama was reading and telling one of her Bible stories, I happened to look up and saw that the bible was upside down. I soon realized that she wasn't reading; she had memorized the entire Bible. I looked up and her face was glowing. It was then that I knew what I had to do. I smiled and asked "Big mama will you help me read the bible?" Knowing that I was the one who would probably be the teacher, I wondered, "how did she memorize the stories of the Bible as they had been read to her over all these years?"

Big Mama smiled and said "yes, Ana Bell," which gave me all the reassurance I needed. It was then that I begin to appreciate the strength and pride women Big Mama's age possessed. I knew that during their youth on the plantations, it was illegal for them to learn to read but, in spite of that, they adapted to the times and memorized those things most important to them - learning and living their life for God!

Mattie Ward is a retired educator who lives in Atoka, TN with her dog, Theo. She is able to continue her love of teaching by mentoring for the Mid-South Literacy program. She also volunteers with the Children's Church and Pulse Health ministries at her church and with the Orpheum Theater in Memphis, TN. Her goal is to complete her daughter's book that she started before her death.

The Loss Of Her

By Kimberly McElreath

That Wednesday started with a pink pig pancake pajama party. In Kindergarten, getting a new weekly letter means a lot. It's another step toward being a member in the secret society known as...readers. With big, innocent eyes, the little ones come to school every day and just wait to be given the next piece of the puzzle.

I never realized how comforting it can be to live in a world of innocence. As an adult, finally having the security of being taken care of, and not having to worry about feeling safe and secure, opened up the world of innocence that I longed to visit. The few months since my wedding allowed me to wallow in self-indulgence and just be content. I felt settled. The constant chaos of my life was gone, and the society shaped stigma of normal seemed to have come at last.

The phone call only lasted a few minutes, and the next half hour was a blur of collecting my belongings, making arrangements for my students, and getting home to Georgia. The lack of emotion and automated planning of a flight and packing my clothes made this event feel like any other trip home from Seattle. I could not allow myself to step outside of the routine and let fear seep in. I just had to get there.

The flight seemed longer than usual. As I gazed at the people around me, I could not help but wonder who else just found out that their own new found innocence was only a mirage? The landing mirrored my bouncing emotions from the past twelve hours. Collecting my baggage was an annoyance, and having to wait for someone to pick me up was irritating. However, I realized that this was happening to me, not them. Everyone orbiting around the situation did not make this happen. They are being affected. I cannot place blame and condemnation on someone for being stuck in traffic. Finally, being in the car and knowing that I was on my way to her settled my nerves. All I had to do was get there.

I did not expect him to be there when I stepped off the elevator. He has the same right as I do. Maybe even more since he is the first born. He should be there. If this is true, then, why are my ears flattening and my fur starting to stand on end? Why am I trying to guard territory that I voluntarily resigned?

A hug seemed to be the right thing to do. I stepped forward and put my arms around him. I missed the expected greeting and proverbial questioning about my flight. The explanation of the stroke changed to hearing one word that had not anticipated. Terminal. A word that carries that much weight and meaning should sound so much more sophisticated. Over the next couple of hours, I found myself using the word as a descriptor of the situation as casually as I would tell someone that the day was chilly. Terminal. The finite understanding of that word would not come to me until hours later after the biopsy and the meetings with the doctors who just shook their heads with pity. Pity for whom? Pity for me for losing the innocence that I just discovered was so precious to me? Pity for him who had never taken care of himself much less someone who was now needing more than the curing cup of soup? Pity for her who remained hopeful that surgery would happen, and she would be fine?

The understanding of the depth of the word came when a nurse touched my arm and preceded to explain to me the different choices I had with choosing an in-home care service. Hospice was a foreign word to me. In-home care? How could I allow someone to come into our world of denial and unacceptance? We were always taught to cover and shield ourselves from onlookers and meddlers, but it was up to me to betray the pact and sign away the independence and self-righteousness of someone who knew no other way of life.

As I sat in the ICU room that night watching the blinking lights and listening to the octaves of beeping machines, I pulled my pink pajama clad knees up to my chest. I wrapped my arms tightly around myself and wished that I could have tasted at least one pancake.

Kimberly McElreath, originally from Georgia, is a middle school administrator in the Seattle area of Washington state. She received her Bachelors of Arts degree in Music Education from Piedmont College in Demorest, Georgia and her Masters of Education degree in School Administration from Central Washington University in Ellensburg, Washington. When not supporting the growth of her students, Kimberly enjoys spending time with her friends and family. Being a novice writer, she looks forward to continuing to explore her voice and style.

My Father

By Paul Petruccelli

At 5:30 a.m., the sun has not quite begun its ascent behind my sister's house, on the other side of the golf course she could never afford to join. It is early June, so the powder blue hydrangeas flanking the back porch steps are reedy and floppy already, and a scattering of petunias has opened up. The new life of the summer season is out in full force.

But my father is dying.

He may have died overnight for all I know. My siblings moved him the other day from the hospital back to his room in the assisted living facility where he and my mother live. So he can spend his last few days in familiar surroundings. This is what we tell ourselves. But the real benefit is that having him there means family and friends can visit him more easily and frequently. Many have done so already. Hospice nurses check on him regularly, adjusting his medications, gently washing his limp body. I doubt he is aware of much of it.

There is really not a lot more anyone can do. My father, who is 87 years old, has suffered from advancing dementia for some time now, relentlessly surrendering hunks of his short-term memory over the past five years or so. He still knows who I am, but not that I've been living in Singapore for the past five years. Or why in the world I would have gone there to begin with. He certainly doesn't remember meeting my fiancée, Lisa, when we were here last fall. I'm not even sure he recalls that Joanne, my first wife, passed away some years ago.

None of this matters. Because those things are really about all of us. And it is most definitely not about us anymore. I'm not sure all of my siblings quite understand this yet. It's not about helping him last as long as possible. Or urging him to keep fighting. Or praying for a miracle recovery – apparently how my devoutly Catholic mother gets through each day.

There are no miracles. And frankly, any improvement short of a 20-year age reversal would be a curse, not a blessing. His life isn't fun. It hasn't been for ages. There are brief moments of happiness, such as when his youngest grandchild visits. But in between these snapshots are countless, terrible periods of confusion, uncertainty, frustration, physical frailty. Surely life loses much of its appeal when you can no longer shower and dress yourself in the morning, or even have the self-awareness to realize that you should; cannot control your bladder or bowels; are unaware that you're drooling; repeatedly rip out your IV and pull the oxygen feed out of your nose and try to get out of bed and go "home," only to fall and injure yourself. Again.

Praying for miracles is a selfish fool's errand. When I first saw him, the day after I landed, his brief, glass-eyed stare offered no hint that he recognized my presence. I was glad to make it home in time to see him, but I would not have wanted him to wait another five seconds for me. I actually prayed on the plane that God would just let his suffering end. And though I knew that was the rational thing to wish for, it struck me as a cold-blooded thought that would horrify my siblings. I am cautious with my comments around the family.

I have never understood what makes me so different from them at times like this. They're the ones who have the active Catholic faith, who go to church every week and take communion and talk about the sermon. They're the ones who have the unshakeable belief in my father's everlasting life in heaven after he dies. Clearly, religious beliefs don't affect how people react to an impending death. If you believe in heaven, I would think you'd want your loved one to get there soonest, no?

I seem to have a chip in my brain that makes me react to death in an unemotional sort of way. Or am missing the portion of my soul that should make me feel a greater sense of loss, grieve more openly. Nor is this new behavior. It's how I have always reacted to these events. Death is a fact of life. And dealing with it – accepting it, even welcoming it on behalf of the dying, making the necessary arrangements, moving forward – is unavoidable. If I think of the person and miss them and grieve over the loss, as I did when Joanne died, it will be later, and likely on my own. Maybe I just don't want my open emotionality to exacerbate someone else's grief, or fancy myself as some sort of pillar they can lean against. I suspect others may see me as unnaturally stoic, or worse, a loveless, soulless bastard. Can't be helped, I guess.

I have always loved my father, probably respected him even more, and as a child often feared him. Diminutive in size, he was nevertheless a forceful man, with a brood that expanded methodically from four kids to ten after I came along. He was constantly working two jobs or taking a night class to qualify for the next hoped-for promotion, leaving my home-maker mother to handle many of the burdens of so much chil-drearing. There was a constant whir of activity in our house, certainly far more yelling and arguing between my parents than was healthy for them or us. And never, ever enough money. I still recall saving up several hundred dollars from my part-time job to pay my overdue high school tuition bill, giving it to my father because he wanted to write a note to accompany it, only to learn a few months later that I had underwritten everyone's Christmas presents that year.

But he was also a genuine hero to me, who taught me my most important life lessons. And frankly, paying for that Christmas was one of them. It taught me to be more cautious and a little less trusting when it came to money. But it also showed me the lengths to which a good, honest person will sometimes have to go to take care of his family. When it developed that one of my uncles had become an alcoholic, my father and his brother-in-law drove several hours down to my uncle's place, cleaned him up, got him into rehab. My father came back home, went to a local finance company, and promptly refinanced all of his outstanding loans in order to free up a few thousand dollars to contribute toward the rehab expenses. This was a guy with ten kids and a medium-paying government job, who was bagging groceries on the side. For sure, it was the last thing in the world he needed at the time. But he was very clear – I remember he talked to me about it – that this was family, and this was simply what you did for family.

Experiences like this one taught me the importance of compassion and forgiveness. Life sometimes makes people do unfortunate, even terrible things – count on it. But don't be too quick to blame people for failings you may one day experience yourself. Consider their motivations, be grateful you aren't the one in such difficult straits, be generous if you can and, unless they repeatedly abuse your kindness, be forgiving if things go south.

There were other lessons, too. When his mother received a letter from another of my uncles, criticizing the scandalous divorce and remarriage of one of her sons, my father was incensed. He composed an eloquent missive, not so much defending his brother as cautioning my uncle against speaking ill of others, and accusing him of a foolish overconfidence where his own children's marriages were concerned. When the bank where I worked as a part-time teller turned down my application for a student loan, he spun off another letter, rebuking them for failing to reward a kid who was putting himself through school and had served them conscientiously for more than four years. I got the loan. As soon as they figured out who wrote the letter – he had neglected to sign it.

Like most kids, I believed my father could do just about anything. He could play any sport; it would be many years before we could hit a softball farther than him, and that was only because his strength waned, not because ours grew. He was a solid bowler, a sharp poker player, a decent golfer. But what really amazed me was his ability to build and fix things. He taught me to measure and saw, hammer nails, operate the hand drill and drive screws. I was barely seven when he started letting me help him build things. First the window bench, so four or five of us kids could sit around the table without the need for more chairs. We made "books" – wooden boxes covered in plastic material and tacked on two sides – so the little kids could sit high enough to eat at the table. We recovered kitchen chairs, removing the seats, carefully fitting new material over them and reattaching them, and we reupholstered the chairs in the living room. We built closets and bookshelves, a bedroom and laundry room. We hung shelves and doors, painted houses and repaired gutters. My father taught me how to mix concrete, frame out a driveway, dig fence posts. And when one of the little kids would flush a toy down the toilet, we'd take it up off the floor so I could snake my skinny little hand around and fish out whatever it was.

I am not at all sure how I ended up being the one who got to do all these things with him. Years later, his kids all grown, I would repay him by expanding his recreation room, tearing down the bedroom we'd built and framing out new walls, putting up new wallboard and trim. He wanted a bar, too, so I promised to build him one. It was by far the most complicated thing I'd ever done, a two-level arrangement with a built-in sink, constructed of walnut and sporting a brass foot rail. He marveled that I would even consider undertaking it. He was in his 60s then, and I was struck by how often he began asking me whether something should be done this way or that. Not because his memory was failing – that was much later. Simply because he had reached the age when you begin to lose the confidence of your own counsel. It saddened me to see that go from him. Still, I couldn't help feeling a little proud that he would seek my advice.

I know he is about to go now. If not today, tomorrow. And I have no clue how to think about that. It seems he has already been gone from me for so long, between his illness and my distance from home. I wish I had the right words for what is about to unfold. Wish I could speak with him one more time, as he really was, and tell him I love him, what a huge presence he has been in my life, the impact he had in this world. I think only Johnny, my brother who died 30 years ago, had the words for him, big enough to capture all of what he was and all of how he affected us. We found the poem in Johnny's papers after he was gone, and I am sure someone will read it at Dad's funeral.

My Father

A Man
Short, Solid as Rock
Massive shoulders and forearms
A hard life
Integrity well-written in his eyes
Old-world class
Smart-lived
Common-sensed.
Wise.
Learned from all.
Presiding now over his offspring.
Respected.
Listened To.
Integrity Passed On.
Loved.

My Father

Rest now, Dad. Well done.

Paul Petruccelli is a retired corporate lawyer, now living and writing in Portland, Oregon.

My Grandfather's Eyes

By Jeffrey James Higgins

I watched my grandfather, known to my family as Baba, as he sat in a wooden chair, appearing uncomfortable and out of place, and stared across the room at his favorite armchair. That over-stuffed, worn chair—the one Baba inhabited every day, the one he wore like a favorite sweater—was occupied by my younger cousin, seemingly unaware of the privilege afforded him.

Baba wore a mustard brown cardigan sweater and an old, grey fedora hat. Black rimmed glasses, hung low on his nose, beneath his dark eyebrows and warm, brown eyes. The corner of a newspaper peeked out from under his sweater, stuffed inside to warm his aging bones. I caught Baba's eye and his bottom lip curled slightly into a sad smile. The wall behind him was covered with family photographs and his own wooden carvings and paintings.

The house busted with activity as Baba's wife, Najla, their three sons and one daughter, their children's spouses, and their grandchildren told stories and laughed. Every Sunday the family gathered in this house where Baba and Najla had raised their children. In the kitchen there was a flurry of activity as Najla made dinner with three generations of family, filling the house with the velvety aroma of tomato sauce and Arabic spices.

I returned my gaze to Baba and I saw him watching the women in the kitchen. I was only a young man with my life in front of me and when I looked at Baba, I saw a man nearing the end of his journey. Much of the man that I was becoming, had come from him, passed down through his genes and learned from his character. My love of writing was his. My respect for my elders and what came before me developed because of him. My strong belief in free expression and in my own convictions mirrored his. My love of family, his.

I sensed Baba knew how I felt, that he realized I understood more of life than my age allowed. Or did he? I was certain he felt my love for him and that was enough. Another cousin walked by and patted Baba on the knee. It was an affectionate gesture, but also patronizing. In the kitchen, I heard two of my aunts talking about Baba as if either he wasn't there or a child unable to understand what they were saying. Again he caught my eye.

"If you only knew me when I was your age, when I thought I could conquer the world," his eyes seem to say. "If only you saw the way I could make girl's swoon. How I won long debates over politics and religion, as my friends and I sipped Turkish coffee and watched the warm nights slip away in Broumana, Lebanon. You should have seen me when I boarded a ship and came to America, full of hope and sadness."

He gave me a look filled with pride and love. His mind was still sharp, hidden behind the stroke-damaged muscles in his face. His look communicated so much. I could almost hear his thoughts.

"I wish you knew how I risked everything to stand up for my ideas. How I printed my own newspaper and delivered copies by hand to people who were closed to new ideas How your grandmother made me suffer for making us outcasts in a small Christian Orthodox town. My secular, philosophical writing almost ruined us. But it didn't. If only you knew me when I was strong."

We crowded around the kitchen table, young and old, and eyed enough food to feed the entire neighborhood. There was baked chicken, grape leaves stuffed with rice and lamb, squash, and fresh, steaming loaves of Syrian bread. There was always warm bread and my mouth watered from the smell. A wooden bowl overflowed with salad, filled with dandelion stems cut in the backyard and vegetables picked from the garden.

That garden. It took up more of his land than the house. Tomato plants were staked with branches, coat hangers, and scraps of wood. Grapevines sprawled across an arbor which my father helped build. The arbor was never needed, but was welcomed as a gift, as an expression of love. The warmth of caring, loyalty, and security was tangible in house and the garden. It enveloped me. It was the gift of a family's love, always present, seemingly infinite. Even now I can feel it.

A small piece of food was stuck on Baba's lower lip. I want to tell him it's there, that it may make him look feeble, but I knew that it didn't. His dignity and his strength was in his eyes, not his failing body. He had earned our respect and love and nothing would change that.

Not long after that, I walked into my parent's house. They lived hundreds of miles away from Baba, but he was never out of our minds. I entered the kitchen and I saw my father standing awkwardly and wearing a strange look.

"What's wrong?" I asked

"Bad news. Baba died today."

"Is Mom okay?" I asked, trying to be strong for my father.

My father always made the effort to talk with Baba about Lebanon and Baba's life in that foreign land. The way he used to be. My father showed him affection the way one strong man respects another.

I drove to a pond near my old high school in the town where I grew up. I sat in my car, staring at the water, surrounded by childhood memories, but all I could see was Baba's face and that loving gaze. The thought warmed me and I could almost hear Baba saying, *"I'm all right. This is the way it happens. You will see one day."*

I was overcome with the grief that accompanies losing someone irreplaceable and the realization that I have to go on without him. I grieved alone because my connection to Baba was mine alone.

As I write this, my breath becomes labored and my eyes burn. I miss him. I let a tear roll down my cheek, because the emotion is real and pardonable, not a source of shame. I loved him and I always will. I feel him with me now. I see him sitting in his chair, with papers sticking out of his sweater, surrounded by family and watching me. I see his curled lip and that sad smile and I wonder if he knows.

Jeffrey James Higgins is a former reporter and a retired supervisory special agent, who now writes creative nonfiction, essays, and novels. Jeffrey recently completed The Narco-Terrorist, a nonfiction book about the first narco-terrorism investigation. Jeffrey is represented by the Inkwell Management Literary Agency and is currently writing his first thriller. Jeffrey has appeared on CNN Newsroom, Discovery ID, CNN Declassified, and other television programs, radio shows, and podcasts. He has been published in the Adelaide Literary Magazine, The Writing Disorder Literary Journal, American Conservative, Trail Runner Magazine, The Washington Times, American Thinker, Police Magazine, and other publications. His recent articles and media appearances can be found at JeffreyJamesHiggins.com.

Blank Stare, No Peach Fuzz

By John Ballantine Jr.

*A memory of my 1967 summer internship with
Osborne Association in the Arkansas Prisons*

Chainsaw Jack did not meet us at the door of Cummins Farm,
as we shook off the red clay kicked up by the state Chevrolet
making its way past the trustees high up on workhorses with
shotguns across their laps. The trustees, with wide cowboy hats,
nudged the horses out of the road and kicked at the line of
men in white work clothes bent over the cotton. The prisoners'
hands were red with blood as they picked, while the trustees
watched stoically over a day's work.

Superintendent Merton greeted us at the flat administration building and let us wander the halls searching out dark
secrets. Our leather shoes slapped on the gray concrete floors;
the steel doors slammed on the prison barracks that were muffled by the afternoon humidity and whirring fan as we walked.
The barracks were dark, with three-story bunks pushed against
each other, blocking out light and humanity. Two or three
bare lightbulbs reached far back to the shadows. Sleeping here
would twist every new inmate forever.

Austin McCormick, now well into his seventies, walked
up to a prison friend standing against the wall and asked where
Jack was—there were no prison guards in sight. The eerie quiet

of the afternoon was strangely reassuring. Chainsaw Jack had trustee privileges—he had been in a long time; the heads he cut off were long forgotten, almost folklore it seemed—he did not have to ride the line in the noonday sun, but watched over the laundry, where contraband was passed back and forth.

Jack told Austin of the Tucker telephone, where the previous warden and bad trustees tortured those they didn't like. A wire to their balls and chest with current rising with the cranked telephone until the lights flickered and eyes shouted. The inmates' hands twitched under the leather straps, and the singed smell of pubic hair filled the room. At least nineteen died on the chair, although many other bodies were found. The dead were buried in one long hole, near an old gravesite, lined up in a series of pits dug over the years and shaded by an oak tree that camouflaged the horror. Jack pointed Austin (and prying reporters) to the trees and graves covered now with the red Arkansas clay and scrub grass.

Gov. Winthrop Rockefeller gave the okay to dig up the bodies and then instructed Superintendent Merton to stop the front-page news stories. *Time* magazine told of nineteen dead inmates tortured at Tucker Farm and Cummins—white and black men separated by color, but not deed. Many more were brutalized. And here I was three months later in the heat of July to see if the new superintendent had cleaned things up. The chair was gone, the green room empty, but the farm still made millions off the backs of these men—in for robbery, armed assault, burglary, and murder.

The peach fuzz disappeared quickly from the seventeen-year-old thieves who were raped repeatedly in the barracks. The sparkle in the eyes of the young boy I met yesterday was gone; his blank stare said he had witnessed his soul's death that night. No exit, no escape now; he was turned and twisted. In the prison corridors, Austin and I asked about the food, the books in the library, the boredom of summer days, and the fear of the night. We pleaded for a little humanity to assuage the screaming souls.

Later I saw men on death row bent over blades of grass, worshiping the air surrounding them. They were let out one by one, once a week for an hour, to see the sun and remember the green. Otherwise they lay prone on steel bunks, staring straight at soiled ceilings and rereading the one book they were allowed again and again. No repentance here, no life for those on death row.

My blond whiskers were barely visible, and soft skin was covered by a light gabardine green suit. We were here to check out the white prison farm of 16,000 acres. The Tucker Farm twenty miles down the road for the blacks was smaller and just as bad. The prisoners picked cotton, dug the potatoes, and harvested rice and soybeans in the sun. The farms made good money for the legislature, $1.4 million—no need to worry about the horrors down here until they made the news. We were five miles from a town of 1,300 and two hours from Little Rock. I did not know what I was doing here in Arkansas, walking the halls and learning the prison business from the best reformer alive. I touched the desperation of being caught and forgot.

Chainsaw Jack told us that things were a bit better. The old warden, Burton, was gone (not murdered in prison like he should have been, but a corrections consultant), the Tucker chair and telephone removed, and the really bad trustees demoted. Merton was tough, fair, and barely in control with forty corrupt prison guards and 150 armed trustees trying to hold a prison of 1,600 together. He made his peace with those running the place, and the price of contraband cigarettes had dropped. But the food was still terrible, the rats still roamed the kitchen, and most of the lights were busted. The young boys were turned over in the barracks of hell each week.

At least now the days were long, hot, and tempers were not as fiery. But more change was needed. Meat at least once a week, a vegetable, lights throughout the barracks, less crowding in each dormitory, fans too, and maybe another book in the library. Spend some of the money the state made off our backs. A simple request really, if only the prison could keep some of the farm profits.

Governor Rockefeller drank late into the night, turned votes in the legislature, not by appealing to the southern humanity, but shame. We don't want to be as bad as Louisiana or Mississippi. No more headlines about dead bodies at Cummins, torture or rape. Just let me run the prisons at breakeven, spend some of the money we make on them, the inmates. And yes, I will integrate the prisons like the schools in due time, soon. Austin wrote a long report about the value of prison programs, why good hot food and lightbulbs were an important first step. And how a library could calm the idle mind. The trustees were a necessary part of prison management, but they did not need to carry shotguns on the line, and breaking the contraband rings took a lot of work. At the very least the new boys should be in a separate dormitory for a couple of months. Let us not make them into psychopaths on the first night.

I stood there in my college suit, watching, shifting from foot to foot and knowing that this was not the worst. My college friends did not see how easy it was to crush hope and destroy. Not with a shiv to the gut, but the collar of servitude and fear. Dulled blue eyes that could not hide the hurt.

I walked the prison halls one hot day after another; listened, walked, and heard story after story. This was not the kindness I imagined in other jails, not the parole my mother meted out in New Jersey and the juvenile furloughs taken into our home. No, this was just a hell that no one could leave. Ever.

John Ballantine - A professor at Brandeis International Business School, John Ballantine took his Bachelor's degree in English at Harvard, with an M.A. from the University of Chicago
and a Ph.D. in Economics from NYU Stern. He has published
economic commentary in Salon and the Boston Globe. His
literary work has appeared in Crack the Spine, Existere, Forge,
Lime Hawk, Penmen Review, Ragazine, Rubbertop Review,
Saint Ann's Review, Santa Fe Literary Review, Slippery Elm,
and SNReview. He writes to understand the world we walk in
and to ouch our complicated lives.

Cakewalk

By Richard Key

"This cake is so easy to make…" declared my wife casually, "…a blind monkey could make this cake."

Here was a challenge I couldn't pass up. I'm the nearest thing to a blind monkey in our household, so I ventured that I might be up to the task. It was my wife's birthday, and this was a chance to make all the other husbands look bad. No, of course, I mean a chance to demonstrate my love. Also, to see if I've learned anything from those cutthroat cooking shows on television.

The recipe for "Mrs. Elkin's chocolate sheath cake" was lovingly handwritten on both sides of a yellow-stained index card, and shared its individual cellophane slot with three other cards in the dessert section of a recipe book. The book was so overstuffed that the front and back covers were permanently stuck in a ninety-degree angle, like a duck having its wisdom teeth extracted.

"Have you ever thought about reworking your recipe book—you know, maybe organize it and make it look less like a forgotten repository of ancient manuscripts dug out of the side of a cave next to the Dead Sea?"

"No, I haven't."

She was serious. I dropped it. One has to know when to back away. Besides, there was work to do. I closed my eyes and tried to channel Mrs. Elkin. I imagined a big, hairy woman with rude manners and a gravelly voice. "You don't need no stinkin' recipe," she growled, "this ain't *Julie and Julia*." She grabbed a handful of butter, dabbed some on her meaty lips, and started coming after me. I was about to plunge under the table when my eyes popped open and she was gone.

After regaining my composure, I dove right in with masculine confidence and just a *dash* of overconfidence. But soon I found out the whole thing had been rigged by years of feminine conspiring. Females will do that. It may take a while to pay off, but they will stack the deck against a male just to watch him squirm. And there I was, up to my elbows in cocoa and flour before I realized I'd been had.

But she played her hand well—tried to be "helpful."

"Oh, I never sift the sugar and cocoa. It's fine to just mix them well."

"The recipe says to sift the sugar and cocoa into a large mixing bowl." I began to softly chew on my upper lip like I do when confronting the illogical maze of modern bureaucracy.

"I know, but I don't."

I'll give her that one. But later, the icing part said *empty a one-pound box of powdered sugar into a mixing bowl.*

"You need to sift that."

"The recipe doesn't say anything about sifting," I pointed out with my Crisco-glazed forefinger, trying to keep a positive outlook. My upper lip was starting to get raw.

"There's not room for every detail on the card," she said, "but everybody knows to sift powdered sugar because you don't want to have sugar lumps in the icing."

Now, I don't think sugar lumps in the icing would necessarily bring about the apocalypse, but if a person thinks this is important they should state so plainly in the recipe.

"So here where you need to sift, there's no mention of sifting, but over here where you don't need to sift, it clearly says to sift."

"Basically, yes."

Well, the logic here was just so pristine, I had to milk it to its source.

"So, perhaps here where it says one half-cup cocoa, that could just as easily mean one half-cup vanilla?"

"Don't be obtuse."

That shut me up. I'm not about to run to the dictionary with cocoa all over my fingers. I was in over my head and I couldn't turn back. The best thing to do was stiffen my spine and forge on ahead. Pure human fortitude got me through the next few steps. There were tablespoons of this, teaspoons of that, reminding me of my dear spouse's slavish devotion to nonmetric measuring systems.

"Is this the cinnamon?" I asked with the humility of a dwarf on the basketball court playing with his shoestrings tied together.

"That's stick cinnamon. Here's the ground cinnamon, but I usually use the Mexican or Vietnamese cinnamon—I keep those over here."

Well, that hit me between the eyes. Each country has its own cinnamon? No wonder we have war after war after war. Can we not even agree on one cinnamon? Let alone currency, and God, and which sport to call football?

My head was still spinning as I mixed in the last of the ingredients. Soon I was pouring the smooth, dark mixture into the greased pan and was ready to pop it into the oven, when…

"Did you preheat the oven?"

"It says, 'cook at four hundred degrees for twenty minutes.'"

"And right now the oven is at room temperature. It doesn't just magically go from seventy degrees to four hundred degrees when you turn the switch on."

So, now she's telling me the oven's not magic. What's next?

I would have pointed out that the instructions would be more complete if they mentioned that detail in the first few steps, but it would have had all the futility of arguing with the umpire. Before long it was in the *preheated* oven, and I was preparing the icing mixture.

After twenty minutes the timer went off for the cake, and I had a saucepan on the stove filled with a hot cocoa and butter mixture. And if you'd have asked me the odds of a timer peril-ously attached to the hood by a flimsy magnet dropping sud-denly into that mixture as I pressed the off button, splashing a third of the hot, brown goo all over the stovetop, the floor, and my front, I would have said the odds were low, because no one would keep a suicidal timer with such a flimsy magnet in the full service of the King's kitchen, would they? Would they?

Well, it was good for a laugh, even if I did use a profane version of the word "fiddlesticks!" to express my intense displea-sure. It was *so* funny. One of us thought it was *extremely* funny. And that person had a birthday cake with very thin icing.

A Blind Night

By Sydney Samone Wright

June 3, 2017. London Bridge, UK at 6:30 PM

"The map says that the nearest tube station is the Borough stop, but that's on the Northern Line, not Bakerloo like we need. But *we could* ride it to Elephant & Castle… Wasn't there a London Bridge stop?"

"But where is Borough stop?"

I didn't want to admit that we were lost, but my fellow study abroad students and I were nothing but just that. We'd had a first day of the study abroad program celebratory cruise down the River Thames and beneath the London Bridge. Afterwards, the program directors set us free to do what we pleased with the evening, or to find our way back to the dorms on Marylebone Road. I was with a group of Southern Mississippi students, mostly theater majors, and it was apparent not one of us had much sense of direction. Or internet connection on our phones.

We could have popped into a nearby McDonalds and try to connect to their wifi, but in my recent experience with that I knew it would take forever to connect and forever to load up any kind of map. So instead, we walked.

The sun was steadily setting behind the London skyline which made the damp streets seem to darken further, and the shadows beneath small road bridges stretched, waking up for the night. I quickly began to regret finishing *Jekyll and Hyde* the previous day. The course I was taking this summer was on Victorian Gothic literature.

"Must be a wild night at the bars," one student said. There were screams floating in the evening air, but no one in our group seemed to be panicked. If we were in Memphis where my home university was, people would be alarmed. We'd learned upon our first night in the dorms that Thursday's were when Londoners began their weekend festivities. So today, Saturday, they were only reaching their peak of weekend raving. Our dorm was on the University of Westminster's campus, which was right next to The Globe bar. There was no air conditioning in the dorms, so at night I'd leave the windows cracked to let cool air flow in. Drunk screams and cheers, and the noise of glass shattering also flowed in on the regular. I would wake up every few hours with a racing heart before falling asleep with the realization of where I was. I was no longer in Memphis.

Tonight's beginnings were different. We were strolling down the sidewalks still soaked with the late afternoon rain, and we were trying our best not to look lost. We arrived at an intersection and squinted into the dimly lit space.

"Shouldn't there be a tube sign somewhere to point us in the right direction? At this point we just need any station so at least we know where we are. We've been walking for a long time."

"We're honestly, *probably* close to the dorms by now," I laughed, knowing my anxiousness was definitely coating the sound, squeezing it back from being light in any way. I didn't really know these theater people from Southern Miss. We'd only just met over an hour of hors d'oeuvres and free drinks. But this is what I always did in new placed I'd gone. I latched on to people, even if I didn't know their names. This way I wouldn't be alone. Sometimes we'd become friends, and sometimes not. On this night I was relieved to be lost with someone and not on my own.

We turned down a street with a little more light. Surely more light meant more populated, which logically would mean a tube station somewhere close. We walked in a loose line so others could walk in the other direction. We tried to stop one lady in a cream-colored business suit. She had sunglasses pushed back on her head that kept her light blonde hair from falling into her face. She was talking to someone on the phone in a fierce manner, so naturally she only glanced at us and continued walking.

A girl in our group groaned out loud. She'd been complaining about food a bit ago, which I couldn't understand considering the mountain of appetizers we'd consumed only thirty minutes ago. "Hey! Is that a bus stop?"

It was. Underneath a dripping bridge there was a bench beside a sign with a bus on it. I didn't know anything about the bus system in London, nor did I know how much it would cost or which direction we should be going. But any form of transportation was better than wandering past bars and restaurants with no intention of entering them. We all sat down on the bench with some hope that we would get home before the night was up. This didn't last very long when buses continued to pass and none stopped where we were seated.

We all stood and jumbled together to discuss our plan of action to get home and a woman and her boyfriend took our seat on the bench. I couldn't help but overhear their conversation. They were both obviously drunk and very upset.

"… well alright then, doesn't matter if I apologize or not if you don't believe a word that leaves my mouth!"

"Sophie, I said I was sorry that I said that. Please lower your voice."

"No! Don't tell me what to do. What I do is now irrelevant to you. I'm no longer your problem."

"Sophie –"

The man tried to touch her arm. She yanked it away and stood up, swinging her metallic purse onto her shoulder and wobbling a few steps away. She was wearing platform sandals and I winced at the sight of the side of her ankles touching the ground with every uneasy step. I imagined she wouldn't make it far, and she didn't. Her boyfriend finally got to hold her arm and she was breathing hard, leaning into the wall of the wet bridge. I couldn't tell if she was crying, but I knew if I was her I would be.

"You can't – you can't just come back now." I wasn't entirely sure that this is what she said because her words seemed to become tired with her body, sluggish and slurred. "What you said really hurt, and then you ignored me for days. I tried – I tried calling and you ignored me. That really hurt. The window to talk ended a long –"

She began to slip again and he grabbed her, pulling her into his side and letting her relax into him. She was undeniably crying now. Her shoulders were shaking just enough that I could tell, and her head was hanging in front of her body like someone had just put the heaviest hat upon her head. They walked away like that, her visibly exhausted and him enduring.

I returned to my group's conversation and realized my eyes had begun to water. I blinked a few times and tried hard to catch up with whatever they'd decided the plan was. It was hard to concentrate on their words, though, so I just followed them as they began to walk. I thought of what it would be like to be Sophie. What had happened between them? What had he said that hurt her so badly? It must have been terrible, I thought. He was obviously blind to some important relationship rule. Maybe it was 'Never go to sleep angry at each other.'

I could definitely see how that would be the case. Or it could have been 'communication is key. Always listen and try to be understanding. Try to reach a compromise, and then move on.' This would be fitting as well. Whatever the case was, I could tell that she was very hurt. The image of her hanging heavily against him, her shoulders shuddering in a continuous rhythm. It made my chest feel tight. That was the worst type of hurt -- hurt from someone that you love and trust with your heart. I'd felt that hurt before, once four years ago. It was nothing more than a scar now. It was a feeling you'd never forget. For Sophie and her beau, I hoped that they would work through whatever they were struggling with. Luckily in relationships, the blind could be cured.

Ahead we finally spotted the brightly lit tube sign -- a giant red, white and blue circle with the words 'Borough' on it. As we walked toward the entrance, there were more screams and echoes of breaking glass. I walked faster to reach the front of the group and tapped my Oyster card to get through the barrier. We hopped on the next tube and headed south for one stop and then switched onto the Bakerloo line at Elephant & Castle to head north until we reached the stop directly outside of our dorms.

We crossed the street and entered the front of Westminster. When I reached my room and the wifi connected to my phone, messages began to spring up on the screen causing it to buzz, buzz, buzz.

'Are you alright' – from Dad

'Tell me you're at home in the dorm?' – from my boyfriend Shola, who lives in South London

'This e-mail is to check in with you following the incidents in London. Please send us a quick e-mail to confirm your safety. We will contact you with updates as we learn more about the situation in London. For now, please follow the advice of the British Studies Faculty and be sure to follow local news so you are informed on the situation. If you have not done so already, please register your travel on STEP at www. state.gov. I look forward to hearing from you. Thank you.' – an email from the British Studies Program Director

I was completely clueless as to what they were talking about. 'I'm okay. In dorm, what happened?' I sent to my dad and boyfriend. Then I pulled up my laptop and typed into Google: London incident. Various articles, videos, and pictures popped onto my screen.

London Terror Attack: Seven Victims Killed, Three Suspects Shot Dead by Police

London Attack: Seven Killed In Vehicle And Stabbing Incidents

London Bridge Terror Incident: What We Know

My throat felt like it was swelling closed. "We were just there," I said to the empty room. "I was just there." I stopped talking for fear that I would begin to cry. I felt so out of control in that moment. I had only been in London a few days, and innocent people had been killed where I'd walked not thirty minutes before. I recalled that walk then: the sun had begun to peek through the clouds that had brought the afternoon drizzle. People stopped to take pictures of the deep gray and light blue bridge architecture that dated back to the early 1800s. Black taxis and tiny cars lumbered by in each direction. The air felt light, free of the humidity that had weighed it down an hour before. It had been a wonderful afternoon. The night had brought more with it than anyone could have predicted.

From: LondonUSCitizenMessages...

United States Embassy London, United Kingdom
Emergency Message for U.S. Citizens:
Security Incidents in London
June 3, 2017 at 7:01 PM

Police in London are reporting that serious security incidents have occurred on the evening of June 3 on London Bridge and at the near by Borough Market. U.S. citizens in London are urged to avoid those areas and to follow local media and other information sources for additional guidance. You can follow police updates directly via Twitter at @metpoliceuk...

Sydney Wright is a Creative Writing graduate student at the University of Memphis specializing in fiction and literature. She has been a Creative Nonfiction editor for The Pinch Literary Journal for two years, and has also read for their literary contest. Sydney was a track and field athlete for the U of M, competing in multiple events during her eligibility.

Nurses In Training

By Katie Toskaner

I took the 5th avenue bus down, all by myself. All by myself, I would be away from home for the first time. I must have carried a suit case but I don't remember doing so. Entering the building on East 98th Street would start my destiny as a student nurse at the Mt. Sinai Hospital. The year was 1947. I was 18.

We were all young, (all but one who must have been in her 30's. It turned out she had entered the training only to get a free operation on a Baker's cyst; once removed, she left as quickly as she could.) Uniforms were given, blue and white checkered with a half white apron. Our feet were examined by a podiatrist and I learned I had flat feet and needed an arch support in the black, Cuban heeled shoes that were issued. We wore no nurses' caps but were told we must wear hair nets. The thin brown mesh strands of netting only pushed my fine, thin hair closer to my scalp. It did nothing for my looks, but I had a nice smile that one patient said made him feel happy.

But that was after we had had classes in anatomy and physiology and long hours spent learning how to make a bed with square cornered sheets (no fitted sheets in those days) with a draw sheet so tightly pulled that a rubber tipped pencil would bounce when dropped onto it. How to make a bed with the patient in it by practicing on each other, remembering never to walk backwards with the linen in hand as you might bump into something or someone. How to give a bed bath after taking the temperature of the water. We practiced this on mannequins. How to make sure there were no bubbles in the syringe filled injection material; then how to quickly thrust the needle forward into the skin by practicing on an orange. How to inject into the buttocks at the right place so as to avoid hitting a nerve. It was a lot to learn and we stayed up many a night after lights out by placing a throw rug against the door jamb so our lamp light would not reveal our misdemeanor.

The day finally came when we were capped. The 'Dutch' style pointed hats were worn with pride. I took mine home and my brother took my picture. We were now allowed on the wards to practice our new skills under the direction of the head nurse. The ward was a room as big as a ball room with at least 20 beds around 3 sides. The 4th side was the wide entrance, at one side of which was the head nurse's desk from which she could see each patient.

Two incidents stand out in my memory, one which taught me a lesson and one which made me proud. The first occurred on a day when my bed making and changing the patients' water glasses had all been accomplished. I went into the utility room where there were some patient glass straws and dirty glasses on the counter. I proceeded to wash them when the head nurse approached. "What are you doing?" she accusingly asked. "I completed my chores and thought…." She glared an answer. "That's not your job. Get a patient's chart and read it. You might learn something."

The second incident occurred when a woman had had surgery and could not pass her urine. We always gave her a bedpan and told her to try before consenting to catheterize her. This went on for days and the women still had had no success even though we would pour water from a pitcher into another pitcher as the sound of running water often caused urination.

She became discouraged and asked that we stop making her try each time. I cajoled her into trying 'just one more time' until she laughed on seeing my approach, bedpan in hand and said, "I know…'just one more time'. This time it worked and I never saw a happier smile as she handed me the fluid filled pan.

I would like to say that I went on to even greater things until I became an RN, but it was not to be.

I was scheduled to go into operating room training the next week and I froze. Or I told myself later that I missed living at home. That seemed better than admitting that I was scared of making a mistake. With my imagination, I thought I might kill somebody. I headed home before I had to face my fear.

For years later, when I had matured, I considered the possibility of returning to training. It was like a virus that would resurface from time to time. It no longer attacks me and I now use my 'imagination' in creating short stories. This one, however, is true.

Katie Toskaner. I started writing as an adult after friends complimented me on my Christmas newsletters and suggested I be a writer. I have taken writing classes and belong to a writing club. A book seemed a daunting task and so I confined myself to short stories and essays but are now working on a book. I have been published in various newspapers and magazines. Writing is a hobby that takes one into another world where troubles are left behind. I highly recommend it.

Still

By Raymond Tatten

I scuffed my boots across the gravel yard, hoping the day had made everything all right. The barn door was open the quarter way it always was. It never closed all the way. I pushed in, letting what was left of late afternoon sunshine spill in over my shoulders, awakening the barn's insides.

"Tex?"

The sudden sunlight stirred the flies to scatter through the sunbeams, crisscrossing, looking for stillness. My eyes struggled with the light, but I heard the whinny and caught the form in the shadow. Tex tried to rise but slumped back to the floor, his head slapping the dirt with a dull thud. He had been waiting.

I rushed to scoop his head while loose hay, swept by thrashing legs, lay in a pattern around him like snow angels on the barn floor. His legs had tried running, and the hair was scraped blood red, his bottom eye caked closed from rubbing the dirt floor.

"Come on Tex," I begged. "You gotta get up!"

I pulled his halter, but his body was tired. I lowered his heavy head, accepting it into my lap.

"Tex, you'll be all right," I lied. "You just gotta rest here for a while to get your strength back. You got to get better; we got a lot of rides to do."

But Tex wasn't listening. Film clouded his eye, maybe in a dream he had left, a contest he was losing. I never really noticed the size of a pony's head. In my lap, it was heavy, like a child – the whole pony in my hands. I mustered tenderness, crafting my touches along Tex's cheek while the dogs moved in and out, sniffing close to my face and then Tex's as if saying goodbyes.

Late afternoon slipped to evening and then to night. Tex's legs thrashed, and he jerked, running or sneaking under the fence at his favorite spot. I hoped I was a comfort, talking low, telling him out loud how I loved him, and remembering – about how he usually let me catch him when I came with the bridle. Thanking him – for never getting grumpy from too many rides when the city kids came and letting the children pat him all they wanted. I told him about the rides we would do – how we'd find the Indian mounds and get a quick jump to beat Hank's Mickey Pony the next time we raced to the pine trees. It was no use to cry.

When the cool night air finally broke the spell, like a fever, I felt the ache in my legs. I should probably go in or maybe just move around some. I stretched and stood straight to look down at the shape. A fly jittered across the pony's black muzzle, while white teeth grinned a snarling smile. The black tail lay stretched behind like a flattened, frayed rope.

I moved with legs stinging with return of blood and almost turned to look back but let the door swing wide behind me as I stepped into the yard. A cloud of mosquitoes slapped my face, but I didn't rush to brush them away.

I walked a little, stopped, and moved again, up the slope toward the house, before turning to gaze back at the stone-still barn. But the mosquitoes were worse now, and all that was left was to go inside.

Raymond Tatten is a forty-year resident of Sterling, Massachusetts and a life-long Yankee living in the beautiful apple country of Central Massachusetts.

His essays and articles have appeared in local publications, including The Worcester Telegram, The Harvard Post, The Bolton Independent, The Landmark and Sterling Meetinghouse News, along with MUSED Bella Online Literary Review and Adelaide Literary Magazine.

Tatten began his writing experience ten years ago while attending a Sterling Conant Library book critique group, and many of his essays are short bursts in response to writing group prompts. Others "just happened" concerning current events or bubbled-up memories. There is sarcasm, humor and honesty in the way Tatten sees the world, and his voice has been called distinct and rich with authority.

As for the work of writing, he says, "I'm finding it takes more effort to ignore an idea. It won't go away but pesters until it's written, and then it pesters more so I'll pick at it and find someone to listen. Then it can finally go in a box with the others."

Tatten's additional work in progress includes an historical fiction account of a sixteen-year-old Lancaster boy's capture by Indians in 1705 along with his own historical narrative as a nine-year-old living on a remote farm in Harvard, Massachusetts.

Raymond shares a home on Rowley Hill with his wife Linda, daughter KT and a three-pound female Yorkie named Dani Dog.

At Law In Lemon Land

By Ellen T. Birrell

After the last fire, we cleared the burned avocados and decided to replant with less fire prone citrus. I stocked up on shocking pink flags at the farm supply figuring they would be really easy to see. I guess the guys were shocked all right, by the time we are all out in the field ready to measure and mark the planting grid, the pink flags had magicly metamorphed into blue ones. No matter. After assessing the minute advantages of slope, drainage and cardinal points, we laid out the planting grid using a long rope knotted at 16-foot intervals. Staking it taut, the knots showed us where to place our small blue flags along that row. We moved the rope over—the width between two knots--and did it all over again until the entire area of the orchard was marked with flags, each flag a future tree. We sat at the top of the slope in a pocket of shade and admire the Christo-graphism of our field of flags, a precise blue grid flapping in the afternoon breeze above the organic undulations of the cleared land. We dreamt abundance, sweetness and money.

The promised "Godzilla" el niño rains came to nothing down here, unlike Northern California where they watched entire dams collapse as reservoirs filled. So much for all our yearning for damp destruction; the sublime gush, a wetness bringing green soaked, wildflower studded landslides, orchards so saturated they simply float off to the sea, the mountain we cling to rising unfettered, sluiced clean of of its pilot-fish road. Oh, and a river, please, one that won't ever run dry. Instead we got another wildfire. If those devil winds had shifted a smidge more to the southeast, it would surely have engulfed us. The river had dried up in early summer, as it has every year since 2012; we would not have had a chance to fight it.

This morning I came across a native California Live Oak seedling growing in a lemon block. The tree is about 2 feet tall and wide and has both glossy green leaves and rosy tender little ones unfurling in dew spangled fuzz, a voluptuous Venus born at the feet of our cloned lemons. Her rude health fills me with optimism. Nothing could be a more artificial environment for a Live Oak than a copiously irrigated lemon orchard, yet she has found her spot here even as the partial shade of her lemon canopy withers. If I were a real farmer, I would rip her out immediately; the seemliness of farming assumes the eradication of "weeds." Admiring Venus's vitality, and her solid claim to this ecological niche--aeons older than mine--I find this perverse.

I am weary of worries. I will concentrate on "what is" and put my energy there. An acre foot is a 12-inch think blanket of water an acre in size—a staggering amount of water--43,560 cubic feet or 326,000 gallons. Our neighbors--our personal "Evil Empire"--have starved our farm of access to sufficient water for years, even before the drought, and they have sued us many times to boot. From one particular November to June they drew over 24-acre feet of water from their newly built and illegal upstream diversion. That translates to seven million, eight hundred twenty-four thousand gallons to our goose egg, or for those who like visual aids: 7,824000-0.

In court during a particularly excruciating moment, I noticed a dark spot on the back of Laser Dude's neck--yes that neck, the one that with its head presents the delicate profile of a North Korean ICBM aimed at my house. A tall man of about 50, his bullet head is covered with scraps of a younger man's hairline--all 15 grizzled strands of it scraped across his pate and gathered down his back into a pencil-dick ponytail. He stands with his shoulders hunched, his arms slightly akimbo and walks with a self-conscious swagger. Today he is in an army green tee shirt that does nothing for his belly, and pre-desert storm camo patterned cargo pants, in purple.

The spot sparked a momentary daydream about my recent visit to the dermatologist; there are a few funny things going on on my skin and I am of an age to be on a strict maintenance program. Without registering, I had identified his body with mine. Why on earth would I extend to L-Dude my instinctive collaborative humanness?

I brought my attention back to court: tediumtedium, a lie, a lie reasserted, tediumtediumtedium, another lie, more tedium, suddenly punctuated with breathtaking slander.

A day goes by. Another. I notice Laser Dude is wearing a shirt with a collar today.

Instructions from the Judge to the opposing counsel--I name them here Chumbucket and Cockroach: "You can't get that into evidence without foundation, objection sustained." And: "I am concerned about your time management." And: "If you did not produce evidence of crop loss in discovery, I am constrained by the rules of evidence to exclude it." And: "We are now at day seven of trial and still only on your second witness."

My gaze returned to Laser Dude's neck as he bent over, and there it was again, peeking out over his shirt collar. This time, instead of feeling concern, I felt the liberation a writer of fiction must feel when they take the reins of a story and ride it anywhere they want to go.

L-Dude is out on his unpermitted pistol range up on the mountain, the one he's positioned so that all the lead bullets fall on and contaminate his neighbor's land, the one the Sheriffs' deputies and Santa Paula Police like to use for target practice. He's bored shooting targets. His attention wanders. An inoffensive brown body screams through the brush, just something small and wild, made of hunger and fright. Suddenly there is also a lot of blood. Satisfied, L-Dude lumbers off to inspect his work.

The pregnant tick hangs out on the very top of a white sage branch, waiting. Unaware of the shooting because she cannot hear, she is unruffled by the trial of boredom-meets-need-and-ends-in-banal-death that L-Dude has wrought around her. She is also sightless, but sensing light and dark, has found her perch by moving toward brightness. She has been there for a while, feeling the bright and the dark come and go countless times. Her signal comes and she simply lets go—there is a warm blooded mammal near. She has let go before and had to make her patient way up to brightness again, but this time her blind leap pays off: she lands bathed in the scent of warm blood and sweat.

A tenacious and cautious champion of mammalian rock climbing, she follows the scent into warm darkness. She slowly makes her way up and up despite the chafing of the purple camo cargo pants and occasional scratching, crosses a furry belly, passing the tempting armpit and finally burying her head for a long suck in the nape of his neck. Unnoticed, she swells and so do her eggs, ripening in anticipation of release. A karmic gotcha story....

The next day, (day eight, day nine?) Laser Dude sits hunched into his shoulders, and I wonder if he found the tick after all because I cannot see it. Suddenly he stretches to examine a document over Chumbucket's shoulder and there it is again, but with my new fiction super powers I see it as not so tick-like—it is too dark, too red, much more like the first melanoma I saw on the scrotum of one of my rescue horses. Red-black, spongy, with a reek of rot, that melanoma was full of maggots. When the vet saw it, he said the maggots were probably a good thing, in that they were keeping the lesion relatively clean. L-Dude has no maggots that I can see. I feel a smug jolt of joy.

The laws of evidence are very arcane. They see documents in our exhibits that will support our contended relationships among the facts. On re-direct, L-Dude's chum, McDummy, lies, siting our exhibit, claiming to have witnessed something that never happened fabricated on the fly to explain our document's inconvenient truths. We break for the day and into a mad scramble to dig out the proof of his lie, photographs, receipts, witnesses, so that on re-cross, we can impeach him. Again.

My inner fiction writer yearns for Perry Mason melodrama: me on the stand in a discreet, but sexy, dark pencil-skirted suit and some kind of wild 50s hat, weeping softly into a white lawn kerchief as I tell my story; them shamed as they confess their trespass against us; the judge delivering a devastating verdict which will bankrupt them and possibly include jail time, their lawyers disbarred: "As a disgrace to the California Bar!"

After two weeks, still on the plaintiff's second witness, trial is continued TBA. The judge has a murder trial coming in, and we might not get on calendar for several months. In open court, Chumbucket declares he has signed on to these disputes for the rest of his lifetime--delays are fine with him: "Besides, your Honor, it doesn't matter what your verdict is. We will never stop."

The tallest building in the county sits to the west and slightly south of where our own Sugar Mountain's grasp of the Pacific exceeds its reach. We cannot see it from our farm, but when we were still on good terms with "Laser Dude," we would ride horses up to what was once the top of the old ranch and survey the entire coast: from southern Santa Barbara County into Ventura County all the way down to the naval base at Port Hueneme, Channel Islands glimmering in the mist offshore. At least that is how I remember it.

I have no recollection of noticing that building from up top, but now as I drive around the county, I wave at it every time I see it. It is where our lawyer's office is, right at the top of the building, and it gives me a reassuring sense that we have lucked into our personal panopticon on the wild west.

When we moved here, Betty C., then regional head of the US Department of Fish and

Game (now named Fish and Wildlife) gave us a tour of the land in a spring drizzle,

narrating its natural features according to her map—a complex of confusing legal decisions that restrict or govern the environment's protections and permitted uses, like The Waters of America Act or The Endangered Species Act, to name just two. Betty was telling us about non-native species in the river bottom that we were required to eradicate: Giant Reed, Castor Bean, Black Mustard, Tree Tobacco, Wild Fennel and on. Turns out we bought several lawsuits along with the farm, but the only one we knew about was the one that brought Betty out here to boss us around. We inherited a judgment against the farm from its previous stewards. They had built a monumental wall along the river bank for flood protection and had assumed their property right trumped busy-body Betty's new-age environmental map.

I pointed out to Betty that her plant list did not include the Eucalyptus we were sheltered under, the tree being a ubiquitous non-native. There was a long pause, and then, employing what I could only hear as the royal "We" she replied: "We have decided that the Eucalyptus is too emotionally significant in the current landscape of California to be a reasonable target for eradication."

We began work on satisfying the judgment, eradicating Betty's non-native species on 42 acres of river-bottom land and donating the cleared area to The Nature Conservancy before permitting and repairing the wall. Our farm shares a well and road improvements with two other parcels. We signed a contract agreeing to certain sharing and maintenance protocols and we kept them infomed about our progress. They never wanted to know much, and certainly resisted any invitation to join us in the judgment to work out a solution. That might have meant money. It took us 4 years to complete the judgement. It felt like a fulfillment of my young scope and ambition: a beautiful old wild place saved, with horses too!

When it was all done, the other parcel owners—Laser Dude and McDummy--decided it would be far more convenient if we no longer had any right to the agricultural water systems at all. Moreover, our parcel could be endlessly burdened with new improvements—wells, pipelines, electrical easements and storage tanks at several sites--to support an enormous expansion of their orchards above us on Sugar Mountain. Not unlike Trump's conviction that Mexico will pay for his border wall, so would we for their improvements. As we went into our first trial with these guys, our real estate lawyer announced: "Now I am not a litigator...." And the problem with that was obvious by the end of the trial 2 days later.

Our current lawyer in the panopticon, a real litigator, is our paid by the hour Mohammed Ali. He keeps winning handily, but L-Dude and McDummy keep suing us. Paying lawyers means, among other things, we don't replace trees in the orchards. Worse, we are paying to protect a right to a water resource that has become increasingly hypothetical. L-Dude, McDummy and their opportunistic lawyers have spread a lot of contamination around as they fish for the big-kill damages. They are our pests--a veritable infestation of them--sucking off our liquid life.

I am reminded of Ahab, tied dead and revenant to the great white whale, or, in a less flattering register, of a boat I laughed about once, set on auto pilot, its crew asleep, burying its prow blindly, obdurately in to the granite face of a Channel Island.

Our judge finalized his decision in our favor and his signed judgment was entered at the County Clerk's office making it a matter of law. It took almost a year after the the last trial ended, because his case work was so backed up. He has awarded us attorney's fees, which we will have to sue in order to receive, and then only if they still have it.

In the guest house on the farm where she came to live some years ago, my elderly mother suddenly complained about shortness of breath, but insisted I attend my niece's wedding far away and without her. I was to wear her lucky dress, as she said, "for both of us." It was the first family event I have attended as part of the oldest generation present.

Not long after casting her first vote for a democrat and for a woman, my mother entered hospice--three thresholds she had never crossed in any other one of her 89 years. "I have to do this for my granddaughters, may your father forgive me." On her fridge was her Do Not Resuscitate order; inside it was a new box of small vials with special instructions for when it gets bad.

My spelling is not coming easily. I take time to pause over each letter as I write these words out. Of course, as any non-native speaker of English can testify, such a strategy does not improve your chances of getting it right: "r-i-g-h-t" not "r-i-t-e." Definitely not "w-r-i-t-e." I take time for the distraction of world news and dictionaries, hoping to tie each granular detail to my space of consciousness. I weave as I walk back and forth to my mom's house, not wanting to arrive anywhere too directly, too quickly. I want no trace of this wobbly passage, please. I must meet each day resolute. I want to stretch the time out thin, to parting; to insist on taking events one at a time, like in books. Rain, send rain, and I will stand out in it and cry.

A box sits next to me on my desk as, yet again, I try to write. Its exterior may include actual wood veneer but my search for any pinning grain fails, drowned as the box is in its many blurring coats of industrially perfect lacquer. It is without seams. It is immaculate and inarguable. I picked it out in the tired and fussy funeral-home show-room hung with waterstained Thomas Kinkade prints. Ambushed by the strangling legal conformities of a hot and rapid conversion to dust, my stalwart siblings and I bore witness to these hideous practicalities without comment or defence.

I remember sitting with you, your feet up, gazing out the window at our mountain. You said: "The only rule of physics that ever stuck with me is that energy is neither made nor destroyed, merely redistributed."

I remembered another wooden box of yours today, one none of us picked for adoption. Our practical friend Lynn took it away somewhere, for consignment. I never liked it much. I dismissed it as all about your small and waspy anglophilia--not your inclusive fluent Spanish. It is old, isn't it? I don't know where you found it; it is not a family piece. Handmade of satin wood I think, with a marquetry sea shell inlay on the top. I think the inlay is slightly heaved out of true from many years of old wood breathing changing air. It has a fussy stand and a little key, but it's warped top makes it useless even as a side table. What I remember liking about it when you first opened it to show me, was its slightly shredded but still tender robin's-egg blue satin--the perfect compliment to the warm patina of the wood--an exuberant lining that had long since abandoned any glued conformity to the small volume of space inside.

I got it back. There among the Beanie Babies, the reproduction "vintage" postcards and the stacks of mismatched plates, its charm was utterly convincing. I am glad and giddy to find it again, a puppy at the pound retrieved before oblivion.

So where are you now, really? We had almost all of our meager allotment of rain, less than half of normal, arrive in March. It made our mountain a green hallucination of a normal spring. Pretty, but not for long. Family news: Bill tore his quadricep apart the day after your memorial and has had surgery and a long convalescence. Laura broke her nose. Amanda lost the diamond in her engagement ring. Both of them have moved. I drove your car into the wall of your house, cracking the windshield with my head just as I was supposed to meet the new people interested in renting it. Your Lady Banksia rose is in full yellow blossomed glory and your artichokes are up. Trump is far worse than we feared. We still are in trial limbo, now paying for appeals.

I have decided to install your marquetry box on the kitchen counter next to the coffee machine. Its chief offense to me always was its preciousness, so I am putting it to work to hold my overflow fresh spices, especially the intense aromatics, freshly dried bay leaves, garam masala and the fresh chipotle pepper powder that we both shared an addiction to.

I am eager to rest a moment in its soothing billowing blue, your blue. Opening it on the counter, I am shocked to find the lining is a tawdry shredded pink, like old polyester underwear--rusted, bruised and falling to dust.

In a little bit, maybe, I will beat the dust out of it and wipe that box clean, but not just now.

My inner fiction super powers have continued to spin my world. In some dystopic future, I am a real farmer. Climate and living things have our algorithmically assigned functions as the wheels of an eventless future, and I have been relieved of my responsibility for the well being of others. I have no ambivalence about the seemliness of the farm. Big Science has devised some mystery fluid, trademarked of course, that I apply. I have attended all the training sessions in its safe application. I am confident that it will live up to its promise and eradicate all of our pestilential weeds.

Oh and I am going back to the dermatologist. I found a strange mole on the back of my neck too.

Ellen Birrell is an artist and lemon farmer. She is on the faculty of the Program in Photography and Media at the California Institute of the Arts, and a cofounder and editor of X-TRA, a quarterly journal of the visual arts based in Los Angeles.

Baby Rhino

By Annina Lavee

On the screen were the malformed bodies of children that resulted from the use of Agent Orange, by the United States
military during the Vietnam War. My phone vibrated, but
I ignored it. The main character a teenage boy, Chau, had
difficulty using his malformed hands, but wanted to be an
artist. The caretakers at the institution told him, "Forget such
a dream." He learned how to paint by holding the paintbrush
in his mouth and by the end of the film he worked as an artist.
Inspiring, this was the first film in a compilation of Academy
Award nominated docs for 2015. A glance at my iPhone
showed Steve's name displayed on the screen and I wondered,
but I placed the phone back into my bag. I was at the movies.

That evening, I pulled into the driveway before the double
gate that led to my parking area. Marks on the wood, those of
a crowbar, told me that someone had tried to get in. I opened
the gates and drove my car under the sunscreen cover. No
light flickered on, as the sensor light had been broken for the
last few days. It was a few minutes before my eyes adjusted to
the darkness, then I approached the interior gate that led to
my house and yard and stood staring at the spilt wood, and
broken lock of the gate. Someone had gotten into the yard. But
why was the first double gate closed? Strangely calm, I lurched

when I remembered that my flash-drive and hard-drive were both sitting near my laptop, if gone I would lose years of work. My chest burned. What would be missing from my house? I walked towards the French doors into the dining room that I use as a main entrance on the side of the house. Plywood covered the door. I yanked my phone from my bag and listened to the message. "There was some excitement around here tonight," said Steve, my neighbor. "Call me." I tapped call back, but with no answer at ten-thirty decided that he'd gone to bed; he must have arranged for the plywood.

My breath was shallow as I entered the other door into the living room, switched on a lamp over the piano, then stepped around the corner into the guestroom. The desktop computer sat unharmed. Nothing seemed out of place, except for the closet door that was ajar. I exhaled, walked into my office where a table and chair were askew and some books on a bookshelf tipped to the side, but my laptop was there. I took in the next grateful breath. Thank you. The door was open to my bedroom but all was fine, just the folding door to the bathroom dangled off the track. I returned to my office where the closet door was partially open; I peered in; hangars with clothing lay in a pile with all of my suitcases askew, as if a tornado sucked everything up into the air then dropped them with glee, helter-skelter.

Inside the dining room, the wooden French door was splintered with two panes of glass scattered over the floor along with the splintered pieces of wood. Where the deadbolt once held it secured into a wood centerpiece, it was ripped open, and the deadbolt, with nothing to hold it in place, hung ajar with the door; the handle below the lock was humped over, frozen in rigor mortis. Steve must have stopped the robbery.

I tapped 911 onto the phone screen. "I've had a break-in." I said.

"Nothing's been reported," the woman said. He didn't call the cops? Five minutes later the phone quacked. I inherited this phone from my best friend, who died around this time last year, in this house, in my living room. She had chosen a duck quack, that I love, as the ringtone. The first time I heard the quack I looked around for the duck, then remembered I was in Tucson. No water, no ducks. I miss water; I miss my friend. I slid my finger across the screen to answer. It was officer Polaski--actually his was another name that brought to mind Stanley from *A Streetcar Named Desire*. Polaski explained, "The perpetrator was arguing with his x-girlfriend up the street from your home where she was living with a friend. A child was involved. We were called by a neighbor and the doofis ran from us over a fence of the neighbors and somehow into your yard. He was heard breaking in the door and was chased into your home. We followed him, with a police dog, and found him barricaded in the closet under a pile of suitcases."

A chase scene from an old silent movie flashed into my mind, the police clumsy, disorganized, tripped over each other, while the man ran room to room searching for a hideout.

Then Polaski told me that a flier, along with a note, was left near the broken-in door which explained my rights as a victim. "I had the plywood put up on your door," he said.

"Thanks. Who do I pay?" I asked.

"Never-mind. I didn't want the door swinging in the breeze.

"Well, thanks."

"He had a knife, has been arrested. He's in prison."

I pictured a man pointing a knife at a woman; his arrival in my house more threatening. I was both grateful that I wasn't home, and wondered if I had been if I would have used my shinai, a bamboo stick from my practice of Kendo, a Japanese martial art.

On top of my filthy outdoor mat, turned upside down, placed on top of a pile of glass was the victim flier. I broomed away the surrounding glass to get to it. Underneath was a handwritten note, no signature, "Call me at this number." The note from Officer Polaski. I could not say the word victim to define myself, although my house felt dirty, violated, but I was grateful that nothing was stolen. I cleaned and straightened up, smudged all the rooms in the house with smoke from burning sage in a seashell. A sweaty black t-shirt that I found in the closet, was thrown in the garbage.

In the morning, I called Steve. "I watched the events," he said. "There must have been ten police and cars with a helicopter circling above, the cops cursing each other while the guy jumped over the fence and broke in your door; the cops fumbled with tools in an attempt to get in through your gate." This added to the silent movie image running in my head. "They wouldn't talk to me."

"I was at the movies," I told him, five minutes away. I wondered why his message hadn't said come home? And why didn't the cops ask if Steve knew the owner?

In the morning, I checked the fence between his house and my other rental property. It lay on the ground. I had to get this all secured before I drove to LA for the year memorial for my dear friend. Could I go? I was supposed to host but I'd have to get my house secured. I called maintenance people. Mel, the maintenance man, assured me that the plywood over the door was secure for now; he'd ordered a new door. The double gate needed a new way to secure it so it wouldn't be simple to open, even if the cops had trouble figuring out that simply lifting the cane and pushing both doors forward was all that was necessary; but the cops sounded confused and unhappy with each other's attempts to apprehend the fugitive. My second line of defense made them work harder—the inside gate. I had arranged this based on the theory that thieves are lazy looking for an easy in and out. Apparently, the vendor, who put up the plywood, closed the double gate behind him giving me the false impression that no one had gotten in.

Mel watched me as I closed and locked the door every time I walked out into my yard. Considering I have a six-foot tall wall around my property it seemed a bit paranoid. "Maybe you could think of this guy as a baby rhino who got loose on your property?" he said. "A unique experience."

I liked the idea. Nothing like this had happened in the twenty-one years I'd lived in this house. It helped to ease my tendency to look over my shoulder and lock doors incessantly.

The rhinoceros, the second largest land mammal, is known to be an aggressive animal, however, if left alone it will rarely attack of its own choice.

The Javan rhinoceros (*Rhinoceros sondaicus*) is one of the most endangered mammals in the world. Only about 60 remain according to a 2015 survey. This rhino has a single horn, and is hairless; it has folds of protective skin around its body. There are only five living species of rhino, two in Africa and three in Asia. The Sumatran rhino is also endangered with only 100 believed to be alive and date back 20 million years ago to the Miocene era. From a branch of the family Hyracodnetidaie, a mammal, a hornless rhino that ranged in size from that of a dog to the Paraceratherium, which could weigh as much as 15 tons and grew 18 feet tall by 26 feet long and is one of the largest land mammals in history dating back to the Oligocene epoch.

The Rhinoceros is endangered and poached for its horn and bought by those of wealth in Asia, China and Viet Nam, where it is ground up into a dust and drunk because it is believed to have medicinal healing qualities, unproven, un-verified scientifically, yet poached and paid for at the same price as gold, by weight. Popular in Vietnam in particular, people pay this price for the rhino horn which is made from keratin, that which produces hair and nails. In 2010, the last Javan rhino in Vietnam was found dead, a bullet wound in his leg and with his horn hacked off." (The Atlantic, May 2013)

I entered and left through another door, which threw off my systems of organization; I now used the piano as a desk where I left my keys, but I'd roam room to room searching for my bag, and glasses every time I tried to leave the house. Everywhere I went I was late.

I drove to LA for the memorial, an extended weekend. When I returned, I received a letter informing me that there would be a court hearing and I could either attend or contact the victim assistant person to stand in for me. I chose to be at the court hearing, in downtown Tucson.

The courtroom scene and everything that went on didn't resemble anything I'd seen on television. I strained to hear the judge who spoke in a low voice while other conversations went on nearby at full volume. It was an oddly relaxed atmosphere with people roaming in and out of the courtroom.

The judge stated the perpetrator's rights; all charges were dropped including criminal trespass; a list of requirements was read to him as conditions for his parole, including restitution to me for the damages to my property. I watched the profile of a short, wiry young man, with a close haircut nod up, then down; he continued to stare at the floor as the judge spoke. Was he remorseful?

The Sumatran rhino is the smallest of the species. During courtship, rhino males and females frequently fight, which sometimes leads to serious wounds, inflicted by their horns. After mating, the pair go their separate ways. Fourteen to eighteen months later a calf is born, who can begin eating vegetation one week after their birth.

The judge asked me if I had anything to say?

"It was a bit of a surprise to find out that Mr. Martell, the police, and a dog were all running around my house. Restitution for the damages would definitely make me happier," I said. What I didn't say was that they ignored my note about taking off their shoes. A Baby Boomer, I had to remind myself to refer to the cops as the police. Mr. Martell turned to me, then said, "I'm sorry."

"Thank you," I responded. Maybe he's not a bad person, just confused?

The judge told him that he must be in drug rehab and must have no contact with his x-girlfriend or me. He was assigned a court date in a month for a review to ascertain if he was keeping his parole agreements. Camila, the victim assistance woman, stepped up to collect the paperwork, and when she returned she handed the pages to me. "I have a strange request," she said.

"What's that?"

He lost his mother's watch in your closet and asked if you could look for it and return it to him?" She laughed.

"I didn't find anything, but I can look for it."

At home, I emptied the suitcases from the closet, packed with my summer clothes, and found the watch in a small plastic bag, at the rear of the closet, next to the sneaker skid marks on the wall. I thought about holding on to the watch until he paid me back for the damages, but I decided to show kindness instead. I arranged a meeting with Camila, near the dumpsters at the back of the courthouse, where I handed over the watch that she would deliver to his lawyer.

When I arrived at the police station, to obtain a copy of the police report and placed my request with the officer behind the desk, she informed me it would cost me five dollars. "As one of the victims I have to pay for the police report?"

"Unless it's a homicide or an assault...."

And a couple of other possible situations. "I see, so if I were dead I wouldn't have to pay?" I said. Stone faced she nodded, then turned and walked through a door into the bowels of the police station to find the paperwork and make a copy.

Forty-five minutes later she returned and handed me a sheaf of pages.

"Here you are," she said.

"Thanks."

When I got to my car and pulled out my key I realized that I'd forgotten and she'd not asked for payment. "Ha," I said out-loud, "victim wins."

Baby rhino and his girlfriend had been arguing when the police were called by a neighbor. He'd left with the baby for two hours earlier in the day and the woman had been frantic. He wanted her to go back to Bisbee, a small town south of Tucson, where they had lived together. He had not threatened his former girlfriend with the knife that was found in his pocket, which the cop had made a point to mention on the phone. I always carry a small pen knife in my own purse.

A month later, I stood in line at the courthouse building a second time to pass through the metal detectors. The judge was behind schedule and I sat on one of the benches for over an hour and a half; a man called out for Mr. Martell during that time. I scanned those seated on the benches, but no one looked like that profile of the twenty-seven-year old, five-foot four-inch male. He was a no show; no show, and no first check of $50 to start his 2 ½ year payback schedule to total the fifteen-hundred dollars I spent for the repairs. Now I felt like that victim. I was sorry that I'd given him back his mother's watch, as he had played me for the damn watch. A warrant was set for his arrest. He'll be put back in jail if and when they find him.

I caught the prosecutor before she left the courtroom. "They'll look for him," she said. I felt foolish for having believed his apology. Maybe he meant it then, but he was running again.

Rhinos can run as fast as thirty-five miles an hour, at a weight of one ton or more their brains are small in comparison to their body weight. They tend to stay together for brief periods except when raising a calf. A temporary association of a group are referred to as a "crash of rhinos".

Meanwhile I purchased security doors to cover my vulnerable French doors and security covers for the deadbolt on my gate. I decided to have both my front and bedroom doors cut down so I could use them for entrance and egress without dragging on the carpet, or the Saltillo tile. It felt good to have all these entrances and exits working again with a new freedom of movement. That last year I hadn't done much since my friend died and now I was on a tear to clean and straighten things up. I threw out a lot of magazines that started off as a ten-dollar sample that cost me over two-hundred dollars, which I hadn't noticed until it was too late. At the time, I was grieving and didn't care about much of anything until recently. So, baby rhino forced me to wake up and take stock, stop procrastinating about life. Did I owe him a thank you?

There are legends about rhinoceros stamping out fires in the forest. These creatures are referred to as badak api, known in India, Burma and Malaysia. There were two scenes in the film, *The Gods Must Be Crazy* showing a rhino performing this act and I wondered about the validity of that behavior. Had I needed the fire of my grieving to be stamped out by baby rhino?

Annina Lavee teaches screenwriting at the University of Arizona. Her work has appeared in The *Literary Journal Brevity, The Adelaide Literary Journal, Sandscript* (winning second prize for poetry), *The Awareness Journal, The Mountain Eagle* and the *Desert Leaf.* She has received grants from the Arizona Arts Commission and the Tucson Pima Arts Council and was a finalist in the Arizona State Poetry Contest-Jorie Graham judge in 2003. She attended the Squaw Valley Community of Writer's program with scholarship and was a semi-finalist for the 2014 Tucson Festival of Books Contest. Lavee worked in film production in New York City including as producer of the short film/video unit at Saturday Night Live. She is a freelance writer and filmmaker.

White Chrysanthemum

By Marianne Song

Deep into the middle night, the section of mp3 of Chinese audio file was being played over and over until that sound of unfamiliar vocabulary could be blending with the reserve of my Shanghai memory. I started to hypnotize myself that I was recalling the forgotten words of my memory box because I happened to be born in the wrong plane instead of Shanghai. The highlight pen between my fingers was hastily drawing circles and lines page after page just under the warmness emitted from the study lamp. The streams of my journey to Chinese started to run spread through my neatly-written notebook as if the yellow leaves of a maple tree falling onto my head. Whenever my pen was sliding down the paper, my heart was soaked into Shanghai nostalgia. Into this autumn-feel studying room came a puff of wind, chilling my face.

My smartphone rang ominously, breaking the serenity of my study room. It was from my dad, known as quiet and reticent, stammering in a tearful voice. "Your brother," paused "died in Vietnam." Suicide was his answer to my question of how he died. That was the first death of my family members in my whole life. From now onwards, I will never be able to see my younger brother in person anymore. After hanging up the phone, I was spaced out.

What drove him to lose the meaning of a given life? Did he feel undervalued by the financial loss from his stock investment? Or from the futility of life where he couldn't generate any hope to cling to. Or he sensed his earthly journey almost coming to an end after experiencing agape with his beautiful son. Maybe he wanted to leave him his perfect image as a wonderful father if he had been fearful of what if his smart boy found his true-self as emotionally unstable.

When I took a glimpse at the photos posted on his wife's Kakao Talk, only tranquility was my impression towards Vietnam, given the photo showing the silhouette of his son gazing at the green rice field through the big window. The porcelain tea cups on the wooden tray next to him added more peaceful atmosphere to this serenity of nature wonders. My brother's extreme decision truly betrayed the blessing from Vietnam's greenery life.

Upon hanging up the phone after exchanging a few comfort words with my dad, the memories of my younger brother started to trickle down deep down to my mind. Particularly, his image as an innocent boy aged five permeated through the whole pictures of him as far as I remembered. His curiosity seemed to be expressed with his fingers whenever he touched the Lego blocks of different colors and sizes. Under his imagination, the blocks were transformed into a variety of figures including castles, submarines, and robots. As soon as he built the castle with those Lego blocks, my sister and I used to bring our Barbie dolls to narrate the happy-ending story of princess and prince. Three of us felt a sense of pride for our each role in this our puppet play: narration for me, doll decoration for my younger sister, and stage setting for my younger brother.

One day he came up to me for help. Although I read the manuals several times, it was beyond my capacity. My help turned out to be a waste of his time and money. Surprisingly, he was smiling at me so beautifully. Given his temperament, yelling and crying must have been followed. This mysterious smile remained an enigma, and this memory faded away gradually as I grow older. Only after this devastating news came to my ears, I started to unravel the enigma of his innocent smile. Maybe he was so satisfied with being togetherness with my attention. The feeling of being cared must have brought him a sense of belonging since he was the only boy, frequently being left alone while my younger sister and I were playing dolls.

Nonetheless of his thirsty for my attention, my face got so blushed into red by neighbor's careless remarks, "Your family has got three kids to have son!" That made me feel that our family was still old-fashioned, still preserving the feudalism. When I was a kindergartner, government started distributing the campaign of "A well-bred daughter is as enviable as ten sons," to staunch the male-dominated society. The fact of having a boy as the youngest son seemed to run counter to modern family.

For this reason, I felt ashamed to be with my youngest brother. When human's primal desire of recognition was frustrated, more aggressive form, deeply subdued in one's subconscious mind, revealed like a dormant volcano erupting suddenly. He tried to fill the sense of isolation with his tantrums, crying, and pranks to get our attention. I was too young to empathize with his ulterior motive behind his devilish mischief. My raised eyebrows were always opposite to his anticipation for sharing laugh and fun with me. I didn't know that his emotional insecurity was just disguised as his naughtiness. For all his spoiled manners, my mother embraced him tightly, which seemed unreasonable to my eyes.

Later, he married a very intelligent career woman, working in a big multinational clothing company. What surprised our family members and relatives was that her face and looked like me. Although a cacophony of his marriage life was often heard and the dark side under the pretense of "Sweet Home" was leaking slowly. For all the emotional wounds being festered and subdued under the name of "Saving Face," it was truly the birth of his lovely son who tied the loose red knots of my younger brother and his wife. However, the hours with his son got him to feel "being together." His way of finding a meaningful life must be the experience of loving and caring his son. I noticed my brother becoming an innocent boy while he was playing with his son. His deeply hidden purity was actualized by his unconditional love towards his own son. Maybe his decision to take his own life was leaving his son only happy moments with him. Maybe he didn't want to be judged by his smart boy, or might have been very fearful about his weakness being laying bare through his son's innocent eyes.

When I met him in the heaven, I want to keep patting him gently on his shoulder and hold his hands tightly, saying, "No need to be fixated on being perfect nor did we ask for your best-self. We are just humans, making a lot of silly mistakes and regrets because God allowed us to be imperfect so we are always searching for love. However, you are so lucky to have true love with your only son. He will remember you as the only father who taught how to love. Your earth journey was so worthy cause. Your life turned out to be so meaningful by sharing love with your son."

The following weekend I searched for my brother's photo with me. There was our memory well-captured in a faded photo, showing our togetherness. On wintery evening, I sang an Italian and Korean song with my music teacher's students on the stage of community center when I was a middle school student. All of my family members gathered around to give me cheers. After the curtain call, my cute brother came up to the stage, handing me out a bouquet of red and yellow roses with foggy flowers. Now I put a white chrysanthemum in a vase in front of my brother's photo, thinking of such a lovely boy, smiling sheepishly in my mind.

"Dear my brother

Most fearful becoming an adult is letting our childlike heart be blunted in a survival-fittest society. To climb the ladder of success in the organization, we forgot what to love, then lying ourselves that success is more important than happiness. When money-related issue fills our heart, no more heart for white snow melting away beneath the black wheels of the cars curelessly in the asphalt road. No more eyes to greet the blue autumn sky and no more ears to whisper to the branches of sweet orange trees. You must have been so sad towards your bluish self-portrait by filling your heart with profits and loss of the balance sheets of the companies you planned to invest. As little prince goes back to his own little planet, you left us to keep the blue bird of happiness flying within your heart so that you could be remaining as an innocent child like Zeze in My Sweet Orange Tree.

Keep warm in the Heaven,"

Marianne Song is an essayist who strives to reproduce the feelings and memories with poetic images through English instead of her mother tongue, Korean to convey her raw emotions as honestly as possible, otherwise might be fabricated by self-consciousness. Her first memoir of My Pearls in Shanghai will be published in March, 2019. My Pearls in Shanghai tells the beautiful story of her journey from a young adult struggling to find her path to a grown, successful woman who has learned who she is. The way she explores her experiences and memories to correlate with social issues corroborate her viewpoint that arts can be far away from reality. Her education in Switzerland and China expanded her capacity of cultural tolerance arising from different ethnics. A variety of people she met, talked to, and shared her feelings with in two countries were well-melt into her memoir. Currently, she is working as a writer and English instructor in Jeju Island, Korea with an unwavering belief that someday her angst and hardships could be transformed into artistic treasure in the same way the natural wonders of Jeju were made from volcanic eruption. Whenever facing a big challenge, she quietly whispers to herself 'Don't be afraid, follow your heart.'

The Howl of An American Psycho: An Introspection into the Destructive America

By Vanya Suchan

To raise the notion that the human being aspires the glamorized "American dream", but remains suppressed in her struggle in a capitalist worldview, we might first examine the works of Ginsberg's beatnick call for the affirmation of life as it appears in his poem, *Howl*. In his convictions, Ginsberg explores the destitution of America and the "best minds of [his] generation [having been] destroyed by madness"(1),"demanding instantaneous lobotom[ies]..."(69). Ginsberg preaches against the all-too modern American business ethic, the endeavor to meet the demanding melee and the fight for success in a stratified, capitalist society. Ginsberg expounds on the human being's struggle to exist in fighting for the realization of the "American dream". This incommensurability that lies at the heart of such platitudes destroys the momentum of her becoming who she *is* and what she initially grasps for in the first place: the forgotten American Dream of life, liberty, and the pursuit of happiness. Ginsberg continually questions the stability of America, inquiring into the nature of that very "American dream". The very drive of commercializing what the human being strives for crushes her sanity. On my reading and as it appears in the text, the human being ventures for what her true American dream is, something destroyed, in the process of her enlightenment, to reveal the source of true happiness. Here, I would like to bring these thought paths of Allen Ginsberg into dialogue with Bret Easton Ellis' "American Psycho" as a way of opening up a hermeneutic understanding of *Howl.* The cinematic adaptation, written by Mary Harron and Guinevere Turner, depicts the mental destruction and the clinging to escapism from what exists as the human being's reality after the confected and dangerously romantic "American dream" comes to fruition. On my reading, the erosion of the human being's spirit, and in turn assimilation into an unnatural, capital and freedom driven existence, ensues in both Ginsberg and Ellis' works. In this way, the polarizing and materialistic idea of freedom, grounded throughout the nation, eradicates that which Allen Ginsberg fights and stands. As such, what remains as the human being is her madness, which I insist on understanding as corresponding with that of Ellis' depiction of the cliché realization of the American dream in the film *American Psycho*: an exaggerated extreme of the American ideal as the creation of freedom fostered in heinous acts of murder.

In exploring these heinous acts of murder, motivated by the American dream ideals, the film adaptation of *American Psycho* follows an elite businessman, Patrick Bateman. As demonstrated in the film, he exists hindered by his binding role as a successful man in a consumer driven society. He prides himself on his wealth, status through his possessions, and physical appearance. Housed in the "American Gardens building on West 81st Street on the 11th floor" his social prestige, although impressive, still leaves him struggling to meet the standards of the social strata of his colleagues. Bateman, routinely mistaken for other men, described as the "boy next door" and " ...a dork...[s]uch a boring, spineless lightweight", struggles with his own masculinity and the fragility of his status. Living wholly obsessed with his self-image and ability to "fit in", he endures a "balanced diet, [and] a rigorous exercise routine" and yet lacks a sense of control. He lives the "American dream", but fails to find pleasures in his routine life, fiancé and luxurious lifestyle. Fabricating an escape from his detrimental regimen of the nine-to-five finds itself in the gruesome killing of his co-workers, prostitutes, and those who impede his success, a pas-time that exclusively exists as his only true coping mechanism. Bateman exists in a detached state with his "self" similar to the Ginsbergian human being. Both variations of this human being exist in the distorted idea of the American dream, forced to carry out the life and ideals of an abstracted vision from which they wish to diverge. In her attempt to survive, she req-uisitely "fad[es] out in vast sordid movies...picks [herself] up out of basements...stumbl[ing] to unemployment offices" (43). The identity in her private discourse and the idea of herself she portrays to the public exist juxtaposed to one another. In this way, she remains in a disconnected state with herself, obligated to juggle between the side in which she will present to the public and the side she discloses to herself and the dark ven-tures in which she chooses to explore. Much like the human being, Bateman exists in, as Heidegger deems the human being as *das unheimlich*, the unhomely way in which she dwells es-tranged to herself, trapped in mediating between a capitalist America and her authentic attunement toward being Bateman, existing in what I call an unhomely comportedness, lies col-located to his, if not sterile, dwindling passion of his pneuma: the vital spirit of his being. As illustrated in film, through the character of Bateman, the human being loses herself in her endeavor for commercial happiness. The core of her being lies deprived of the forgotten American dream, becoming an idea, a routine, as she lives "hug[ing] and kiss[ing] America under [her] bed sheets" (127) "while it coughs all night and won't let [her] sleep", the same America that Ginsberg laments. (128) Ginsberg's verdict on the sickliness of America we understand is epitomized in the character Bateman, as he broods on his actuality that "there is an idea of Patrick Bateman, some kind of abstraction, but there is no real [him]". Bateman flees towards an escape from the tortures of his dying core to an existence of control through animalistic behaviour. The indulgent pleasures of sex and drugs, such as that of his colleagues, inefficiently quenches Bateman's yearning to kill, a symptom of the ailment which afflicts this kind of American society.

Reaching for a diversion from this lifestyle, Ginsberg similarly presents the human being taking on her own methods to reaching an escape from the incarceration of her societal roles that she insists on playing. She takes part in the external pleasures of "drugs… alcohol and cock" (11), a hubristic act in an attempt to reach happiness before she is forcefully shocked herself out of her "natural" ecstasy by Moloch, the Canaanite demon in "Howl" that I would like to see as that very fallenness of contemporary America. She diverts herself from the constructs of societal norms, extending to the divine in an "ancient heavenly connection"(3) in a moment of flooding freedom, clinging to her daily sojourn. In this way, the human being has the ability to achieve a moment of peace without dragging the body of the taboo and monstrous lifestyle similarly to Patrick Bateman. Comparable to the human beings diversion in *Howl*, *American Psycho* invokes these occuring themes and motifs as well. Throughout the film, similarly Ginsberg's motifs, drugs, sex, and alcohol exist as a crutch, even a prevailing mechanism for the most elite in the business world. These imperious characters spend their free time worrying about how "good [a] bathroom [is] to do coke in" and a woman "who will satisfy all sexual demands... without being too slutty about things." Their domineering traits, employed by the demands of a competitive and hyper masculine culture, force them to escape to a realm that Ginsberg identifies as a "starry dynamo in the machinery of night" (3), unable to find happiness in their own realities. On my reading, these men, much like the human being, cling to any escape from her actuality and the mockery of her simple existence. She lives detached from her self, existing as "some kind of abstraction...", a conceptual version of who she really exists as. Through the human being's process of seeking the fundamental life of the "American dream" she finds herself in a tortured state of being. The shallow ideology that supports the capitalistic "American dream", destructive in nature, embeds itself in her and manifests into a bitter existence. Her "self" and who she once lived as subsists in disunity, emblematic of an eristic existence. Her life is now one of dischord and friction between who she wants to be and who she is forced to routinely dwell as. She now remains as an imitation of herself, her past ideals forgotten, clocked-out of her pneuma, living solely for the tasks she must complete. Although she has reached a point of supposed success, what was seemingly her goal, she remains yearning and pining to bridge her existence to that of the forgotten American dream. In this way, the divide between attaining the "American dream" and the happiness beyond the bounds of that notion exists as a liminal space she cannot cross. Here, the human being finds herself forced to remain trapped by the societal duties of the "American dream" or live detached from this reverie eternally. She remains fastened between the two, struggling, possibly even failing to mediate between them. This detrimental life she leads which Ginsberg diagnoses as "the narcotic haze of capitalism" (51), which blinds her as she takes a proverbial drag from that cigarette of an inescapable and monstrous ideals of a capitalistic driven democracy. What she was once in awe of now embodies that of her nemesis. She lives howling for those who "bared their brains to Heaven..." (4) and howls for the "ancient heavenly connection"(3) and "though [she] can hide [her] cold gaze, and you can shake [her] hand, [she] is simply not there." In the human being's attempt to sprout form the soil of the forgotten American dream, she diverges from her once un-tainted desires to a corrupted agenda. Only when she realizes that this seeded perversion has bloomed like a "sunflower...on top of a pile of ancient sawdust" (4), does she have the choice to escape.

Vanya Suchan is a student who attends Lakehill Preparatory in Dallas, Texas where she studies and excels in deep textual analyzation of literature and poetics. Her work mainly focuses on the human being's existence in dialogue with other texts. She hopes to be able to share her work with others and to help readers be as passionate about literature as she is.

Remembering José Guadalupe Posada

By Emily Peña Murphey

If anyone has ever wondered about the origins of the "iconic" skull or skeleton figures that are so often used as emblems of Mexican culture, it wasn't the Pixar Studios! I will tell you a bit about the man credited with first creating them. He was an engraver and print maker named José Guadalupe Posada.

Posada was born in Aguascalientes ("Hot Waters") in Mexico's North and lived and worked in Mexico City for most of his creative life. His main period of productivity was during the two decades preceding the Mexican Revolution (which, as many of us know, started in 1910.)

This was a time when printed broadsheets bearing *corrido* ballads, poetry about current events, accounts of the exploits of outlaws, etc., were peddled on the streets for *centavos* to keep people informed and entertained. Posada's imagery was prominently featured on many of these, frequently making use of the symbolism of the *calavera*, a Spanish word for "skull" which has a secondary meaning of a wild or roguish person.

Perhaps he sensed the approaching demise of Mexico's long-standing political and cultural elite, for the major themes of Posada's *calavera* figures was the futility of all human endeavor and the inevitability of death, without regard to privilege or earthly possessions. Thus political figures, the clergy, the wealthy, or simply common Mexican "types" were portrayed as skeletons pursuing their ordinary activities as if unaware of their fated mortality. The dark humor of this became popular and soon spread to the folk arts such as *papel picado* (paper cuttings), pastry and candy-making, ceramics, and *papier maché*. Today these crafts and Posada's imagery are strongly associated with the celebration of the Day of the Dead, *El Día de los Muertos*, which takes place on the first and second days of November each year.

Perhaps the most famous Posada *calavera* image is the one known as "*La Catrina*." A *catrín* or *catrina* is a vain and ambitious person of low social class who attempts to convey an appearance of glamour or wealth, as a household servant might by dressing up in her mistress's cast-off clothing. *La Catrina* is portrayed in Posada's image wearing a showy hat with ostrich plumes, ostentatious earrings, and sometime even a feather boa. To me, her fleshless face bears an expression of exuberance and voraciousness as she cavorts through life. But to what end?

Indeed. the vanity of ambition is an underlying theme to much of the traditional humor and folk wisdom of Mexico. It is this force of nature, among so many other great challenges, that is defied by valiant families of immigrants in their *cruzando la frontera* seeking a better life *por el otro lado*? Perhaps this death consciousness engenders a willingness to make the ultimate sacrifice in the struggle.

There are myriad *calaveras*-related images viewable online, and they're fun to look at. I encourage my readers to explore!

Work Cited

Ginsberg, Allen. *Howl.* The Norton Anthology of American Literature, W.W. Norton and Company, 2012. p. 492-500. Print.

Harron, Mary *American Psycho.* (2000). [DVD].

Ginsberg, Allen. *Sunflower Sutra.* The Norton Anthology of American Literature, W.W. Norton and Company, 2012. Print.

Emily Peña Murphey is a retired psychotherapist with academic training in psychology, social work, and Jungian psychoanalysis. She has family roots in Texas' Río Grande Valley and the Smoky Mountains of North Carolina, and sings and plays the traditional music of both regions. She has published short fiction in several online journals, and enjoys writing from a cross-cultural perpective. Her current projects include a collection of short stories and a trilogy of trans-border novels. She lives in Philadelphia.

Trumped!

By Jeffrey Kass

"You don't think Trump's a racist, do you?"

Regina and I were on our second date and the African American couple next to us at Kazoku Sushi in Lakewood, Colorado was discussing the issue of Trump's racism rather loudly over a tray of yellowtail, eel and salmon sushi rolls. I only noticed because eel creeps me out. I must've smirked or had some other visible facial reaction when Regina came at me hard with this question. We had such a nice first date and I really had no reason to suspect Regina was a hard core Trump supporter.

Our first date was at a quaint place just outside of downtown Denver. I remember it well. Regina stood up to hug me when I arrived five minutes late. She was an inch taller than me, at almost 5'10, had alluring dark eyes, long eyelashes and a stunning body. She gave me a peck on the cheek. "So nice to meet you," she said with an approving smile. "You're cute!" I was flattered. I guess my working out and eating right the past six months was paying off. We had met on an online dating app so that was the first time either of us saw more than pictures. Regina and I talked and talked and talked for almost two hours. About our families. College. Our jobs. Things we like to do. It couldn't have gone better. She was gorgeous, nice and smart. The perfect combo! We set a second date before we said our goodbyes. "I'd like to see you before you go out of town this Friday, Jeffrey." "How about this Thursday?" I asked. She checked her phone and the date was booked.

"Well, of course I think he's racist," I responded in a calm tone to her question about Trump.

This is when things went south. And I mean really south.

"Why the fucking hell would you think that," she asked me in an angry tone, the decibel rising with each word.

I'm not sure why Trump supporters feel the need to respond with such vigor, volume and anger. While I try to avoid these type of discussions in general, I definitely had noticed a pattern of more aggressive reactions when anything related to Trump comes up. I actually usually just refer to him as 45 by the way. I never had so much disdain for any president until him so I can't always muster the word "President" in connection with Trump.

I continued in my calm tone, despite wanting to turn up the volume to match hers.

"First, Trump hired Steve Bannon to be one of his top advisors after he was elected. Bannon is the chairman of the far right wing racist and anti-Semitic publication Breitbart News. That was enough to raise my eyebrows."

It only took this one statement for the-defend-him-at-all-costs irrational response to follow.

"Trump probably didn't even know about his connection to that publication," she yelled at me and then stared with piercing eyes. "Anyway, he's doing a great job as president."

I remained relaxed reminding her that I wasn't commenting about the job he was doing or not doing.

"Didn't know Bannon was head of a racist publication?" I retorted. "Even I knew in Denver, Colorado. And I'm nobody."

"He's an important man. I'm sure someone else was handling it for him. President Trump doesn't have time for all that." She continued with her adamant defense.

"C'mon, it was in every newspaper in America," I shrugged. "Plus, who hired the person allegedly handling it for him? Trump? Or another handler?"

Realizing her initial line of defense might have sounded a bit off, she switched gears.

"Anyway, how do you know that publication is racist? You can't believe everything you read on the Internet. Everyone knows that!"

I almost couldn't contain myself but I proceeded even more calmly than I started despite her loud defenses. Other patrons in the restaurant had begun to stare.

"Um… I was just going by what his alt-right publication says in opposing multi-culturalism and immigration and their claim about Jewish conspiracies for white genocide. You can read the articles yourself. It's their own words. I'm not making this shit up."

"Well, I try to avoid reading stuff on the Internet," she exclaimed as if she got me and somehow there was another mysterious source for all this information I was missing out on.

Just to make sure she knew it wasn't just one thing, I couldn't hold back further.

"Trump's also said that some people marching along Nazis in Charlottesville were very fine people. He called African countries shit holes. One of his speech writers is a regular attendee at alt-right conferences. The American Nazi Party and David Duke are among his supporters…"

She couldn't take it anymore, even though I wasn't finished with my long list.

"It's not his fault bad people support him. How's he supposed to control that?" she interrupted.

I couldn't believe I had to explain more to this highly intelligent educated woman.

"All he had to do was forcefully disavow these hate groups. He's never done so in any meaningful way. Instead, choosing people from their ranks. He knows they voted for him. He knows they're part of his base. He'll gladly take their votes even if it means giving them a voice."

"I think you should get the check," as she threw her napkin on the table in disgust. "Or maybe we should just agree to disagree."

"What is it exactly we are agreeing to disagree on?" I asked sarcastically, but still in my now annoying calm tone.

I motioned for the waiter and handed him my credit card before asking for the check. She demanded to split the bill, but it's not my style so I paid for dinner anyway and we headed to our respective cars. The waiter gave me an "I feel for you" look as she had heard almost the entire exchange. I imagine half the restaurant did.

"Well, I know it didn't work out, but I wish you the best," I told her and then headed to my car without so much as a handshake goodbye.

A text message popped up on my phone minutes later.

"You obviously are someone who cannot handle someone with different views."

I couldn't help but laugh since my friend circle always included people across the political spectrum.

I should've let it go but I texted back.

"So the thing is, racism isn't a different view. I'm great friends with people with different opinions on economics, the environment, foreign policy, taxes etc. I don't do well with racism. It's a disease, not a viewpoint. Best of luck to you."

I suppose I owe 45 a little thanks. Three days later, the love of my life asked to try making it work with me again and Regina wasn't in the way. Maybe Trump serves a good purpose after all.

Busia Josie

By Donna Stramella

When I remember Grandma Josie, she is not the blind woman with the swirls in her eyes. She is not the frail woman fitfully trying to sleep as her amputated leg mysteriously aches. She is not the woman in the nursing home, in the lonely morning hours before her family visits.

The Grandma Josie I remember is holding me on her hip, dancing a polka. Her head drops back as she laughs, her bright eyes an impossible shade of blue. My *Busia* is soft and plump and lovable. She is moving from person to person, giving hugs and kisses to the people crammed inside her tiny, neat home--passionate people whose ideas, opinions, stories echo off the walls. They talk about their favorite subjects—politics, family, and faith.

She is the one neighbors visit—for food, for homemade herbal remedies, for prayer, for compassion. She is the conductor of a spirited orchestra, knowing what to ask of whom, smiling as everyone gives the maestro their best, and in turn, she gives her best to them. Her appearance is humble, but her presence is royal. Yet she is more servant than queen. She is in this place not merely through fate, but through courage and the countless tiny decisions that swept her across thousands of miles at sea, from a land that held every answer, to a land that held only questions.

Josie Czaja was just 12 when she made the passage with her mother, father, and siblings to Ellis Island, their names neatly signed on the ship's manifest. I don't know why the Czajas left their homeland. The early 1900s were turbulent political times, but it would be nearly a decade before World War I ravaged Polish lands.

They arrived in 1905, among the first of three waves of Polish immigrants who settled in *Polonias*—Polish communities across the United States, including Baltimore. By 1940, nearly 9,000 Polish immigrants lived in the city.

The family settled in the growing neighborhood of Canton, a place with brick and flagstone row houses where the children sat outside with friends on spotless marble steps that their mothers scrubbed clean each weekend.

I have no details about how Grandma Josie's parents made their living in Poland, but since they opened a confectionary store in Baltimore, I assume they had business experience. At the same time Josie was helping her parents at the shop in Baltimore, her future husband Walter was making the same journey from his native Poland to Ellis Island. I pictured him pulling a scratched, dented trunk onboard the ship. The trunk held his past. His shirt pocket held his future--five dollars and a slip of paper with his brother's address in New Jersey. Eventually, Walter Koros settled in Baltimore and met Josie.

The couple married when they were in their mid-20s and their celebration would be a grand affair. They would carry on the same traditions they saw at their parents' weddings, traditions continued at my mother and father's wedding, and at my own. My grandmother's lovely long veil was replaced with a lace *czypeck*—a small caplet that indicated the bride's role had changed. The groom's hat, a wish for fun and laughter in the marriage, was hand-made. My own husband's hat was adorned with large yellow roses. "Necklaces" fashioned with ribbons and tiny plastic babies were placed around the bride and groom's necks—an acknowledgement that children would be welcomed into the family.

In their wedding photo, my grandparents reflect movie star good looks. Josie holds a massive bouquet of white roses tied with a thick white ribbon, fit for a Hollywood wedding. In their eyes, I see a flash of light that reflects their joy—and resolve.

The newlyweds bought a large corner row home in Canton, divided in two. The first half was for living. The second half, walled off from the residence, contained their corner grocery store.

In the half where they lived, there was a cozy living room where all five children, spouses and grandchildren squeezed in, sometimes all at once. I remember trying to find space on the floor to sit. No one had to tell us that the chairs were reserved for the grownups.

The small kitchen was often filled with neighborhood friends. The Polish women with fair skin, high cheekbones and toothy smiles played cards, drank coffee, talked, and laughed loudly. The men with the weathered faces and crinkled eyes watched Orioles baseball or Colts football games on the small television as they smoked cigars and drank vodka, the clink of their glasses echoed as they toasted, *Sto Lat*—a phrase we sang on birthdays to wish *100 years*.

Often, the Saturday night card games of pinochle or pitch continued all night and ended in time for the family to dress for church.

On the other side of the row house was Walter Koros Groceries, the family's name painted professionally on the large storefront window. The deli case held homemade kielbasa, stuffed into casings by my grandfather who used a machine kept just above the store, in the hall outside my grandparents' bedroom.

Each week, Grandma Josie negotiated prices with the man in the straw hat, whose horse drawn wagon delivered soft golden mushrooms, sweet onions, and firm brown potatoes for the pierogis; cabbage for the sauerkraut.

We often visited my grandparents on Sundays, when the store was closed. Sometimes the living quarters seemed manic with so many loud people crammed in such tight space.

When we opened the door between the two parts of the rowhome, we entered a different world. Inside this new world, there were only muted sounds from next door. The aisles were empty, the cans stacked neatly, all labels uniformly facing front. As children, our eyes were drawn to canned colas, peanut butter treats, and chocolate candy bars. The floor's immaculate tiles reflected our saddle shoes.

The ledger sat directly next to the register. I never looked inside, but my father told me the books kept an account of money owed. Most customers, who worked at the American Can Company and other Baltimore factories, brought their accounts up-to-date on payday, but some took longer. My grandparents continued to give them food, even as bills accumulated.

Life was simple. To escape the summer heat of the city, the family took day trips to "the shore" – beaches on Chesapeake Bay tributaries just a short drive from the city. Sometimes my father and uncle would gather up nets and chicken livers for bait, then launch a small rowboat to go crabbing. They built a fire on the beach and boiled water, tossing in the live crabs with handfuls of spices. Josie covered splintered picnic tables with newspapers, spreading out the steamed crabs for lunch.

As a child, I thought Grandma Josie's life was perfect. Now I know that life is never perfect, even when it's good.

When I was older, I learned that Grandpa Walter was seriously ill for many years before Tuberculosis finally took his life. I learned that Grandma Josie simultaneously ran the grocery store and worked at The Packing House in Baltimore, canning tomatoes and green beans. She stood long hours on the assembly line so she could collect Social Security checks when she turned 62.

My grandparents buried two sons. One was still a baby and the other, Michael was 18 months old. At that time, birth and death were revealed in the same place—at home. Mothers delivered their babies in their bedrooms. The deceased were presented in coffins in the living room for visitors to pray over, so God would accept them into heaven.

Grandma Josie dressed her two sons for eternity, in simple white garments. As she raised their small heads to put on the clothing, threaded their tiny arms through the sleeves, did she think of the first time she dressed them? The same family and friends who visited the house in joy to welcome the new children would be the same people who came to grieve their loss.

Eventually, years after Grandpa Walter died, Grandma sold the house and store. She left years of memories behind. In this home, she had tended two sons, then kept vigil over their tiny, still bodies. Was this the hardest memory to release?

She moved in with her eldest daughter, my Aunt Irene who lived just a block from a large community beach in the Maryland suburbs, a short drive from where my family lived. In the winter, we danced the Polka on tile floors in the basement. In the summer, we swam in the Magothy River or took turns jetting out on my Uncle's boat. My cousins and I separated into age groupings to talk about music and boys.

I remember family barbecues in the summer, grandma still wearing a simple housedress as she sat in the sunshine. She wasn't strong enough to walk down to the beach, but she made sure she talked to everyone. On each visit, she seemed more fragile. Eventually, she needed continuous care and moved to a new nursing home in a location that was central for all family members. In the eight years that she lived in Caton Manor, she had visitors nearly every day.

She was completely blind now and one of her legs had been amputated, both from complications of diabetes.

Our family visits were each Sunday after church. As a teen, I'd sometimes argue with my parents about spending part of my weekend at the nursing home. Occasionally my parents relented, but most times they insisted I go with the family. When I think back, I'm grateful for those visits and I'm ashamed I thought spending time with my friends was more valuable. I have vivid memories of my Sundays with grandma, but I can't remember a single detail about the Sundays I spent with my friends.

Grandma Josie was too weak to attend my wedding. My aunts removed my veil to add the lace *czypeck*, then placed the funny hat on my husband's head. We wore ribbons with tiny baby dolls around our necks. I was twirled so quickly around the floor during the apron dance that I felt dizzy.

Soon after our honeymoon, my husband and I visited Grandma in the nursing home. She wanted to hear every detail about the wedding ceremony and the reception. If she was sad that her circumstances didn't allow her to be with us that day, she didn't show it.

She asked about each member of the family, what they said, what they wore, if they had a good time. She asked me if I danced the Polka. When I named all the relatives I danced with at the wedding, she tilted her head back and laughed. It was cloudy outside, but sunlight seemed to wash across her face.

Donna Koros Stramella is a writer from Maryland whose fiction and nonfiction pieces have been published in *Adelaide Lit-*

erary Magazine, Scarlet Leaf Review, Columbia Magazine, and the Baltimore Sun. She is a previous award-winning journalist and a graduate of the University of Tampa MFA in Creative Writing. Currently, she is seeking representation for her first novel, *Coffee Killed My Mother* and is working on her second, *Among the Bones.*

First Kiss

By Kevin Drzakowski

The girl in the red skirt hung upside down on the monkey bars, brazenly putting her underwear on display for all to see. From where I sat across the playground, I regarded her with interest, shoving a clump of grass in my mouth and chewing it thoughtfully. Curious, I thought. Her underwear did not have a picture of He-Man. In fact, none of the Masters of the Universe were on those panties, not even Moss Man or Ram Man. Instead, her underwear had pictures of little daisies. I did not know such underwear existed in the world.

For the life of me, I cannot remember that girl's name, but I will never forget those daisies. I hoped she would stay like that, hanging upside down forever. For a reason I couldn't understand, I didn't want to look at anything other than those daisies ever again.

My wish was not granted. The girl bent her waist, swinging herself up and grabbing hold of another monkey bar. Her legs slipped off the first bar, and that red skirted floated back down to the earth, coming all the way down to her knees. Someone called my name. The other toddler boys were climbing up the ladder of the slide, pretending they were cowboys. The fact that cowboys would have been unlikely to encounter slides in the Old West was no deterrent to their imagination. They called for me to join them, but I kept looking at the girl in the red skirt. She was wearing a white blouse, the red skirt, knee-high white socks, and red sneakers. She looked like a candy cane. And I loved candy canes.

I watched her make her way across the playground. She passed the sandbox, the swing set, and ended up at the tunnel, a piece of playground equipment that was really no more than a long piece of industrial tubing. She got down on her hands and knees and crawled into the gaping darkness. Just before she disappeared, I caught one more glimpse of those daisies. I ate another handful of grass, then went over to the tunnel and crawled in.

The inside was thick with the tart aroma of urine, most likely the product of Donny, the kid whose singular goal in life was peeing on anything and everything. I ignored the smell, though, and crawled toward the middle of the tunnel, where she sat waiting, wrapped in shadows. She looked back at me, as though she had been waiting for me all this time. I stopped next to her. She smiled, and leaned toward me. I leaned toward her. Our lips met. Trying my best to replicate the technique I had learned from my mom when she kissed me goodnight, I allowed a small amount of pressure to build up between our two pairs of lips before they separated with the sound of a tiny pop. At some point, my eyes had closed, and when I opened them again I could just make out her lips in the darkness. They were still smiling. She turned around and crawled toward the other end of the tunnel, casting a few glances over her shoulder, as though beckoning me. I followed, my heart full of daisies.

When I emerged from the end of the tunnel, she was crying. She ran over to one of the teachers, pointing at me and rubbing her arm. She told the teacher I had hit her. I was baffled. The teacher was a rather unattractive woman named

Miss Smith. All the prettier younger preschool teachers, most of them teenagers, went by their first names: Miss Sandy, Miss Allison, Miss Gina, Miss Whatever. Miss Smith was of another ilk. I did not like her. She stomped over to me, her flabby arms crossed and a scowl on her face. She asked if I had hit the girl in the red skirt. I told her I did not. Miss Smith asked me what we were doing in the tunnel. Based on my understanding, the girl in the red skirt and I had just had sex, and I did not think this was something proper to reveal. So, instead of offering up the truth, I uttered the one phrase guaranteed to solidify guilt: "I don't know."

Miss Smith made me sit on the side of the sandbox, where all the bad kids were put. I sadly watched my friends playing on the slide. It appeared they were now pretending to be cavemen, which again didn't necessarily lend itself to incorporation of a playground slide, but, in the mind of a child, there are no boundaries to what cowboys or cavemen can do. Their fun was too painful for me to watch, so I turned to the sandbox. I traced a heart, a shape I had just learned how to make, into the sand. The girl in the red skirt was on the swing set, soaring higher and higher, laughing and singing with the other girls. I smeared out the heart in the sand, replacing it with another shape I knew, one I saw frequently on the top of my hand-writing assignments: a frowny-face.

Kevin Drzakowski is the chair of the English and Philosophy Department at the University of Wisconsin-Stout, where he teaches creative writing and composition. His plays have been performed in the Midwest and in New York City, and his po-etry and prose have appeared in magazines such as *Spectrum, Five2One, Adelaide, and The Wisconsin Review.* He serves as one of the editors for the online journal *HitchLit.*

www.ingramcontent.com/pod-product-compliance
Lightning Source LLC
Chambersburg PA
CBHW022349020726
47500CB00002B/194